O

AUTHORIZED BIBLE
VINDICATED

BENJAMIN G. WILKINSON, Ph. D.
Dean of Theology, Washington Missionary College
TAKOMA PARK, D. C.

———

TEACH Services, Inc.
New York

Facsimile Reproduction

2007 08 09 10 11 12 · 5 4 3 2 1

Copyright © 2006 TEACH Services, Inc.
ISBN-13: 978-1-57258-401-3
ISBN-10: 1-57258-401-7
Library of Congress Control Number: 2005936419

Published by
TEACH Services, Inc.
www.TEACHServices.com

FOREWORD

This volume is written in the fervent hope that it will confirm and establish faith in God's Word, which through the ages has been preserved inviolate. In these days when faith is weakening and the Bible is being torn apart, it is vital that we enter into fields which can yield up their evidence of how God, through the centuries, intervened to transmit to us a perfect Bible. Much of the material given in this book was collected in response to the needs of the author's classroom work. In pursuing this line of study, he has been astounded and thrilled to find in historical situations, where he least expected it, evidences of special intervention and special purposes of God with regard to His Holy Word. His faith in the inspiration of the Bible has been deeply strengthened as he has perceived how down through the ages God's true Bible has constantly triumphed over erroneous versions.

With regard to the different versions, it is necessary, while confirming the glorious inspiration of the Bible, to warn the people against Bibles which include false books, and, especially at the present time, against the dangers of false readings in genuine books. There are versions of the Bible, prepared by men of scholarship, with certain books and readings we cannot accept. Such versions may be of use for reference or for comparison. In certain passages, they may give a clearer rendering. But it is unthinkable that those who use such versions would be unwilling to have the public informed of their dangers.

This work has been written under great pressure. In addition to the author's tasks in the Theological Department of the College, and his evangelical work as pastor of a city church, he wrote this book in response to urgent requests. It may be possible that there are a few technical mistakes. The author has strong confidence, however, that the main lines of argument are timely, and that they stand on a firm foundation.

It is possible to know what is the true Word of God. The author sends forth this book with a fervent prayer that it may aid the earnest seeker after truth to find the answer to this all-important question.

B. G. WILKINSON

Takoma Park, D. C.,
    June, 1930.

CONTENTS

CHAPTER I

Fundamentally, Only Two Different Bibles

"There is the idea in the minds of some people that scholarship demands the laying aside of the Authorized Version of the Bible and taking up the latest Revised Version. This is an idea, however, without any proper basis. This Revised Version is in large part in line with what is known as modernism, and is peculiarly acceptable to those who think that any change, anywhere or in anything, is progress. Those who have really investigated the matter, and are in hearty sympathy with what is evangelical, realize that this Revised Version is a part of the movement to 'modernize' Christian thought and faith and do away with the established truth." *The Herald and Presbyter (Presbyterian), July 16, 1924, p. 10.*

I N ONE of our prominent publications, there appeared in the winter of 1928, an article entitled, "Who Killed Goliath?" and in the spring of 1929, an article named, "The Dispute About Goliath." Attention was called to the fact that in the American Revised Version, *II Samuel 21:19*, we read that Elhanan killed Goliath. A special cablegram from the "most learned and devout scholars" of the Church of England, said in substance, that the Revised Version was correct, that Elhanan and not David killed Goliath; that there were many other things in the Bible which were the product of exaggeration, such as the story of Noah and the ark, of Jonah and the whale, of the Garden of Eden, and of the longevity of Methuselah. The first article says that these modern views have been held and taught in practically all American theological seminaries of standing, and that young ministers being graduated from them, have rejected the old beliefs about these events whether the public knew it or not. This publication aroused a national interest and its office was "inundated," as the editor says, with letters as to whether this Revised Version is correct, or whether, as we have always believed, according to the Authorized Version, David killed Goliath. [1]

Is the American Revised Version correct on this point, or is the Bible, which has led the Protestant world for three hundred years, correct? Is the Revised Version correct in thousands of other changes made, or is the King James Version correct?

Back of this and other changes lie the motives and events which, in 1870, brought into existence the Committees which produced the Revised Versions—both the English and the American. During the three hundred and fifty years following the Reformation, repeated attempts were made to set aside the Greek New Testament, called the Received Text, from which the New Testament of the King James in English and other Protestant Bibles in other languages were translated. Many individual efforts produced different Greek New Testaments. Likewise furious attacks were made upon the Old Testament in Hebrew, from which the King James and other Bibles had been translated. None of these assaults, however, met with any marked success until the Revision Committee was appointed by the southern half of the Church of England under the Archbishop of Canterbury,—although the same church in the northern half of England under the Archbishop of York, refused to be a party to the project. This Revision Committee, besides the changes in the Old Testament, made over 5000 changes in the Received Text of the New Testament and so produced a new Greek New Testament. This permitted all the forces hostile to the Bible to gather themselves together and pour through the breach. Since then, the flood gates have been opened and we are now deluged with many different kinds of Greek New Testaments and with English Bibles translated from them, changed and mutilated in bewildering confusion.

---

[1] *The Literary Digest*, Dec. 29, 1928; Mar. 9, 1929.

Again, in the story of the dark hour when Jesus hung on the cross, the King James Bible declares that the darkness which was over the whole land from the sixth to the ninth hour was produced because the *sun was darkened*. This reason offers the Christian believer a testimony of the miraculous interposition of the Father in behalf of His son, similar to the darkness which afflicted Egypt in the plagues upon that nation. In the New Testament, as translated by Moffatt and certain other modern Bibles, we are told that the darkness was caused by an *eclipse of the sun*. Of course, a darkness caused by an eclipse of the sun is very ordinary; it is not a miracle. Moreover, Christ was crucified at the time of the Passover which always occurred when the moon was full. At the time of a full moon, no eclipse of the sun is possible. Now which of these two records in Greek did God write: the miraculous, as recorded in the King James Bible and which we have believed for three hundred years; or the unnatural and impossible, as recorded in Moffatt's translation? Moffatt and the Revisers both used the same manuscript.

Some of those who had part in these Revised and Modern Bibles were higher critics of the most pronounced type. At least one man sat on the Revision Committee of 1881 who had openly and in writing denied the divinity of our Lord and Saviour Jesus Christ. On this account, their chairman of high standing absented himself almost from the first.[2] Also, men sat on the Revision Committee who, openly and in a critical hour when their word was of weight, had defended the great movement to Romanize the Church of England.

It is too late to beguile us with soothing words that all versions and all translations are of equal value; that nowhere is doctrine affected. Doctrine is seriously affected. So wrote Dr. G. V. Smith, a member of the English New Testament Revision Committee:

---

[2] Samuel Hemphill, A History of the Revised Version, pp. 36, 37.

"Since the publication of the revised New Testament, it has been frequently said that the changes of translation which the work contains are of little importance from a doctrinal point of view. . . . To the writer, any such statement appears to be in the most substantial sense contrary to the facts of the case." [3]

Life is bigger than logic. When it comes to the philosophy of life, scholarship and science are not the all which counts. It is as true to-day as in the days of Christ, that "the common people heard him gladly." If it be a question of physics, of chemistry, of mathematics, or of mechanics, there, scientists can speak with authority. But when it is a question of revelation, of spirituality, or of morality, the common people are as competent judges as are the product of the schools. And in great crises, history has frequently shown that they were safer.

Experience also determines issues. There are those among us now who would change the Constitution of the United States, saying: "Have we not men to-day who have as great intellect as Washington, Adams, Jefferson, and the others? Have we not much more light than they? Why must we be tied to what they taught?" We will not deny that there are men now living as brilliant as the founding fathers. But no men to-day ever went through the same experience as the framers of the Constitution. Those pioneers were yet witnesses of the vicious principles of the Dark Ages and their cruel results. They were called upon to suffer, to endure, to fight, that principles of a different nature might be established. Experience, not reading or philosophizing, had thoroughly wrought in them the glorious ideals incorporated into the fundamental document of the land.

Experience can throw some light also upon the relative value of Bible Versions. The King James Bible was translated when England was fighting her way out from Catholicism to Protestantism; whereas, the Revised Ver-

---

[3] Dr. G. Vance Smith, Texts and Margins of the Revised N. T., p. 45.

sion was born after fifty years (1833-1883) of terrific Romanizing campaigns, when one convulsion after another rocked the mental defenses of England and broke down the ascendency of the Protestant mentality in that empire. The King James Version was born of the Reformation; the Revised Versions and some modern Bibles were born of Higher Criticism and Romanizing activities, as this treatise will show.

We hear a great deal to-day about the Sunday Law of the Roman Emperor Constantine, 321 A. D. Why is it that we do not hear about the corrupt Bible which Constantine adopted and promulgated, the version which for 1800 years has been exploited by the forces of heresy and apostasy? This Bible, we regret to say, lies at the bottom of many versions which now flood the publishing houses, the schools, the churches, yes, many homes, and are bringing confusion and doubt to untold millions. Down through the centuries, the pure Bible, the living Word of God, has often faced the descendants of this corrupt Version, robed in splendor and seated on the throne of power. It has been a battle and a march, a battle and a march. God's Holy Word has always won; to its victories we owe the very existence of Christian civilization and all the happiness we now have and hope for in eternity. And now, once again, in these last days, the battle is being renewed, the affections and the control of the minds of men are being contended for by these two rival claimants.

Devotion to error can never produce true righteousness. Out of the present confusion of Bibles, I propose to trace the situation back to its origin, that our hearts may be full of praise and gratitude to God for the marvelous manner in which He has given to us and preserved for us the Holy Scriptures.

THE HEBREW TEXT OF THE OLD TESTAMENT

For the present, the problem revolves mostly around the thousands of different readings in the Greek New

Testament manuscripts. By the time of Christ, the Old Testament was in a settled condition. Since then, the Hebrew Scriptures had been carried down intact to the day of printing (about 1450 A. D.) by the unrivalled methods of the Jews in transmitting perfect Hebrew manuscripts. Whatever perplexing problems there are in connection with the Old Testament, these have largely been produced by translating it into Greek and uniting that translation to the Greek New Testament. It is around the problems of the Greek New Testament that the battle for centuries has been fought. We must, therefore, confine ourselves largely to the Christian Era; for the experience which befell the New Testament and the controversies that raged around it, also befell the Old Testament. Moreover, the Revisers, themselves, would have no one think for an instant that they used any other MSS. in revising the Old Testament than the Massoretic text, the only reliable Hebrew Bible. Dr. Ellicott, chairman of the English New Testament Committee, repeatedly recommends the story of the Old Testament Revision by Dr. Chambers. Dr. Chambers says:—

"The more sober critics with one consent hold fast the Massoretic text. This has been the rule with the authors of the present revision. Their work is based throughout upon the traditional Hebrew. In difficult or doubtful places, where some corruption seems to have crept in or some accident to have befallen the manuscript, the testimony of the early versions is given in the margin, but never incorporated with the text." [4]

THE APOSTASY OF THE EARLY CHRISTIAN CHURCH PREPARES THE WAY FOR CORRUPTING THE MANUSCRIPTS

Inspired by the unerring Spirit of God, chosen men brought forth the different books of the New Testament, these originally being written in Greek. For a few years, under the guidance of the noble apostles, believers in

---

[4] Dr. Chambers, Companion to the Revised O. T., p. 74. Dr. Chambers was a member of the American O. T. Revision Committee.

Christ were privileged to have the unadulterated Word of God.

But soon the scene changed; the fury of Satan, robbed of further opportunity to harass the Son of God, turned upon the written Word. Heretical sects, warring for supremacy, corrupted the manuscripts in order to further their ends. "Epiphanius, in his polemic treatise the 'Panarion,' describes not less than eighty heretical parties." [5] The Roman Catholics won. The true church fled into the wilderness, taking pure manuscripts with her.

When the apostle Paul foretold the coming of the great apostasy in his sermon and later in his epistle to the Thessalonians, he declared that there would "come a falling away," *II Thess. 2:3;* and then he added that the "mystery of iniquity doth already work." *II Thess. 2:7.*

Later when he had gathered together, on his journey to Jerusalem, the bishops, those who were over the church of Ephesus, he said, "Of your own selves shall men arise, speaking perverse things, to draw away disciples after them. Therefore watch, and remember, that by the space of three years I ceased not to warn every one night and day with tears." *Acts 20:30,31.*

Though there are many important events in the life of the great apostle which have been left unrecorded, the Holy Spirit deemed it of high importance to put on record this prophecy, to warn us that even from among the elders or bishops there would arise perverse leadership. This prophecy would be fulfilled,—was fulfilled. Until we sense the importance of this great prediction of the Holy Spirit and come to recognize its colossal fulfillment, the Bible must in many things remain a sealed book.

When Paul was warned of the coming apostasy, he aroused the Thessalonians not to be soon shaken or troubled in spirit "by letter as from us." *II Thess. 2:2.* It would have been bold at any time to write a letter to a

---

[5] G. P. Fisher, History of Christian Doctrine, p. 19.

church and sign to it the apostle's name. But how daring must have been that iniquity which would commit that forgery even while the apostle was yet alive! Even in Paul's day, the apostasy was built on lawless acts.

Later in his labors, Paul specifically pointed out three ways in which the apostasy was working; 1, by exalting man's knowledge above the Bible; 2, by spiritualizing the Scriptures away; and lastly, 3, by substituting philosophy for revelation.

I—*False Knowledge Exalted Above Scripture*

Of the first of these dangers we read as follows: "O Timothy, keep that which is committed to thy trust, avoiding profane and vain babblings, and oppositions of science falsely so called." *I Tim. 6:20.*

The Greek word in this verse which is translated "science" is "gnosis." "Gnosis" means knowledge. The apostle condemned, not knowledge in general, but false knowledge. False teachers were placing their own interpretations on Christian truth by reading into it human ideas. This tendency grew and increased until a great system bearing the name of Christianity, known as Gnosticism, was established. To show that this religion was not a theory without an organization among men, but that it had communities and was widespread, I quote from Milman:

"The later Gnostics were bolder, but more consistent innovators on the simple scheme of Christianity. . . . In all the great cities of the East in which Christianity had established its most flourishing communities, sprang up this rival which aspired to a still higher degree of knowledge than was revealed in the Gospel, and boasted that it soared almost as much above the vulgar Christianity as the vulgar paganism."[6]

The mysterious theories of these Gnostics have reappeared in the works of theologians of our day. The following words from the *Americana*, will prove the tend-

---

[6] History of Christianity, Vol. II., p. 107.

ency of this doctrine to break out in our times. Note the place of "æons" in their system:

"There have been no Gnostic sects since the fifth century; but many of the principles of their system of emanations reappear in later philosophical systems, drawn from the same sources as theirs. Plato's lively representation had given to the idea of the Godhead, something substantial, which the Gnostics transferred to their æons." [1]

In fact, the æons system has found a treatment in the Revised Version. Bishop Westcott who was one of the dominating minds of the English New Testament Revision Committee advocates that the Revised New Testament be read in the light of the modern æon theories of the Revisers. He comments thus on the revised reading of Eph. 3:21:

"Some perhaps are even led to pause on the wonderful phrase in Eph. 3:21, margin, 'for all the generations of the age of the ages,' which is represented in English (A. V.) by 'to all generations forever and ever;' and to reflect on the vision so open of a vast æon of the which the elements are æons unfolding, as it were, stage after stage, the manifold powers of one life fulfilled in many ways, each æon the child (so to speak) of that which has gone before." [8]

J. H. Newman, the Oxford divine, who was made a Cardinal after he had left the Church of England for the Church of Rome, and whose doctrines, in whole or in part, were adopted by the majority of the Revisers, did more to influence the religion of the British Empire than any other man since the Reformation. He was invited to sit on the Revision Committee. Dr. S. Parkes Cadman speaks thus, referring to his Gnosticism:

"From the fathers, Newman also derived a speculative angelology which described the unseen universe as inhabited by hosts of intermediate beings who were

[1] Americana (1914), Art., "Gnostics."
[8] Bishop Westcott, Some Lessons of the R. V., pp. 186, 187.

spiritual agents between God and creation. . . . Indeed, Newman's cosmogony was essentially Gnostic, and echoed the teachings of Cerinthus, who is best entitled to be considered as the link between the Judaizing and Gnostic sects." [9]

The following quotation from a magazine of authority gives a description of this modern species of Gnosticism which shows its Romanizing tendency. It also reveals how Bishop Westcott could hold this philosophy, while it names Dr. Philip Schaff, President of both American Committees of Revision, as even more an apostle of this modern Gnosticism:

"The roads which lead to Rome are very numerous. . . . Another road, less frequented and less obvious, but not less dangerous, is the philosophical. There is a strong affinity between the speculative system of development, according to which every thing that is, is true and rational, and the Romish idea of a self-evolving infallible church. . . . No one can read the exhibitions of the Church and of theology written even by Protestants under the influence of the speculative philosophy, without seeing that little more than a change of terminology is required to turn such philosophy into Romanism. Many distinguished men have already in Germany passed, by this bridge, from philosophical skepticism to the Romish Church. A distinct class of the Romanizing portion of the Church of England belongs to this philosophical category. Dr. Nevin had entered this path long before Dr. Schaff came from Germany to point it out to him." [10]

II—*Spiritualizing the Scriptures Away*

The next outstanding phase of the coming apostasy,— spiritualizing the Scriptures away,—is predicted by the apostle:

"But shun profane and vain babblings; for they will increase unto more ungodliness. And their word will eat

---

[9] S. Parkes Cadman, Three Religious Leaders of Oxford, pp. 481, 482.
[10] *Princeton Review*, Jan., 1854, pp. 152, 153.

as doth a canker: of whom is Hymenaeus and Philetus; who concerning the truth have erred, saying that the resurrection is past already; and overthrow the faith of some." *II Tim. 2:16-18.*

The Bible teaches the resurrection as a future event. One way these prominent teachers, full of vanity, could say that it was past, was to teach, as some of their descendants do to-day, that the resurrection is a spiritual process which takes place, say, at conversion. The prediction of the apostle was fulfilled in a great system of Bible spiritualizing or mystifying which subverted the primitive faith. Turning the Scriptures into an allegory was a passion in those days. In our day, allegorizing is not only a passion, but is also a refuge from truth for many leaders with whom we have to do.

III—*Substituting Philosophy for Scripture*

The third way in which the apostasy came, was predicted by the apostle thus:

"Beware lest any man spoil you through philosophy and vain deceit, after the tradition of men, after the rudiments of the world, and not after Christ." *Col. 2:8.*

The philosophy condemned in this passage is not the philosophy found in the sacred Word, but the philosophy which is "after the tradition of men." Even before the days of Christ, the very existence of the Jewish religion was threatened by intellectual leaders of the Jews who were carried away with the subtleties and glamour of pagan philosophy. This same temptress quickly ensnared multitudes who bore the name of Christian.

"Greek philosophy exercised the greatest influence not only on the Christian mode of thought, but also through that on the institutions of the Church. In the completed church we find again the philosophic schools." [11]

The greatest enemies of the infant Christian church, therefore, were not found in the triumphant heathenism which filled the world, but in the rising flood of heresy

---

[11] Harnack, History of Dogma, Vol. I., p. 128.

which, under the name of Christianity, engulfed the truth for many years. This is what brought on the Dark Ages. This rising flood, as we shall see, had multiplied in abundance copies of the Scriptures with bewildering changes in verses and passages within one hundred years after the death of John (100 A. D.). As Irenæus said concerning Marcion, the Gnostic:

"Wherefore also Marcion and his followers have betaken themselves to mutilating the Scriptures, not acknowledging some books at all; and, curtailing the Gospel according to Luke, and the epistles of Paul, they assert that these alone are authentic, which they have themselves shortened." [12]

FUNDAMENTALLY, THERE ARE ONLY TWO STREAMS OF BIBLES

Anyone who is interested enough to read the vast volume of literature on this subject, will agree that down through the centuries there were only two streams of manuscripts.

The first stream which carried the Received Text in Hebrew and Greek, began with the apostolic churches, and reappearing at intervals down the Christian Era among enlightened believers, was protected by the wisdom and scholarship of the pure church in her different phases; by such as the church at Pella in Palestine where Christians fled, when in 70 A. D. the Romans destroyed Jerusalem;[13] by the Syrian Church of Antioch which produced eminent scholarship; by the Italic Church in northern Italy; and also at the same time by the Gallic Church in southern France and by the Celtic Church in Great Britain; by the pre-Waldensian, the Waldensian, and the churches of the Reformation. This first stream appears, with very little change, in the Protestant Bibles of many languages, and in English, in that Bible known as the King James Version, the one which

---

[12] Ante-Nicene Fathers (Scribner's) Vol. I, pp. 484, 485.
[13] G. T. Stokes, Acts of the Apostles, Vol. II, p. 439.

has been in use for three hundred years in the English speaking world. These MSS. have in agreement with them, by far the vast majority of numbers. So vast is this majority that even the enemies of the Received Text admit that nineteen-twentieths and some ninety-nine one-hundredths of all Greek MSS. are of this class; while one hundred per cent of the Hebrew MSS. are for the Received Text.

The second stream is a small one of a very few manuscripts. These last MSS. are represented:

(a)　In Greek:—The Vatican MS., or Codex B, in the library at Rome; and the Sinaitic, or Codex Aleph (ℵ), its brother. We will fully explain about these two MSS. later.

(b)　In Latin:—The Vulgate or Latin Bible of Jerome.

(c)　In English:—The Jesuit Bible of 1582, which later with vast changes is seen in the Douay, or Catholic Bible.

(d)　In English again:—In many modern Bibles which introduce practically all the Catholic readings of the Latin Vulgate which were rejected by the Protestants of the Reformation; among these, prominently, are the Revised Versions.

So the present controversy between the King James Bible in English and the modern versions is the same old contest fought out between the early church and rival sects; later between the Waldenses and the Papists from the fourth to the thirteenth centuries; and later still, between the Reformers and the Jesuits in the sixteenth century.

The Apostle Paul Prepares to Preserve the Truth Against Coming Apostasy

In his later years, the apostle Paul spent more time in preparing the churches for the great future apostasy than in pushing the work farther on. He foresaw that this apostasy would arise in the west. Therefore, he spent years laboring to anchor the Gentile churches of

Europe to the churches of Judea. The Jewish Christians had back of them 1500 years of training. Throughout the centuries God had so molded the Jewish mind that it grasped the idea of sin; of an invisible Godhead; of man's serious condition; of the need for a divine Redeemer. But throughout these same centuries, the Gentile world had sunk lower and lower in frivolity, heathenism, and debauchery. It is worthy of notice that the apostle Paul wrote practically all of his epistles to the Gentile churches,—to Corinth, to Rome, to Philippi, etc. He wrote almost no letters to the Jewish Christians. Therefore, the great burden of his closing days was to anchor the Gentile churches of Europe to the Christian churches of Judea. In fact, it was to secure this end that he lost his life.

"St. Paul did his best to maintain his friendship and alliance with the Jerusalem Church. To put himself right with them, he traveled up to Jerusalem, when fresh fields and splendid prospects were opening up for him in the West. For this purpose he submitted to several days restraint and attendance in the Temple, and the results vindicated his determination." [14]

This is how Paul used churches in Judea as a base,— "For ye, brethren, became followers of the churches of God which in Judea are in Christ Jesus: for ye also have suffered like things of your own countrymen, even as they have of the Jews." *I Thess. 2:14.*

"There is not a word here of the church of Rome being the model after which the other churches were to be formed; it had no such preëminence:—this honor belonged to the churches of Judea; it was according to them, not the church at Rome, that the Asiatic churches were modeled. The purest of all the apostolic churches was that of the Thessalonians, and this was formed after the Christian churches in Judea. Had any preëminence or authority belonged to the church of Rome, the apostle would have

---

[14] Stokes, The Acts of the Apostles, Vol. II, p. 439.

proposed this as a model to all those which he formed, either in Judea, Asia Minor, Greece, or Italy." [15]

EARLY CORRUPTION OF BIBLE MSS.

The last of the apostles to pass away was John. His death is usually placed about 100 A. D. In his closing days, he coöperated in the collecting and forming of those writings we call the New Testament.[16] An ordinary careful reading of Acts, Chapter 15, will prove the scrupulous care with which the early church guarded her sacred writings. And so well did God's true people through the ages agree on what was Scripture and what was not, that no general council of the church, until that of Trent (1645) dominated by the Jesuits, dared to say anything as to what books should comprise the Bible or what texts were or were not spurious.[17]

While John lived, heresy could make no serious headway. He had hardly passed away, however, before perverse teachers infested the Christian Church. The doom of heathenism, as a controlling force before the superior truths of Christianity, was soon foreseen by all. These years were times which saw the New Testament books corrupted in abundance.

Eusebius is witness to this fact. He also relates that the corrupted manuscripts were so prevalent that agreement between the copies was hopeless; and that those who were corrupting the Scriptures, claimed that they really were correcting them.[18]

When the warring sects had been consolidated under the iron hand of Constantine, this heretical potentate adopted the Bible which combined the contradictory versions into one, and so blended the various corruptions with the bulk of pure teachings as to give sanction to the great apostasy now seated on the throne of power.

Beginning shortly after the death of the apostle John,

[15] Dr. Adam Clarke, Commentary on N. T., Vol. II, p. 544.
[16] Eusebius, Eccles. History, Book III, Chap. 24.
[17] Dean Stanley, Essays on Church and State, p. 136.
[18] Eusebius, Eccles. History, Book V., Chap. 28.

four names stand out in prominence whose teachings contributed both to the victorious heresy and to the final issuing of manuscripts of a corrupt New Testament. These names are, 1, Justin Martyr, 2, Tatian, 3, Clement of Alexandria, and 4, Origen. We shall speak first of Justin Martyr.

The year in which the apostle John died, 100 A. D., is given as the date in which Justin Martyr was born. Justin, originally a pagan and of pagan parentage, afterward embraced Christianity and although he is said to have died at heathen hands for his religion, nevertheless, his teachings were of a heretical nature. Even as a Christian teacher, he continued to wear the robes of a pagan philosopher.

In the teachings of Justin Martyr, we begin to see how muddy the stream of pure Christian doctrine was running among the heretical sects fifty years after the death of the apostle John. It was in Tatian, Justin Martyr's pupil, that these regrettable doctrines were carried to alarming lengths, and by his hand committed to writing. After the death of Justin Martyr in Rome, Tatian returned to Palestine and embraced the Gnostic heresy. This same Tatian wrote a Harmony of the Gospels which was called the Diatessaron, meaning four in one. The Gospels were so notoriously corrupted by his hand that in later years a bishop of Syria, because of the errors, was obliged to throw out of his churches no less than two hundred copies of this Diatessaron, since church members were mistaking it for the true Gospel. [19]

We come now to Tatian's pupil known as Clement of Alexandria, 200 A. D. [20] He went much farther than Tatian in that he founded a school at Alexandria which instituted propaganda along these heretical lines. Clement expressly tells us that he would not hand down Christian teachings, pure and unmixed, but rather clothed with precepts of pagan philosophy. All the writings

---

[19] Encyclopedias, "Tatian."
[20] J. Hamlyn Hill, The Diatessaron of Tatian, p. 9.

of the outstanding heretical teachers were possessed by Clement, and he freely quoted from their corrupted MSS. as if they were the pure words of Scripture.[21] His influence in the depravation of Christianity was tremendous. But his greatest contribution, undoubtedly, was the direction given to the studies and activities of Origen, his famous pupil.

When we come to Origen, we speak the name of him who did the most of all to create and give direction to the forces of apostasy down through the centuries. It was he who mightily influenced Jerome, the editor of the Latin Bible known as the Vulgate. Eusebius worshiped at the altar of Origen's teachings. He claims to have collected eight hundred of Origen's letters, to have used Origen's six-column Bible, the Hexapla, in his Biblical labors. Assisted by Pamphilus, he restored and preserved Origen's library. Origen's corrupted MSS. of the Scriptures were well arranged and balanced with subtlety. The last one hundred years have seen much of the so-called scholarship of European and English Christianity dominated by the subtle and powerful influence of Origen.

Origen had so surrendered himself to the furore of turning all Bible events into allegories that he, himself, says, "The Scriptures are of little use to those who understand them as they are written." [22]   In order to estimate Origen rightly, we must remember that as a pupil of Clement, he learned the teachings of the Gnostic heresy and like his master, lightly esteemed the historical basis of the Bible. As Schaff says, "His predilection for Plato (the pagan philosopher) led him into many grand and fascinating errors."[23]   He made himself acquainted with the various heresies and studied under the heathen Ammonius Saccas, founder of Neo-Platonism.

He taught that the soul existed from eternity before it

---

[21] Dean Burgon, The Revision Revised, p. 336.
[22] McClintock and Strong, Art. "Origen."
[23] Dr. Schaff, Church History, Vol. II, p. 791.

inhabited the body, and that after death, it migrated to a higher or a lower form of life according to the deeds done in the body; and finally all would return to the state of pure intelligence, only to begin again the same cycles as before. He believed that the devils would be saved, and that the stars and planets had souls, and were, like men, on trial to learn perfection. In fact, he turned the whole law and Gospel into an allegory.

Such was the man who from his day to this has dominated the endeavors of destructive textual critics. One of the greatest results of his life, was that his teachings became the foundation of that system of education called Scholasticism, which guided the colleges of Latin Europe for nearly one thousand years during the Dark Ages.

Origenism flooded the Catholic Church through Jerome, the father of Latin Christianity. "I love. . . the name of Origen," says the most distinguished theologian of the Roman Catholic Church since 1850, "I will not listen to the notion that so great a soul was lost." [24]

A final word from the learned Scrivener will indicate how early and how deep were the corruptions of the sacred manuscripts:

"It is no less true to fact than paradoxical in sound, that the worst corruptions to which the New Testament has ever been subjected, originated within a hundred years after it was composed; that Irenæus (A.D. 150), and the African Fathers, and the whole Western, with a portion of the Syrian Church, used far inferior manuscripts to those employed by Stunica, or Erasmus, or Stephens thirteen centuries later, when moulding the Textus Receptus." [25]

The basis was laid to oppose a mutilated Bible to the true one. How these corruptions found their way down the centuries and reappear in our revised and modern Bibles, the following pages will tell.

----

[24] Dr. Newman, Apologia pro vita sua, Chapter VII, p. 282.
[25] Scrivener, Introduction to N. T. Criticism, 3rd Edition, p. 511.

CHAPTER II

The Bible Adopted by Constantine and the Pure Bible of the Waldenses

CONSTANTINE became emperor of Rome in 312 A.D. A little later he embraced the Christian faith for himself and for his empire. As this so-called first Christian emperor took the reins of the civil and spiritual world to bring about the amalgamation of paganism and Christianity, he found three types of manuscripts, or Bibles, vying for supremacy: the Textus Receptus or Constantinopolitan, the Palestinian or Eusebio-Origen, and the Egyptian of Hesychius.[1] The adherents of each claimed superiority for their manuscript. Particularly was there earnest contention between the advocates of the Textus Receptus and those of the Eusebio-Origen text.[2] The defenders of the Textus Receptus were of the humbler class who earnestly sought to follow the early church. The Eusebio-Origen text was the product of the intermingling of the pure word of God and Greek philosophy in the mind of Origen. It might be called the adaptation of the Word of God to Gnosticism.

As the Emperor Constantine embraced Christianity, it became necessary for him to choose which of these Bibles he would sanction. Quite naturally he preferred the one edited by Eusebius and written by Origen, the outstanding intellectual figure that had combined Christianity with Gnosticism in his philosophy, even as Constantine himself was the political genius that was seeking to unite Christianity with pagan Rome. Constantine regarded himself as the director and guardian of this anomalous world church, and as such he was responsible for selecting the Bible for the great Christian centers. His pre-

[1] N. B. Swete, Introduction to the Old Testament in Greek, pp. 76-86.
[2] Hort's Introduction, p. 138.

dilection was for the type of Bible whose readings would give him a basis for his imperialistic ideas of the great state church, with ritualistic ostentation and unlimited central power. The philosophy of Origen was well suited to serve Constantine's religio-political theocracy.

Eusebius was a great admirer of Origen and a deep student of his philosophy. He had just edited the fifth column of the Hexapla which was Origen's Bible. Constantine chose this, and asked Eusebius to prepare fifty copies for him. Dr. Ira M. Price refers to the transaction as follows:

"Eusebius of Cæsarea (260-340), the first church historian, assisted by Pamphilus or *vice versa,* issued with all its critical marks the fifth column of the Hexapla, with alternative readings from the other columns, for use in Palestine. The Emperor Constantine gave orders that fifty copies of this edition should be prepared for use in the churches." [3]

Thus we see that Constantine chose the Hexapla Bible of Origen, one of the Eusebio-Origen type. This Bible, chosen by Constantine, was thereby given prestige and influence over the other Bibles, wherever Constantine's authority was recognized. While the Hexapla was the work of Origen, Dr. Price makes it plain that Eusebius and Pamphilus edited this work.

The Vaticanus Manuscript (Codex B) and the Siniaticus Manuscript (Codex Aleph ℵ) belong to the Eusebio-Origen type, and many authorities believe that they were actually two of the fifty copies prepared for Constantine by Eusebius. Dr. Robertson singles out these two manuscripts as possibly two of the fifty Constantine Bibles. He says:

"Constantine himself ordered fifty Greek Bibles from Eusebius, Bishop of Cæsarea, for the churches in Constantinople. It is quite possible that Aleph (ℵ) and B are two of these fifty." [4]

Both these manuscripts were written in Greek, each

[3] Dr. Ira M. Price, The Ancestry of Our English Bible, p. 70.
[4] A. T. Robertson, Introduction to Textual Criticism of N. T., p. 80.

containing the whole Bible, we think, though parts are missing in them now. The Vatican MS. is in the Papal Museum at Rome; the Sinaitic MS. is in the Soviet Museum at Moscow, Russia.

Dr. Gregory, a recent scholar in the field of manuscripts, also thinks of them in connection with the fifty. We quote from him:

"This Manuscript (Vaticanus) is supposed, as we have seen, to have come from the same place as the Sinaitic Manuscript. I have said that these two show connections with each other, and that they would suit very well as a pair of the fifty manuscripts written at Cæsarea for Constantine the Great." [5]

The following quotation is given as evidence that the Sinaitic Manuscript was the work of Origen:

"It (Sinaitic MS.) seems to have been at one time at Cæsarea; one of the correctors (probably of seventh century) adds this note at the end of Esdras, (Ezra): 'This Codex was compared with a very ancient exemplar which had been corrected by the hand of the holy martyr Pamphilus (d. 309); which exemplar contained at the end, the subscription in his own hand: "Taken and corrected according to the Hexapla of Origen: Antonius compared it: I, Pamphilus, corrected it" '. . . . The text of Aleph (ℵ) bears a very close resemblance to that of B." [6]

Two outstanding scholars, Burgon and Miller, thus express their belief that in the Vaticanus and Sinaiticus MSS. we have two of the Bibles prepared by Eusebius for the Emperor:

"Constantine applied to Eusebius for fifty handsome copies, among which it is not improbable that the manuscripts B and Aleph (ℵ) were to be actually found. But even if this is not so, the Emperor would not have selected Eusebius for the order, if that Bishop had not been in the habit of providing copies: and Eusebius in fact carried on the work which he had commenced under his

[5] Dr. Gregory, The Canon and Text of the N. T., p. 345.
[6] Catholic Encyclopedia, Vol. IV, p. 86.

friend Pamphilus, and in which the latter must have followed the path pursued by Origen. Again, Jerome is known to have resorted to this quarter." [7]

Both admirers and foes of the Vaticanus and Sinaiticus Manuscripts admit and contend that these two Codices are remarkably similar. They are so near together as to compel one to believe that they were of common origin. Dr. Philip Schaff says:

"The Roman editors contend, of course, for the primacy of the Vatican against the Sinaitic MS., but admit that they are not far apart." [8]

Eusebius, the author of the Vaticanus, was a great admirer of Origen as noted above, transmitted his views, and preserved and edited his works. Whether or not the Vaticanus and Sinaiticus were actually two of the fifty Bibles furnished by Eusebius for Constantine, at least they belonged to the same family as the Hexapla, the Eusebio-Origen type. So close were the relations of Origen, Eusebius, and Jerome, that Dr. Scrivener says:

"The readings approved by Origen, Eusebius, and Jerome should closely agree." [9]

It is evident that the so-called Christian Emperor gave to the Papacy his indorsement of the Eusebio-Origen Bible. It was from this type of manuscript that Jerome translated the Latin Vulgate which became the authorized Catholic Bible for all time.

The Latin Vulgate, the Sinaiticus, the Vaticanus, the Hexapla, Jerome, Eusebius, and Origen, are terms for ideas that are inseparable in the minds of those who know. The type of Bible selected by Constantine has held the dominating influence at all times in the history of the Catholic Church. This Bible was different from the Bible of the Waldenses, and, as a result of this difference, the Waldenses were the object of hatred and cruel persecution, as we shall now show. In studying this

---

[7] Burgon and Miller, The Traditional Text, p. 163.
[8] Dr. Philip Schaff, Companion to the Greek Testament, p. 115, N. 1.
[9] Dr. Scrivener, Introduction to the Criticism of the N. T., Vol. II, p. 270.

history, we shall see how it was possible for the pure manuscripts, not only to live, but actually to gain the ascendancy in the face of powerful opposition.

A CHANNEL OF COMMUNICATION FROM THE CHURCHES IN JUDEA CARRIED PURE MANUSCRIPTS TO THE PRIMITIVE CHRISTIANS IN WESTERN LANDS

Attentive observers have repeatedly been astonished at the unusual phenomenon exhibited in the meteoric history of the Bible adopted by Constantine. Written in Greek, it was disseminated at a time when Bibles were scarce, owing to the unbridled fury of the pagan emperor, Diocletian. We should naturally think that it would therefore continue long. Such was not the case.

The echo of Diocletian's warfare against the Christians had hardly subsided, when Constantine assumed the imperial purple. Even so far as Great Britain, had the rage of Diocletian penetrated. One would naturally suppose that the Bible which had received the promotion of Constantine, especially when disseminated by that emperor who was the first to show favor to the religion of Jesus, would rapidly have spread everywhere in those days when imperial favor meant everything. The truth is, the opposite was the outcome. It flourished for a short space. The span of one generation sufficed to see it disappear from popular use as if it had been struck by some invisible and withering blast. We turn with amazement to discover the reason for this phenomenon.

This chapter will show that the Textus Receptus was the Bible in possession and use in the Greek Empire, in the countries of Syrian Christianity, in northern Italy, in southern France, and in the British Isles in the second century. This was a full century and more before the Vaticanus and the Sinaiticus saw the light of day.[10] When the apostles of the Roman Catholic Church entered these countries in later centuries they found the people using the Textus Receptus; and it was not without difficulty

---

[10] Burgon, Revision Revised, p. 27.

and a struggle that they were able to displace it and to substitute their Latin Vulgate. This chapter will likewise show that the Textus Receptus belongs to the type of these early apostolic manuscripts that were brought from Judea, and its claim to priority over the Vaticanus and Sinaiticus will be established.

EARLY GREEK CHRISTIANITY—WHICH BIBLE?

First of all, the Textus Receptus was the Bible of early Eastern Christianity. Later it was adopted as the official text of the Greek Catholic Church. There were local reasons which contributed to this result. But, probably, far greater reasons will be found in the fact that the Received Text had authority enough to become, either in itself or by its translation, the Bible of the great Syrian Church; of the Waldensian Church of northern Italy; of the Gallic Church in southern France; and of the Celtic Church in Scotland and Ireland; as well as the official Bible of the Greek Catholic Church. All these churches, some earlier, some later, were in opposition to the Church of Rome and at a time when the Received Text and these Bibles of the Constantine type were rivals. They, as represented in their descendants, are rivals to this day. The Church of Rome built on the Eusebio-Origen type of Bible; these others built on the Received Text. Therefore, because they, themselves, believed that the Received Text was the true apostolic Bible, and further, because the Church of Rome arrogated to itself the power to choose a Bible which bore the marks of systematic depravation, we have the testimony of these five churches to the authenticity and the apostolicity of the Received Text. The following quotation from Dr. Hort is to prove that the Received Text was the Greek New Testament of the East. Note that Dr. Hort always calls it the Constantinopolitan or Antiochian text:

"It is no wonder that the traditional Constantinopolitan text, whether formally official or not, was the Antiochian text of the fourth century. It was equally natural that the text recognized at Constantinople should eventually become in practice the standard New Testament of the East." [11]

EARLY SYRIAN CHRISTIANITY—WHICH BIBLE?

It was at Antioch, capital of Syria, that the believers were first called Christians. And as time rolled on, the Syrian-speaking Christians could be numbered by the thousands. It is generally admitted, that the Bible was translated from the original languages into Syrian about 150 A.D.[12] This version is known as the Peshitto (the correct or simple). This Bible even to-day generally follows the Received Text.[12]

One authority tells us that,—

"The Peshitto in our days is found in use amongst the Nestorians, who have always kept it, by the Monophysites on the plains of Syria, the Christians of St. Thomas in Malabar, and by the Maronites, on the mountain terraces of Lebanon." [14]

Having presented the fact, that the Bible of early Greek Christianity and early Syrian Christianity was not of the Eusebio-Origen or Vaticanus type, but the Received Text, we shall now show that the early Bible of northern Italy, of southern France, and of Great Britain was also the Received Text.

The type of Christianity which first was favored, then raised to leadership by Constantine was that of the Roman Papacy. But this was not the type of Christianity that first penetrated Syria, northern Italy, southern France, and Great Britain.[15] The ancient records of the first believers in Christ in those parts, disclose a Christianity which is not Roman but apostolic. These lands were first penetrated by missionaries, not from Rome, but from Palestine and Asia Minor. And the Greek

[11] Hort's Introduction, p. 143. See also Burgon Revision Revised, p. 134.
[12] Burgon, Revision Revised, p. 27. Note.
[14] Burgon and Miller, The Traditional Text, p. 128.
[15] Dr. T. V. Moore, The Culdee Church, Chapters 3 and 4.

New Testament, the Received Text they brought with
them, or its translation, was of the type from which the
Protestant Bibles, as the King James in English, and the
Lutheran in German, were translated.   We shall pres-
ently see that it differed greatly from the Eusebio-Origen
Greek New Testament.

EARLY ENGLAND—WHICH BIBLE?

Onward then pushed those heroic bands of evangelists
to England, to southern France, and northern Italy. The
Mediterranean was like the trunk of a tree with branches
running out to these parts, the roots of the tree being in
Judea or Asia Minor, from whence the sap flowed westward to fertilize the distant lands.   History does not
possess any record of heroism superior to the sacrifices
and sufferings of the early Christians in the pagan West.
The first believers of ancient Britain nobly held their
ground when the pagan Anglo-Saxons descended on the
land like a flood.   Dean Stanley holds it against Augustine, the missionary sent by the Pope in 596 A.D. to convert England, that he treated with contempt the early
Christian Britons.[16] Yes, more, he connived with the
Anglo-Saxons in their frightful extermination of that
pious people.   And after Augustine's death, when those
same pagan Anglo-Saxons so terrified the papal leaders in
England that they fled back to Rome, it was the British
Christians of Scotland who occupied the forsaken fields.
It is evident from this that British Christianity did not
come from Rome. Furthermore, Dr. Adam Clarke claims
that the examination of Irish customs reveals that they
have elements which were imported into Ireland from
Asia Minor by early Christians.[18]

Since Italy, France, and Great Britain were once provinces of the Roman Empire, the first translations of the
Bible by the early Christians in those parts were made
into Latin.   The early Latin translations were very dear

---

[16] Dean Stanley, Historic Memorials of Canterbury, pp. 33, 34. Quoted in
Cathcart, Ancient British and Irish Churches, p. 12.
[18] Dr. Clarke, Commentaries. Comment on Matt. 1:18.

to the hearts of these primitive churches, and as Rome did not send any missionaries toward the West before 250 A.D., the early Latin Bibles were well established before these churches came into conflict with Rome. Not only were such translations in existence long before the Vulgate was adopted by the Papacy, and well established, but the people for centuries refused to supplant their old Latin Bibles by the Vulgate. "The old ·Latin versions were used longest by the western Christians who would not bow to the authority of Rome—e. g., the Donatists; the Irish in Ireland, Britain, and the Continent; the Albigenses, etc." [19]

God in His wisdom had invested these Latin versions by His Providence with a charm that outweighed the learned artificiality of Jerome's Vulgate. This is why they persisted through the centuries. A characteristic often overlooked in considering versions, and one that cannot be too greatly emphasized, needs to be pointed out in comparing the Latin Bible of the Waldenses, of the Gauls, and of the Celts with the later Vulgate. To bring before you the unusual charm of those Latin Bibles, I quote from the *Forum* of June, 1887:

"The old Italic version into the rude Low Latin of the second century held its own as long as Latin continued to be the language of the people. The critical version of Jerome never displaced it, and only replaced it when the Latin ceased to be a living language, and became the language of the learned. The Gothic version of Ulfilas, in the same way, held its own until the tongue in which it was written ceased to exist. Luther's Bible was the first genuine beginning of modern German literature. In Germany, as in England, many critical translations have been made, but they have fallen stillborn from the press. The reason of these facts seems to be this: that the languages into which these versions were made, were almost perfectly adapted to express the broad, generic simplicity of the original text. Microscopic accuracy of phrase and classical nicety of expression may be very

---

[19] Jacobus, Catholic and Protestant Bibles Compared, p. 200, Note 15.

well for the student in his closet, but they do not represent the human and divine simplicity of the Scriptures to the mass of those for whom the Scriptures were written. To render that, the translator needs not only a simplicity of mind rarely to be found in companies of learned critics, but also a language possessing in some large measure that broad, simple, and generic character which we have seen to belong to the Hebrew and to the Greek of the New Testament. It was partly because the Low Latin of the second century, and the Gothic of Ulfilas, and the rude, strong German of Luther had that character in a remarkable degree, that they were capable of rendering the Scriptures with a faithfulness which guaranteed their permanence." [20]

For nine hundred years, we are told, the first Latin translations held their own after the Vulgate appeared.[21] The Vulgate was born about 380 A.D. Nine hundred years later brings us to about 1280 A.D. This accords well with the fact that at the famous Council of Toulouse, 1229 A.D., the Pope gave orders for the most terrible crusade to be waged against the simple Christians of southern France and northern Italy who would not bow to his power. Cruel, relentless, devastating, this war was waged, destroying the Bibles, books, and every vestige of documents to tell the story of the Waldenses and Albigenses. Since then, some authorities speak of the Waldenses as having as their Bible, the Vulgate. We regret to dispute these claims. But when we consider that the Waldenses were, so to speak, in their mountain fastnesses, on an island in the midst of a sea of nations using the Vulgate, without doubt they knew and possessed the Vulgate; but the Italic, the earlier Latin, was their own Bible, the one for which they lived and suffered and died. Moreover, to the east was Constantinople, the center of Greek Catholicism, whose Bible was the Received Text; while a little farther east, was the noble Syrian Church which also had the Received Text. In

---

[20] Fulton in the *Forum*, June, 1887.
[21] Jacobus, Catholic and Protestant Bibles, p. 4.

touch with these, northern Italy could easily verify her text.

It is very evident that the Latin Bible of early British Christianity not only was not the Latin Bible of the Papacy, that is, the Vulgate, but it was at such variance with the Vulgate as to engender strife. The following quotation from Dr. Von Dobschutz will verify these two facts:

"When Pope Gregory found some Anglo-Saxon youths at the slave market of Rome and perceived that in the North there was still a pagan nation to be baptized, he sent one of his monks to England, and this monk, who was Saint Augustine, took with him the Bible and introduced it to the Anglo-Saxons, and one of his followers brought with him from Rome pictures showing the Biblical history, and decorated the walls of the church in the monastery of Wearmouth. We do not enter here into the difficult question of the relations between this newly founded Anglo-Saxon church and the old Iro-Scottish church. Differences of Bible text had something to do with the pitiful struggles which arose between the churches and ended in the devastation of the older one." [22]

Famous in history among all centers of Bible knowledge and Bible Christianity was Iona, on the little island of Hy, off the northwest coast of Scotland. Its most historic figure was Columba. Upon this island rock, God breathed out His Holy Spirit and from this center, to the tribes of northern Europe. When Rome awoke to the necessity of sending out missionaries to extend her power, she found Great Britain and northern Europe already professing a Christianity whose origin could be traced back through Iona to Asia Minor. About 600 A.D. Rome sent missionaries to England and to Germany, to bring these simple Bible Christians under her dominion, as much as to subdue the pagans. D'Aubigne has furnished us this picture of Iona and her missions:

"D'Aubigne says that Columba esteemed the cross of Christ higher than the royal blood which flowed in his

---

[22] Von Dobschutz, The Influence of the Bible on Civilization, pp. 61, 62.

veins, and that *precious manuscripts were brought to Iona,* where a theological school was founded and the Word was studied. 'Erelong a missionary spirit breathed over this ocean rock, so justly named "the light of the Western world." ' British missionaries carried the light of the gospel to the Netherlands, France, Switzerland, Germany, yea, even into Italy, and did more for the conversion of central Europe than the half-enslaved Roman Church." [23]

EARLY FRANCE—WHICH BIBLE?

In southern France, when in 177 A.D. the Gallic Christians were frightfully massacred by the heathen, a record of their suffering was drawn up by the survivors and sent, not to the Pope of Rome, but to their brethren in Asia Minor.[24] Milman claims that the French received their Christianity from Asia Minor.

These apostolic Christians in southern France were undoubtedly those who gave effective help in carrying the Gospel to Great Britain.[25] And as we have seen above, there was a long and bitter struggle between the Bible of the British Christians and the Bible which was brought later to England by the missionaries of Rome. And as there were really only two Bibles,—the official version of Rome, and the Received Text,—we may safely conclude that the Gallic (or French) Bible, as well as the Celtic (or British), were the Received Text. Neander claims, as follows, that the first Christianity in England, came not from Rome, but from Asia Minor, probably through France:

"But the peculiarity of the later British church is evidence against its origin from Rome; for in many ritual matters it departed from the usage of the Romish Church, and agreed much more nearly with the churches of Asia Minor. It withstood, for a long time, the authority of the Romish Papacy. This circumstance would seem to indicate, that the Britons had received their

---

[23] J. N. Andrews and L. R. Conradi, History of the Sabbath, pp. 581, 582.
[24] See Cathcart, Ancient British and Irish Churches, p. 16.
[25] Idem, p. 17.

Christianity, either immediately, or through Gaul, from Asia Minor,— a thing quite possible and easy, by means of the commercial intercourse. The later Anglo-Saxons, who opposed the spirit of ecclesiastical independence among the Britons, and endeavored to establish the church supremacy of Rome, were uniformly inclined to trace back the church establishments to a Roman origin; from which effort many false legends as well as this might have arisen." [26]

THE WALDENSES IN NORTHERN ITALY—WHICH BIBLE?

That the messengers of God who carried manuscripts from the churches of Judea to the churches of northern Italy and on, brought to the forerunners of the Waldenses a Bible different from the Bible of Roman Catholicism, I quote the following:

"The method which Allix has pursued, in his History of the Churches of Piedmont, is to show that in the ecclesiastical history of every century, from the fourth century, which he considers a period early enough for the enquirer after apostolical purity of doctrine, there are clear proofs that doctrines, unlike those which the Romish Church holds, and conformable to the belief of the Waldensian and Reformed Churches, were maintained by theologians of the north of Italy down to the period, when the Waldenses first came into notice. Consequently the opinions of the Waldenses were not new to Europe in the eleventh or twelfth centuries, and there is nothing improbable in the tradition, that the Subalpine Church persevered in its integrity in an uninterrupted course from the first preaching of the Gospel in the valleys." [27]

There are many earlier historians who agree with this view. [28] It is held that the pre-Waldensian Christians of northern Italy could not have had doctrines purer than Rome unless their Bible was purer than Rome's; that is, was not of Rome's falsified manuscripts. [29]

---

[26] Neander, History of the Christian Religion and Church, Vol. 1, pp. 85, 86.
[27] Gilly, Waldensian Researches, pp. 118, 119.
[28] Allix, Leger, Gilly, Comba, Nolan.
[29] Comba, the Waldenses of Italy, p. 188.

It is inspiring to bring to life again the outstanding history of an authority on this point. I mean Leger. This noble scholar of Waldensian blood was the apostle of his people in the terrible massacres of 1655, and labored intelligently to preserve their ancient records. His book, the "General History of the Evangelical Churches of the Piedmontese Valleys," published in French in 1669, and called "scarce" in 1825, is the prized object of scholarly searchers. It is my good fortune to have that very book before me. Leger, when he calls Olivetan's French Bible of 1537 "entire and pure," says:

"I say 'pure' because all the ancient exemplars, which formerly were found among the Papists, were full of falsifications, which caused Beza to say in his book on Illustrious Men, in the chapter on the Vaudois, that one must confess it was by means of the Vaudois of the Valleys that France today has the Bible in her own language. This godly man, Olivetan, in the preface of his Bible, recognizes with thanks to God, that since the time of the apostles, or their immediate successors, the torch of the gospel has been lit among the Vaudois (or the dwellers in the Valleys of the Alps, two terms which mean the same), and has never since been extinguished." [30]

The Waldenses of northern Italy were foremost among the primitive Christians of Europe in their resistance to the Papacy. They not only sustained the weight of Rome's oppression but they were successful in retaining the torch of truth until the Reformation took it from their hands and held it aloft to the world. Veritably they fulfilled the prophecy of Revelation concerning the church which fled into the wilderness where she hath a place prepared of God. *Revelation 12:6,14.* They rejected the mysterious doctrines, the hierarchal priesthood and the worldly titles of Rome, while they clung to the simplicity of the Bible.

The agents of the Papacy have done their utmost to calumniate their character, to destroy the records of their

---

[30] Leger, General Hist. of the Vaudois Churches, p. 165.

noble past, and to leave no trace of the cruel persecution they underwent. They went even farther,—they made use of words written against ancient heresies to strike out the name of the heretics and fill the blank space by inserting the name of the Waldenses. Just as if, in a book written to record the lawless deeds of some bandit, like Jessie James, his name should be stricken out and the name of Abraham Lincoln substituted. The Jesuit Gretser in a book written against the heretics of the twelfth and thirteenth centuries, put the name Waldenses at the point where he struck out the name of these heretics.[31] Nevertheless, we greet with joy the history of their great scholars who were ever a match for Rome.

In the fourth century, Helvidius, a great scholar of northern Italy, accused Jerome, whom the Pope had empowered to form a Bible in Latin for Catholicism, with using corrupt Greek manuscripts.[32] How could Helvidius have accused Jerome of employing corrupt Greek MSS. if Helvidius had not had the pure Greek manuscripts? And so learned and so powerful in writing and teaching was Jovinian, the pupil of Helvidius, that it demanded three of Rome's most famous fathers—Augustine, Jerome, and Ambrose—to unite in opposing Jovinian's influence. Even then, it needed the condemnation of the Pope and the banishment of the Emperor to prevail. But Jovinian's followers lived on and made the way easier for Luther.

History does not afford a record of cruelty greater than that manifested by Rome toward the Waldenses. It is impossible to write fully the inspiring history of this persecuted people, whose origin goes back to apostolic days and whose history is ornamented with stories of gripping interest. Rome has obliterated the records. Dr. DeSanctis, many years a Catholic official at Rome, some time official Censor of the Inquisition and later a convert to Protestantism, thus reports the conversation

---

[31] W. S. Gilly, Waldensian Researches, p. 8, note.
[32] Post-Nicene Fathers, Vol. VI. p. 338 (Christian Lit. Ed.)

of a Waldensian scholar as he points out to others the ruins of Palatine Hill, Rome:

" 'See,' said the Waldensian, 'a beautiful monument of ecclesiastical antiquity. These rough materials are the ruins of the two great Palatine libraries, one Greek and the other Latin, where the precious manuscripts of our ancestors were collected, and which Pope Gregory I, called the Great, caused to be burned.' " [33]

The destruction of Waldensian records beginning about 600 A.D. by Gregory I, was carried through with thoroughness by the secret agents of the Papacy.

"It is a singular thing," says Gilly, "that the destruction or rapine, which has been so fatal to Waldensian documents, should have pursued them even to the place of security, to which all, that remained, were consigned by Morland, in 1658, the library of the University of Cambridge. The most ancient of these relics were ticketed in seven packets, distinguished by letters of the alphabet, from A to G. The whole of these were missing when I made inquiry for them in 1823." [34]

ANCIENT DOCUMENTS OF THE WALDENSES

There are modern writers who attempt to fix the beginning of the Waldenses from Peter Waldo, who began his work about 1175. This is a mistake. The historical name of this people as properly derived from the valleys where they lived, is Vaudois. Their enemies, however, ever sought to date their origin from Waldo. Waldo was an agent, evidently raised up of God to combat the errors of Rome. Gilly, who made extensive research concerning the Waldenses, pictures Waldo in his study at Lyon, France, with associates, a committee, "like the translators of our own Authorized Version." [35] Nevertheless the history of the Waldenses, or Vaudois, begins centuries before the days of Waldo.

There remains to us in the ancient Waldensian language, "The Noble Lesson" (La Nobla Leyçon), written

---

[33] DeSanctis, Popery, Puseyism, Jesuitism, p. 53.
[34] Gilly, Waldensian Researches, p. 80.
[35] Comba, Waldenses of Italy, p. 169, note 596.

about the year 1100 A. D., which assigns the first opposition of the Waldenses to the Church of Rome to the days
of Constantine the Great, when Sylvester was Pope. This
may be gathered from the following extract:

"All the Popes, which have been from Sylvester to the
present time." (Que tuit li papa, que foron de Silvestre
en tro en aquest.) [36]

Thus when Christianity, emerging from the long persecutions of pagan Rome, was raised to imperial favor
by the Emperor Constantine, the Italic Church in northern Italy—later the Waldenses—is seen standing in opposition to papal Rome. Their Bible was of the family
of the renowned Itala. It was that translation into
Latin which represents the Received Text. Its very name
"Itala" is derived from the Italic district, the regions of
the Vaudois. Of the purity and reliability of this version,
Augustine, speaking of different Latin Bibles (about 400
A.D.) says:

"Now among translations themselves the Italian
(Itala) is to be preferred to the others, for it keeps closer
to the words without prejudice to clearness of expression." [37]

The old Waldensian liturgy which they used in their
services down through the centuries contained "texts of
Scripture of the ancient Version called the Italick." [38]

The Reformers held that the Waldensian Church was
formed about 120 A.D., from which date on, they passed
down from father to son the teachings they received
from the apostles. [39] The Latin Bible, the Italic, was
translated from the Greek not later than 157 A.D. [40] We
are indebted to Beza, the renowned associate of Calvin,
for the statement that the Italic Church dates from 120
A.D. From the illustrious group of scholars which gathered round Beza, 1590 A.D., we may understand how the

---

[36] Gilly, Excursions to the Piedmont, Appendix II, p. 10.
[37] Nicene and Post-Nicene Fathers (Christian Lit. Ed.), Vol. II, p. 542.
[38] Allix, Churches of Piedmont (1690), p. 37.   [39] Idem, p. 177.
[40] Scrivener's Introduction, Vol. II, p. 43.

Received Text was the bond of union between great historic churches. As the sixteenth century is closing, we see in the beautiful Swiss city of Geneva, Beza, an outstanding champion of Protestantism, the scholar Cyril Lucar, later to become the head of the Greek Catholic Church, and Diodati, also a foremost scholar. As Beza astonishes and confounds the world by restoring manuscripts of that Greek New Testament from which the King James is translated, Diodati takes the same and translates into Italian a new and famous edition, adopted and circulated by the Waldenses.[41] Leger, the Waldensian historian of his people, studied under Diodati at Geneva. He returned as pastor to the Waldenses and led them in their flight from the terrible massacre of 1655.[42] He prized as his choicest treasure the Diodati Bible, the only worldly possession he was able to preserve. Cyril Lucar hastened to Alexandria where Codex A, the Alexandrian Manuscript, is lying, and laid down his life to introduce the Reformation and the Reformers' pure light regarding the books of the Bible.

At the same time another group of scholars, bitterly hostile to the first group, were gathered at Rheims, France. There the Jesuits, assisted by Rome and backed by all the power of Spain, brought forth an English translation of the Vulgate. In its preface they expressly declared that the Vulgate had been translated in 1300 into Italian and in 1400 into French, "the sooner to shake out of the deceived people's hands, the false heretical translations of a sect called Waldenses." This proves that Waldensian Versions existed in 1300 and 1400. It was the Vulgate, Rome's corrupt Scriptures against the Received Text—the New Testament of the apostles, of the Waldenses, and of the Reformers.

That Rome in early days corrupted the manuscripts while the Italic Church handed them down in their apostolic purity, Allix, the renowned scholar, testifies. He

---

[41] McClintock & Strong, Encycl., Art. "Waldenses."
[42] Gilly, Researches, pp. 79, 80.

reports the following as Italic articles of faith: "They receive only, saith he, what is written in the Old and New Testament. They say, that the Popes of Rome, and other priests, have depraved the Scriptures by their doctrines and glosses." [43]

It is recognized that the Itala was translated from the Received Text (Syrian, Hort calls it) ; that the Vulgate is the Itala with the readings of the Received Text removed." [44]

WALDENSIAN BIBLES

Four Bibles produced under Waldensian influence touched the history of Calvin: namely, a Greek, a Waldensian vernacular, a French, and an Italian. Calvin himself was led to his great work by Olivetan, a Waldensian. Thus was the Reformation brought to Calvin, that brilliant student of the Paris University. Farel, also a Waldensian, besought him to come to Geneva and open up a work there. Calvin felt that he should labor in Paris. According to Leger, Calvin recognized a relationship to the Calvins of the valley of St. Martin, one of the Waldensian Valleys. [45]

Finally, persecution at Paris and the solicitation of Farel caused Calvin to settle at Geneva, where, with Beza, he brought out an edition of the Textus Receptus,—the one the author now uses in his college class rooms, as edited by Scrivener. Of Beza, Dr. Edgar says that he "astonished and confounded the world" with the Greek manuscripts he unearthed. This later edition of the Received Text is in reality a Greek New Testament brought out under Waldensian influence. Unquestionably, the leaders of the Reformation, German, French, and English, were convinced that the Received Text was the genuine New Testament, not only by its own irresistible history and internal evidence, but also because it matched with

---

[43] Allix, Churches of Piedmont, pp. 288, 11.
[44] Kenyon, Our Bible and the Ancient Manuscripts, pp. 169, 176.
[45] Leger, History of the Vaudois, p. 167.

the Received Text which in Waldensian form came down from the days of the apostles.

The other three Bibles of Waldensian connection were due to three men who were at Geneva with Calvin, or, when he died, with Beza, his successor, namely, Olivetan, Leger, and Diodati. How readily the two streams of descent of the Received Text, through the Greek East and the Waldensian West, ran together, is illustrated by the meeting of the Olivetan Bible and the Received Text. Olivetan, one of the most illustrious pastors of the Waldensian Valleys, a relative of Calvin, according to Leger,[46] and a splendid student, translated the New Testament into French. Leger bore testimony that the Olivetan Bible, which accorded with the Textus Receptus, was unlike the old manuscripts of the Papists, because they were full of falsification. Later, Calvin edited a second edition of the Olivetan Bible. The Olivetan in turn became the basis of the Geneva Bible in English, which was the leading version in England in 1611 when the King James appeared.

Diodati, who succeeded Beza in the chair of Theology at Geneva, translated the Received Text into Italian. This version was adopted by the Waldenses, although there was in use at that time a Waldensian Bible in their own peculiar language. This we know because Sir Samuel Morland, under the protection of Oliver Cromwell, received from Leger the Waldensian New Testament which now lies in the Cambridge University library. After the devastating massacre of the Waldenses in 1655, Leger felt that he should collect and give into the hands of Sir Samuel Morland as many pieces of the ancient Waldensian literature as were available.

It is interesting to trace back the Waldensian Bible which Luther had before him when he translated the New Testament. Luther used the Tepl Bible, named from Tepl, Bohemia. This Tepl manuscript represented a translation of the Waldensian Bible into the German

---

[46] Leger, History of the Vaudois, p. 167.

which was spoken before the days of the Reformation."
Of this remarkable manuscript, Comba says:

"When the manuscript of Tepl appeared, the attention
of the learned was aroused by the fact that the text it
presents corresponds word for word with that of the first
three editions of the ancient German Bible. Then Louis
Keller, an original writer, with the decided opinions of
a layman and versed in the history of the sects of the
Middle Ages, declared the Tepl manuscript to be Waldensian. Another writer, Hermann Haupt, who belongs to
the old Catholic party, supported his opinion vigorous-
ly." [48]

From Comba we also learn that the Tepl manuscript
has an origin different from the version adopted by the
Church of Rome; that it seems to agree rather with the
Latin versions anterior to Jerome, the author of the Vulgate; and that Luther followed it in his translation,
which probably is the reason why the Catholic Church
reproved Luther for following the Waldenses. [49] Another
peculiarity is its small size, which seems to single it out
as one of those little books which the Waldensian evangelists carried with them hidden under their rough
cloaks. [50] We have, therefore, an indication of how much
the Reformation under Luther as well as Luther's Bible
owed to the Waldenses.

Waldensian influence, both from the Waldensian
Bibles and from Waldensian relationships, entered into
the King James translation of 1611. Referring to the
King James translators, one author speaks thus of a Waldensian Bible they used:

"It is known that among modern versions they consulted was an Italian, and though no name is mentioned,
there cannot be room for doubt that it was the elegant
translation made with great ability from the original
Scriptures by Giovanni Diodati, which had only recently
(1607) appeared at Geneva." [51]

---

[47] Comba, The Waldenses of Italy, p. 191.   [48] Idem, p. 190.
[49] Idem, p. 192.   [50] Idem, p. 191, note 679.
[51] Dr. Benjamin Warfield of Princeton University, Collections of Opinions
and Reviews, Vol. II, p. 99.

It is therefore evident that the translators of 1611 had before them four Bibles which had come under Waldensian influences: the Diodati in Italian, the Olivetan in French, the Lutheran in German, and the Genevan in English. We have every reason to believe that they had access to at least six Waldensian Bibles written in the old Waldensian vernacular.

Dr. Nolan, who had already acquired fame for his Greek and Latin scholarship, and researches into Egyptian chronology, and was a lecturer of note, spent twenty-eight years to trace back the Received Text to its apostolic origin. He was powerfully impressed to examine the history of the Waldensian Bible. He felt certain that researches in this direction would demonstrate that the Italic New Testament, or the New Testament of those primitive Christians of northern Italy whose lineal descendants the Waldenses were, would turn out to be the Received Text. He says:

"The author perceived, without any labor of inquiry, that it derived its name from that diocese, which has been termed the Italick, as contradistinguished from the Roman. This is a supposition, which receives a sufficient confirmation from the fact,—that the principal copies of that version have been preserved in that diocese, the metropolitan church of which was situated in Milan. The circumstance is at present mentioned, as the author thence formed a hope, that some remains of the primitive Italick version might be found in the early translations made by the Waldenses, who were the lineal descendants of the Italick Church; and who have asserted their independence against the usurpations of the Church of Rome, and have ever enjoyed the free use of the Scriptures. In the search to which these considerations have led the author, his fondest expectations have been fully realized. It has furnished him with abundant proof on that point to which his inquiry was chiefly directed; as it has supplied him with the unequivocal testimony of a truly apostolical branch of the primitive church, that the celebrated text of the heavenly witnesses was adopted in the version which prevailed in the Latin Church, previously to the introduction of the modern Vulgate." [52]

How the Bible Adopted by Constantine Was Set Aside

Where did this Vaudois Church amid the rugged peaks of the Alps secure these uncorrupted manuscripts? In the silent watches of the night, along the lonely paths of Asia Minor where robbers and wild beasts lurked, might have been seen the noble missionaries carrying manuscripts, and verifying documents from the churches in Judea to encourage their struggling brethren under the iron heel of the Papacy. The sacrificing labors of the apostle Paul were bearing fruit. His wise plan to anchor the Gentile churches of Europe to the churches of Judea, provided the channel of communication which defeated continually and finally the bewildering pressure of the Papacy. Or, as the learned Scrivener has beautifully put it:

"Wide as is the region which separates Syria from Gaul, there must have been in very early times some remote communication by which the stream of Eastern testimony, or tradition, like another Alpheus, rose up again with fresh strength to irrigate the regions of the distant West." [53]

We have it now revealed how Constantine's Hexapla Bible was successfully met. A powerful chain of churches, few in number compared with the manifold congregations of an apostate Christianity, but enriched with the eternal conviction of truth and with able scholars, stretched from Palestine to Scotland. If Rome in her own land was unable to beat down the testimony of apostolic Scriptures, how could she hope, in the Greek speaking world of the distant and hostile East, to maintain the supremacy of her Greek Bible? The Scriptures of the apostle John and his associates, the traditional text, —the Textus Receptus, if you please,—arose from the

---

[52] Dr. Frederick Nolan, Integrity of the Greek Vulgate, pp. xvii, xviii.
[53] Scrivener, Introduction, Vol. II, pp. 299, 300.

place of humiliation forced on it by Origen's Bible in the hands of Constantine and became the Received Text of Greek Christianity. And when the Greek East for one thousand years was completely shut off from the Latin West, the noble Waldenses in northern Italy still possessed in Latin the Received Text.

To Christians preserving apostolic Christianity, the world owes the Bible. It is not true, as the Roman Church claims, that she gave the Bible to the world. What she gave was an impure text, a text with thousands of verses so changed as to make way for her unscriptural doctrines. While upon those who possessed the veritable Word of God, she poured out through long centuries her stream of cruel persecution. Or, in the words of another writer:

"The Waldenses were among the first of the peoples of Europe to obtain a translation of the Holy Scriptures. Hundreds of years before the Reformation, they possessed the Bible in manuscript in their native tongue. They had the truth unadulterated, and this rendered them the special objects of hatred and persecution. . . . Here for a thousand years, witnesses for the truth maintained the ancient faith. . . . In a most wonderful manner it (the Word of Truth) was preserved uncorrupted through all the ages of darkness." [54]

The struggle against the Bible adopted by Constantine was won. But another warfare, another plan to deluge the Latin west with a corrupt Latin Bible was preparing. We hasten to see how the world was saved from Jerome and his Origenism.

NOTE: The two great families of Greek Bibles are well illustrated in the work of that outstanding scholar, Erasmus. Before he gave to the Reformation the New Testament in Greek, he divided all Greek MSS. into two classes: those which agreed with the Received Text and those which agreed with the Vaticanus MS. [55]

[54] E. G. White, Great Controversy, pp. 65, 66, 69.
[55] Nolan, Inquiry p. 413.

THE TWO PARALLEL STREAMS OF BIBLES

Apostles (Original).	Apostates (Corrupted Originals).
Received Text (Greek).	Sinaiticus and Vaticanus Bible (Greek).
Waldensian Bible (Italic).	Vulgate (Latin). Church of Rome's Bible.
Erasmus (Received Text Restored).	Vaticanus (Greek).
Luther's Bible, D u t c h, French, I t a l i a n, etc., (from Received Text).	French, Spanish, Italian, etc., (from Vulgate).
Tyndale, (English) 1535 (from Received Text).	Rheims (English) from Vulgate (Jesuit Bible of 1582).
King James, 1611 (from Received Text).	Oxford Movement.
	Wescott and Hort (B and Aleph). English Revised 1881.
	Dr. Philip Schaff (B and Aleph). American Revised 1901.

The King James from the Received Text has been the Bible of the English speaking world for 300 years. This has given the Received Text, and the Bibles translated from it into other tongues, standing and authority. At the same time, it neutralized the dangers of the Catholic manuscripts and the Bibles in other tongues translated from them.

CHAPTER III

The Reformers Reject the Bible of the Papacy

THE Papacy, defeated in her hope to control the version of the Bible in the Greek world when the Greek New Testament favored by Constantine was driven into retirement, adopted two measures which kept Europe under its domination. First, the Papacy was against the flow of Greek language and literature to Western Europe. All the treasures of the classical past were held back in the Eastern Roman Empire, whose capital was Constantinople. For nearly one thousand years, the western part of Europe was a stranger to the Greek tongue. As Doctor Hort says:

"The West became exclusively Latin, as well as estranged from the East; with local exceptions, interesting in themselves and valuable to us but devoid of all extensive influence, the use and knowledge of the Greek language died out in Western Europe." [1]

When the use and knowledge of Greek died out in Western Europe, all the valuable Greek records, history, archæology, literature, and science remained untranslated and unavailable to western energies. No wonder, then, that this opposition to using the achievements of the past brought on the Dark Ages (476 A.D. to 1453 A.D.).

This darkness prevailed until the half-century preceding 1453 A.D. when refugees, fleeing from the Greek world threatened by the Turks, came west introducing Greek language and literature. After Constantinople fell in 1453, thousands of valuable manuscripts were secured by the cities and centers of learning in Europe.

---

[1] Hort's Introduction, p. 142.

Europe awoke as from the dead, and sprang forth to newness of life. Columbus discovered America. Erasmus printed the Greek New Testament. Luther assailed the corruptions of the Latin Church. Revival of learning and the Reformation followed swiftly.

The second measure adopted by the Pope which held the Latin West in his power was to stretch out his hands to Jerome (about 400 A.D.), the monk of Bethlehem, reputed the greatest scholar of his age, and appeal to him to compose a Bible in Latin similar to the Bible adopted by Constantine in Greek. Jerome, the hermit of Palestine, whose learning was equaled only by his boundless vanity, responded with alacrity. Jerome was furnished with all the funds that he needed and was assisted by many scribes and copyists.

THE ORIGENISM OF JEROME

By the time of Jerome, the barbarians from the north who later founded the kingdoms of modern Europe, such as England, France, Germany, Italy, etc., were overrunning the Roman Empire. They cared nothing for the political monuments of the empire's greatness, for these they leveled to the dust. But they were overawed by the external pomp and ritual of the Roman Church. Giants in physique, they were children in learning. They had been trained from childhood to render full and immediate submission to their pagan gods. This same attitude of mind they bore toward the Papacy, as one by one they substituted the saints, the martyrs, and the images of Rome for their former forest gods. But there was danger that greater light might tear them away from Rome.

If, in Europe, these children fresh from the north were to be held submissive to such doctrines as the papal supremacy, transubstantiation, purgatory, celibacy of the priesthood, vigils, worship of relics, and the burning of daylight candles, the Papacy must offer, as a record of revelation, a Bible in Latin which would be as Origenistic as the Bible in Greek adopted by Constantine. Therefore, the Pope turned to Jerome to bring forth a new version in Latin.

Jerome was devotedly committed to the textual criticism of Origen, "an admirer of Origen's critical principles," as Swete says.[2] To be guided aright in his forthcoming translation, by models accounted standard in the semi-pagan Christianity of his day, Jerome repaired to the famous library of Eusebius and Pamphilus at Cæsarea, where the voluminous manuscripts of Origen had been preserved.[3] Among these was a Greek Bible of the Vaticanus and Sinaiticus type.[4] Both these versions retained a number of the seven books which Protestants have rejected as being spurious. This may be seen by examining those manuscripts. These manuscripts of Origen, influenced Jerome more in the New Testament than in the Old, since finally he used the Hebrew text in translating the Old Testament. Moreover, the Hebrew Bible did not have these spurious books. Jerome admitted that these seven books—Tobith, Wisdom, Judith, Baruch, Ecclesiasticus, 1st and 2nd Maccabees—did not belong with the other writings of the Bible. Nevertheless, the Papacy endorsed them,[5] and they are found in the Latin Vulgate, and in the Douay, its English translation.

The existence of those books in Origen's Bible is sufficient evidence to reveal that tradition and Scripture were on an equal footing in the mind of that Greek theologian. His other doctrines, as purgatory, transubstantiation, etc., had now become as essential to the imperialism of the Papacy as was the teaching that tradition had equal authority with the Scriptures. Doctor Adam Clarke indicates Origen as the first teacher of purgatory.

THE VULGATE OF JEROME

The Latin Bible of Jerome, commonly known as the Vulgate, held authoritative sway for one thousand years.

---

[2] Swete, Introduction to Greek O. T., p. 86.
[3] Jacobus, Cath. and Prot. Bibles, p. 4.   [4] Price, Ancestry, pp. 69, 70,
[5] Jacobus, p. 6.

The services of the Roman Church were held at that time in a language which still is the sacred language of the Catholic clergy, the Latin.

Jerome in his early years had been brought up with an enmity to the Received Text, then universally known as the Greek Vulgate.* The word Vulgate means, "commonly used," or "current." This word Vulgate has been appropriated from the Bible to which it rightfully belongs, that is, to the Received Text, and given to the Latin Bible. In fact, it took hundreds of years before the common people would call Jerome's Latin Bible, the Vulgate.' The very fact that in Jerome's day the Greek Bible, from which the King James is translated into English, was called the Vulgate, is proof in itself that, in the church of the living God, its authority was supreme. Diocletian (302-312 A.D.), the last in the unbroken line of pagan emperors, had furiously pursued every copy of it, to destroy it. The so-called first Christian emperor, Constantine, chief of heretical Christianity, now joined to the state, had ordered (331 A.D.) and under imperial authority and finances had promulgated a rival Greek Bible. Nevertheless, so powerful was the Received Text that even until Jerome's day (383 A.D.) it was called the Vulgate.*

The hostility of Jerome to the Received Text made him necessary to the Papacy. The Papacy in the Latin world opposed the authority of the Greek Vulgate. Did it not see already this hated Greek Vulgate, long ago translated into Latin, read, preached from, and circulated by those Christians in Northern Italy who refused to bow beneath its rule? For this reason it sought the great reputation Jerome enjoyed as a scholar. Moreover, Jerome had been taught the Scriptures by Gregory Nazianzen, who, in turn, had been at great pains with two other scholars of Cæsarea to restore the library of Eusebius in that city. With that library Jerome was well acquaint-

---

⁶ Hort's Introduction, p. 138.   ⁷ Jacobus, p. 203.
⁸ Swete's Introduction, pp. 85, 86.

ed; he describes himself as a great admirer of Eusebius. While studying with Gregory, he had translated from Greek into Latin the Chronicle of Eusebius. And let it be remembered, in turn, that Eusebius in publishing the Bible ordered by Constantine, had incorporated in it the manuscripts of Origen.[9]

In preparing the Latin Bible, Jerome would gladly have gone all the way in transmitting to us the corruptions in the text of Eusebius, but he did not dare. Great scholars of the West were already exposing him and the corrupted Greek manuscripts.[10] Jerome especially mentions Luke 2:33 (where the Received Text read: "And Joseph and his mother marvelled at those things which were spoken of him," while Jerome's text read: "His father and his mother marvelled," etc.) to say that the great scholar Helvidius, who from the circumstances of the case was probably a Vaudois, accused him of using corrupted Greek manuscripts.[11]

Although endorsed and supported by the power of the Papacy, the Vulgate—which name we will now call Jerome's translation—did not gain everywhere immediate acceptance. It took nine hundred years to bring that about.[12] Purer Latin Bibles than it, had already a deep place in the affections of the West. Yet steadily through the years, the Catholic Church has uniformly rejected the Received Text wherever translated from the Greek into Latin and exalted Jerome's Vulgate. So that for one thousand years, Western Europe, with the exception of the Waldenses, Albigenses, and other bodies pronounced heretics by Rome, knew of no Bible but the Vulgate. As Father Simon, that monk who exercised so powerful an influence on the textual criticism of the last century, says:

"The Latins have had so great esteem for that father

[9] Price, Ancestry, p. 70.
[10] W. H. Green, The Text of O. T., p. 116.
    Post-Nicene Fathers, Vol. 6, p. 338.
[11] Jerome against Helvidius.   [12] Jacobus, p. 4.

(Jerome) that for a thousand years they used no other version." [13]

Therefore, a millenium later, when Greek manuscripts and Greek learning were again general, the corrupt readings of the Vulgate were noted. Even Catholic scholars of repute, before Protestantism was fully under way, pointed out its thousands of errors. As Doctor Fulke in 1583 writing to a Catholic scholar, a Jesuit, says:

"Great friends of it and your doctrine, Lindanus, bishop of Ruremond, and Isidorus Clarius, monk of Casine, and bishop Fulginatensis: of which the former writeth a whole book, discussing how he would have the *errors, vices, corruptions, additions, detractions, mutations, uncertainties, obscurities, pollutions, barbarisms, and solecisms of the vulgar Latin translation corrected and reformed;* bringing many examples of every kind, in several chapters and sections: the other, Isidorus Clarius, giving a reason of his purpose, in castigation of the said vulgar Latin translation, confesseth that it was *full of errors almost innumerable;* which if he should have reformed all according to the Hebrew verity, he could not have set forth the vulgar edition, as his purpose was. Therefore in many places he retaineth the accustomed translation, but in his annotations admonisheth the reader, how it is in the Hebrew. And, notwithstanding this moderation, he acknowledgeth that about *eight thousand places* are by him so noted and corrected." (Italics mine). [14]

EVEN WYCLIFFE'S TRANSLATION WAS FROM THE VULGATE

Wycliffe, that great hero of God, is universally called "The morning star of the Reformation." He did what he could and God greatly blessed. Wycliffe's translation of the Bible into English was two hundred years before the birth of Luther. It was taken from the Vulgate and like its model, contained many errors. Therefore the Reformation lingered. Wycliffe, himself, nominally a Catholic to the last, had hoped that the needed reform

[13] Quoted in Nolan, Inquiry, p. 33.
[14] Fulke, Defence of Translations of the Bible (1583), p. 62.

would come within the Catholic Church. Darkness still enshrouded Western Europe and though bright stars shone out brilliantly for a while, only to disappear again into the night, the Reformation still lingered. Then appeared the translation into English of Tyndale from the pure Greek text of Erasmus.

Speaking of Tyndale, Demaus says:

"He was of course aware of the existence of Wycliffe's Version; but this, as a bald translation from the Vulgate into obsolete English, could not be of any assistance (even if he had possessed a copy) to one who was endeavoring, 'simply and faithfully, so far forth as God had given him the gift of knowledge and understanding' to render the New Testament from its original Greek into 'proper English.' " [15]

Again: "For, as became an accomplished Greek scholar, Tyndale was resolved to translate the New Testament from the original language, and not as Wycliffe had done, from the Latin Vulgate; and the only edition of the Greek text which had yet appeared, the only one at least likely to be in Tyndale's possession, was that issued by Erasmus at Basle." [16]

THE REFORMERS OBLIGED TO REJECT JEROME'S VULGATE

The Reformation did not make great progress until after the Received Text had been restored to the world. The Reformers were not satisfied with the Latin Vulgate.

The papal leaders did not comprehend the vast departure from the truth they had created when they had rejected the lead of the pure teachings of the Scriptures. The spurious books of the Vulgate opened the door for the mysterious and the dark doctrines which had confused the thinking of the ancients. The corrupt readings of the genuine books decreased the confidence of people in inspiration and increased the power of the priests. All were left in a labyrinth of darkness from which there was no escape. Cartwright, the famous Puritan scholar, described the Vulgate as follows:

---

[15] Demaus, William Tyndale, p. 105.   [16] Idem, p. 73.

"As to the Version adopted by the Rhemists (Cartwright's word for the Jesuits), Mr. Cartwright observed that all the soap and nitre they could collect would be insufficient to cleanse the Vulgate from the filth of blood in which it was originally conceived and had since collected in passing so long through the hands of unlearned monks, from which the Greek copies had altogether escaped." [17]

More than this, the Vulgate was the chief weapon relied upon to combat and destroy the Bible of the Waldenses. I quote from the preface of the New Testament translated by the Jesuits from the Vulgate into English, 1582 A.D.:

"It is almost three hundred years since James, Archbishop of Genoa, is said to have translated the Bible into Italian. More than two hundred years ago, in the days of Charles V the French king, was it put forth faithfully in French, the sooner to shake out of the deceived people's hands, the false heretical translations of a sect called Waldenses."

Such was the darkness and so many were the errors which the Reformers had to encounter as they started on their way. They welcomed the rising spirit of intelligence which shone forth in the new learning, but the priests loudly denounced it. They declared that the study of Greek was of the devil and prepared to destroy all who promoted it. [18] How intrenched was the situation may be seen in the following quotation of a letter written by Erasmus:

"Obedience (writes Erasmus) is so taught as to hide that there is any obedience due to God. Kings are to obey the Pope. Priests are to obey their bishops. Monks are to obey their abbots. Oaths are exacted, that want of submission may be punished as perjury. It may happen, it often does happen, that an abbot is a fool or a drunkard. He issues an order to the brotherhood in the name of holy obedience. And what will such order be? An order to observe chastity? An order to be sober? An

[17] Brook's Memoir of Life of Cartwright, p. 276.
[18] Froude, Life and Letters of Erasmus, pp. 232, 233.

order to tell no lies? Not one of these things. It will be that a brother is not to learn Greek; he is not to seek to instruct himself. He may be a sot. He may go with prostitutes. He may be full of hatred and malice. He may never look inside the Scriptures. No matter. He has not broken any oath. He is an excellent member of the community. While if he disobeys such a command as this from an insolent superior there is stake or dungeon for him instantly." [19]

It was impossible, however, to hold back the ripening harvest. Throughout the centuries, the Waldenses and other faithful evangelicals had sown the seed. The fog was rolling away from the plains and hills of Europe. The pure Bible which long had sustained the faith of the Vaudois, was soon to be adopted by others so mighty that they would shake Europe from the Alps to the North Sea.

"The light had been spreading unobserved, and the Reformation was on the point of being anticipated. The demon Innocent III was the first to descry the streaks of day on the crest of the Alps. Horror-stricken, he started up, and began to thunder from his pandemonium against a faith which had already subjugated provinces, and was threatening to dissolve the power of Rome in the very flush of her victory over the empire. In order to save the one-half of Europe from perishing by heresy, it was decreed that the other half should perish by the sword." [20]

It must be remembered that at the time (about 400 A.D.) when the Empire was breaking up into modern kingdoms, the pure Latin was breaking up into the Spanish Latin, the French Latin, the African Latin, and other dialects, the forerunners of many modern languages. Into all those different Latins the Bible had been translated, in whole or in part. Some of these, as the Bible of the Waldenses, had come mediately or immediately from the Received Text and had great influence.

When the one thousand years had gone by, strains of new gladness were heard. Gradually these grew in crescendo until the whole choir of voices broke forth as

---

[19] Idem, p. 64.   [20] Wylie, The Papacy, p. 92.

Erasmus threw his first Greek New Testament at the feet of Europe. Then followed a full century of the greatest scholars of language and literature the world ever saw. Among them were Stephens and Beza, each contributing his part to establishing and fortifying the Received Text. The world stood amazed as these two last mentioned scholars brought forth from hidden recesses, old and valuable Greek manuscripts.

ERASMUS RESTORES THE RECEIVED TEXT

The Revival of Learning produced that giant intellect and scholar, Erasmus. It is a common proverb that "Erasmus laid the egg and Luther hatched it." The streams of Grecian learning were again flowing into the European plains, and a man of caliber was needed to draw from them their best and throw it upon the needy nations of the West. Endowed by nature with a mind that could do ten hours work in one, Erasmus, during his mature years in the earlier part of the sixteenth century, was the intellectual dictator of Europe. He was ever at work, visiting libraries, searching in every nook and corner for the profitable. He was ever collecting, comparing, writing and publishing. Europe was rocked from end to end by his books which exposed the ignorance of the monks, the superstitions of the priesthood, the bigotry, and the childish and coarse religion of the day. He classified the Greek MSS. and read the Fathers.

It is customary even to-day with those who are bitter against the pure teachings of the Received Text, to sneer at Erasmus. No perversion of facts is too great to belittle his work. Yet while he lived, Europe was at his feet. Several times the King of England offered him any position in the kingdom, at his own price; the Emperor of Germany did the same. The Pope offered to make him a cardinal. This he steadfastly refused, as he would not compromise his conscience. In fact, had he been so minded, he perhaps could have made himself Pope. France and Spain sought him to become a dweller in their realm; while Holland prepared to claim her most distinguished citizen.

Book after book came from his hand. Faster and faster came the demands for his publications. But his crowning work was the New Testament in Greek. At last after one thousand years, the New Testament was printed (1516 A.D.) in the original tongue. Astonished and confounded, the world, deluged by superstitions, coarse traditions, and monkeries, read the pure story of the Gospels. The effect was marvelous. At once, all recognized the great value of this work which for over four hundred years (1516 to 1930) was to hold the dominant place in an era of Bibles. Translation after translation has been taken from it, such as the German, and the English, and others. Critics have tried to belittle the Greek manuscripts he used, but the enemies of Erasmus, or rather the enemies of the Received Text, have found insuperable difficulties withstanding their attacks. Writing to Peter Baberius August 13, 1521, Erasmus says:

"I did my best with the New Testament, but it provoked endless quarrels. Edward Lee pretended to have discovered 300 errors. They appointed a commission, which professed to have found bushels of them. Every dinner-table rang with the blunders of Erasmus. I required particulars, and could not have them." [21]

There were hundreds of manuscripts for Erasmus to examine, and he did; but he used only a few. What matters? The vast bulk of manuscripts in Greek are practically all the Received Text. If the few Erasmus used were typical, that is, after he had thoroughly balanced the evidence of many and used a few which displayed that balance, did he not, with all the problems before him, arrive at practically the same result which only could be arrived at to-day by a fair and comprehensive investigation? Moreover, the text he chose had such an outstanding history in the Greek, the Syrian, and the Waldensian Churches, that it constituted an irresistible

---

[21] Froude, Erasmus, p. 267.

argument of God's providence. God did not write a hundred Bibles; there is only one Bible, the others at best are only approximations. In other words the Greek New Testament of Erasmus, known as the Received Text, is none other than the Greek New Testament which successfully met the rage of its pagan and papal enemies.

We are told that testimony from the ranks of our enemies constitutes the highest kind of evidence. The following statement which I now submit, is taken from the defense of their doings by two members of that body so hostile to the Greek New Testament of Erasmus,—the Revisers of 1870-1881. This quotation shows that the manuscripts of Erasmus coincide with the great bulk of manuscripts.

"The manuscripts which Erasmus used, differ, for the most part, only in small and insignificant details from the bulk of the cursive manuscripts,—that is to say the manuscripts which are written in running hand and not in capital or (as they are technically called) uncial letters. The general character of their text is the same. By this observation the pedigree of the Received Text is carried up beyond the individual manuscripts used by Erasmus to a great body of manuscripts of which the earliest are assigned to the ninth century."

Then after quoting Doctor Hort, they draw this conclusion on his statement:

"This remarkable statement completes the pedigree of the Received Text. That pedigree stretches back to a remote antiquity. The first ancestor of the Received Text was, as Dr. Hort is careful to remind us, at least contemporary with the oldest of our extant manuscripts, if not older than any one of them." [22]

TYNDALE'S TOWERING GENIUS IS USED TO TRANSLATE ERASMUS INTO ENGLISH

God who foresaw the coming greatness of the English-speaking world, prepared in advance the agent who early would give direction to the course of its thinking. One

---

[22] Two Members of the N. T. Company on the Revisers and the Greek Text, pp. 11, 12.

man stands out silhouetted against the horizon above all others, as having stamped his genius upon English thought and upon the English language.   That man was William Tyndale.

The Received Text in Greek, having through Erasmus reassumed its ascendancy in the West of Europe as it had always maintained it in the East, bequeathed its indispensable heritage to the English.   It meant much that the right genius was engaged to clamp the English future within this heavenly mold.   Providence never is wanting when the hour strikes.   And the world at last is awakening fully to appreciate that William Tyndale is the true hero of the English Reformation.

The Spirit of God presided over Tyndale's calling and training.   He early passed through Oxford and Cambridge Universities.   He went from Oxford to Cambridge to learn Greek under Erasmus, who was teaching there from 1510 to 1514.   Even after Erasmus returned to the Continent, Tyndale kept informed on the revolutionizing productions which fell from that master's pen.   Tyndale was not one of those students whose appetite for facts is omnivorous but who is unable to look down through a system.   Knowledge to him was an organic whole in which, should discords come, created by illogical articulation, he was able to detect them at once.   He had a natural aptitude for languages, but he did not shut himself into an air-tight compartment with his results, to issue forth with some great conclusion which would chill the faith of the world.   He had a soul.   He felt everywhere the sweetness of the life of God, and he offered himself as a martyr, if only the Word of God might live.

Herman Buschius, a friend of Erasmus and one of the leaders in the revival of letters, spoke of Tyndale as "so skilled in seven languages, Hebrew, Greek, Latin, Italian, Spanish, English, French, that whichever he spoke you would suppose it his native tongue." [23]   "Modern Catholic Versions are enormously indebted to Tyndale," says

---

[23] Demaus, Life of Tyndale, p. 130.

Dr. Jacobus. From the standpoint of English, not from the standpoint of doctrine, much work has been done to approximate the Douay to the King James.

When he left Cambridge, he accepted a position as tutor in the home of an influential landowner. Here his attacks upon the superstitions of Popery threw him into sharp discussions with a stagnant clergy, and brought down upon his head the wrath of the reactionaries. It was then that in disputing with a learned man who put the Pope's laws above God's laws, that he made his famous vow, "If God spare my life, ere many years, I will cause a boy that driveth a plough shall know more of the Scripture than thou doest."

From that moment until he was burnt at the stake, his life was one of continual sacrifice and persecution. The man who was to charm whole continents and bind them together as one in principle and purpose by his translation of God's Word, was compelled to build his masterpiece in a foreign land amid other tongues than his own. As Luther took the Greek New Testament of Erasmus and made the German language, so Tyndale took the same immortal gift of God and made the English language. Across the sea, he translated the New Testament and a large part of the Old. Two-thirds of the Bible was translated into English by Tyndale, and what he did not translate was finished by those who worked with him and were under the spell of his genius. The Authorized Bible of the English language is Tyndale's, after his work passed through two or three revisions.

So instant and so powerful was the influence of Tyndale's gift upon England, that Catholicism, through those newly formed papal invincibles, called the Jesuits, sprang to its feet and brought forth, in the form of a Jesuit New Testament, the most effective instrument of learning the Papacy, up to that time, had produced in the English language. This newly invented rival version advanced to the attack, and we are now called to consider how a crisis in the world's history was met when the Jesuit Bible became a challenge to Tyndale's translation.

CHAPTER IV

The Jesuits
and the Jesuit Bible of 1582

I HAVE now before my eyes, on a shelf of my library, a book entitled "The Black Pope." There are two Popes, the White Pope and the Black Pope. The world little realizes how much that fact means. The White Pope is the one we generally know and speak of as the Pope, but the real power is in the hand of that body directed by the Black Pope. The Black Pope, which name does not refer to color, is the head of the Jesuits, —an organization which, outside of God's people, is the mightiest that history has ever known. On the other hand, it is the most subtle and intolerant. It was formed after the Reformation began and for the chief purpose of destroying the Reformation.

The Catholic Church has 69 organizations of men, some of which have been in existence for over one thousand years. Of these we might name the Augustinians, the Benedictines, the Capuchins, the Dominicans, and so on. The Benedictines were founded about 540 A.D. Each order has many members, often reaching into the thousands, and tens of thousands. The Augustinians, for example, (to which order Martin Luther belonged), numbered 35,000 in his day. The men of these orders never marry but live in communities, or large fraternity houses known as monasteries which are for men what the convents are for women. Each organization exists for a distinct line of endeavor, and each, in turn, is directly under the order of the Pope. They overrun all countries and constitute the army militant of the Papacy. The monks are called the regular clergy, while the priests, bishops, etc., who conduct churches, are called the secular clergy. Let us see why the Jesuits stand predominantly above all these, so that the general of the Jesuits has great authority within all the vast ranks of the Catholic clergy, regular and secular.

Within thirty-five years after Luther had nailed his thesis upon the door of the Cathedral of Wittenberg, and launched his attacks upon the errors and corrupt practices of Rome, the Protestant Reformation was thoroughly established. The great contributing factor to this spiritual upheaval was the translation by Luther of the Greek New Testament of Erasmus into German. The medieval Papacy awakened from its superstitious lethargy to see that in a third of a century, the Reformation had carried away two-thirds of Europe. Germany, England, the Scandinavian countries, Holland, and Switzerland had become Protestant. France, Poland, Bavaria, Austria, and Belgium were swinging that way.

In consternation, the Papacy looked around in every direction for help. If the Jesuits had not come forward and offered to save the situation, to-day there might not be a Catholic Church. What was the offer, and what were these weapons, the like of which man never before had forged?

The founder of the Jesuits was a Spaniard, Ignatius Loyola, whom the Catholic Church has canonized and made Saint Ignatius. He was a soldier in the war which King Ferdinand and Queen Isabella of Spain were waging to drive the Mohammedans out of Spain, about the time that Columbus discovered America.

Wounded at the siege of Pampeluna (1521 A.D.), so that his military career was over, Ignatius turned his thoughts to spiritual conquests, and spiritual glory. Soon afterwards, he wrote that book called "Spiritual Exercises," which did more than any other document to erect a new papal theocracy and to bring about the establishment of the infallibility of the Pope. In other words, Catholicism since the Reformation is a new Catholicism. It is more fanatical and more intolerant.

Ignatius Loyola came forward and must have said in

substance to the Pope: Let the Augustinians continue
to provide monasteries of retreat for contemplative
minds; let the Benedictines give themselves up to the
field of literary endeavor; let the Dominicans retain their
responsibility for maintaining the Inquisition; but we,
the Jesuits, will capture the colleges and the universities.
We will gain control of instruction in law, medicine,
science, education, and so weed out from all books of instruction, anything injurious to Roman Catholicism. We
will mould the thoughts and ideas of the youth. We will
enroll ourselves as Protestant preachers and college professors in the different Protestant faiths. Sooner or
later, we will undermine the authority of the Greek New
Testament of Erasmus, and also of those Old Testament
productions which have dared to raise their heads
against the Old Testament of the Vulgate and against
tradition. And thus will we undermine the Protestant
Reformation.

We now quote a few words to describe their spirit and
their methods from a popular writer:

"Throughout Christendom, Protestantism was men-
aced by formidable foes. The first triumphs of the
Reformation past, Rome summoned new forces, hoping to
accomplish its destruction. At this time, the order of
the Jesuits was created, the most cruel, unscrupulous,
and powerful of all the champions of Popery. . . . To
combat these forces, Jesuitism inspired its followers with
a fanaticism that enabled them to endure like dangers,
and to oppose to the power of truth all the weapons of
deception. There was no crime too great for them to
commit, no deception too base for them to practice, no
disguise too difficult for them to assume. Vowed to perpetual poverty and humility, it was their studied aim to
secure wealth and power, to be devoted to the overthrow
of Protestantism, and the reëstablishment of the papal
supremacy.

"When appearing as members of their order, they wore
a garb of sanctity, visiting prisons and hospitals, minis-
tering to the sick and the poor, professing to have re-
nounced the world, and bearing the sacred name of

Jesus, who went about doing good. But under this blameless exterior the most criminal and deadly purposes were often concealed. It was a fundamental principle of the order that the end justifies the means. By this code, lying, theft, perjury, assassination, were not only pardonable but commendable, when they served the interests of the church. Under various disguises the Jesuits worked their way into offices of state, climbing up to be the counselors of kings, and shaping the policy of nations. They became servants, to act as spies upon their masters. They established colleges for the sons of princes and nobles, and schools for the common people; and the children of Protestant parents were drawn into an observance of popish rites." [1]

How well the Jesuits have succeeded, let the following pages tell. Soon the brains of the Catholic Church were to be found in that order. About 1582, when the Jesuit Bible was launched to destroy Tyndale's English Version, the Jesuits dominated 287 colleges and universities in Europe.

Their complete system of education and of drilling was likened, in the constitution of the order itself, to the reducing of all its members to the placidity of a corpse, whereby the whole could be turned and returned at the will of the superior. We quote from their constitution:

"As for holy obedience, this virtue must be perfect in every point—in execution, in will, in intellect—doing what is enjoined with all celerity, spiritual joy, and perseverance; persuading ourselves that everything is just; suppressing every repugnant thought and judgment of one's own, in a certain obedience; . . . and let every one persuade himself that he who lives under obedience should be moved and directed, under Divine Providence, by his superior, just as if he were a corpse (*perinde ac si cadaver esset*), which allows itself to be moved and led in any direction." [2]

That which put an edge on the newly forged mentality was the unparalleled system of education impressed upon

---

[1] E. G. White, The Great Controversy, pp. 234, 235.
[2] R. W. Thompson, Ex-Secretary of Navy, U. S. A., The Footprints of the Jesuits, p. 51.

the pick of Catholic youth.   The Pope, perforce, virtually
threw open the ranks of the many millions of Catholic
young men and told the Jesuits to go in and select the
most intelligent.   The initiation rites were such as to
make a lifelong impression on the candidate for admission.   He never would forget the first trial of his faith.
Thus the youth are admitted under a test which virtually
binds forever the will, if it has not already been en-
slaved.   What matters to him?   Eternal life is secure,
and all is for the greater glory of God.

Then follow the long years of intense mental training,
interspersed with periods of practice.   They undergo
the severest methods of quick and accurate learning.
They will be, let us say, shut up in a room with a heavy
Latin lesson, and expected to learn it in a given period
of hours.   Of the results achieved by means of this policy
and the methods, Macaulay says:

"It was in the ears of the Jesuit that the powerful,
the noble, and the beautiful, breathed the secret history
of their lives.   It was at the feet of the Jesuit that the
youth of the higher and middle classes were brought up
from childhood to manhood, from the first rudiments to
the courses of rhetoric and philosophy.   Literature and
science, lately associated with infidelity or with heresy,
now became the allies of orthodoxy.   Dominant in the
south of Europe, the great order soon went forth con-
quering and to conquer.   In spite of oceans and deserts,
of hunger and pestilence, of spies and penal laws, of
dungeons and racks, of gibbets and quartering-blocks,
Jesuits were to be found *under every disguise,* and in
every country; scholars, physicians, merchants, serving
men; in the hostile court of Sweden, in the old manor-
house of Cheshire, among the hovels of Connaught; arguing, instructing, consoling, stealing away the hearts of
the young, animating the courage of the timid, holding
up the crucifix before the eyes of the dying.   Nor was it
less their office to plot against the thrones and lives of
the apostate kings, to spread evil rumors, to raise tu-
mults, to inflame civil wars, to arm the hand of the as-
sassin.   Inflexible in nothing but in their fidelity to the

Church, they were equally ready to appeal in her cause to the spirit of loyalty and to the spirit of freedom. Extreme doctrines of obedience and extreme doctrines of liberty, the right of rulers to misgovern the people, the right of every one of the people to plunge his knife in the heart of a bad ruler, were inculcated by the same man, according as he addressed himself to the subject of Philip or to the subject of Elizabeth." [3]

And again: "If Protestantism, or the semblance of Protestantism, showed itself in any quarter, it was instantly met, not by petty, teasing persecution, but by persecution of that sort which bows down and crushes all but a very few select spirits. Whoever was suspected of heresy, whatever his rank, his learning, or his reputation, knew that he must purge himself to the satisfaction of a severe and vigilant tribunal, or die by fire. Heretical books were sought out and destroyed with similar rigor." [4]

THE CATHOLIC COUNCIL OF TRENT (1545-1563) CALLED TO DEFEAT THE REFORMATION. HOW THE COUNCIL REFUSED THE PROTESTANT ATTITUDE TOWARD THE SCRIPTURES AND ENTHRONED THE JESUIT

"The Society came to exercise a marked influence to which their presence in the Council of Trent, as the Pope's theologians, gave signal testimony. It was a wise stroke of policy for the Papacy to entrust its cause in the Council so largely to the Jesuits." [5]

The Council of Trent was dominated by the Jesuits. This we must bear in mind as we study that Council. It is the leading characteristic of that assembly. "The great Convention dreaded by every Pope" was called by Paul III when he saw that such a council was imperative if the Reformation was to be checked. And when it did assemble, he so contrived the manipulation of the program and the attendance of the delegates, that the Jesuitical conception of a theocratic Papacy should be incorporated into the canons of the church.

---

[3] Macaulay, Essays, pp. 480, 481.   [4] Idem, pp. 482, 483.
[5] Hulme, Renaissance and Reformation, p. 428.

So prominent had been the Reformers' denunciations of the abuses of the church, against her exactions, and against her shocking immoralities, that we would naturally expect that this council, which marks so great a turning point in church history, would have promptly met the charges. But this it did not do. The very first propositions to be discussed at length and with intense interest, were those relating to the Scriptures. This shows how fundamental to all reform, as well as to the great Reformation, is the determining power over Christian order and faith, of the disputed readings and the disputed books of the Bible. Moreover, these propositions denounced by the Council, which we give below, the Council did not draw up itself. They were taken from the writings of Luther. We thus see how fundamental to the faith of Protestantism is their acceptance; while their rejection constitutes the keystone to the superstitions and to the tyrannical theology of the Papacy. These four propositions which first engaged the attention of the Council, and which the Council condemned, are:

They Condemned: I—"That Holy Scriptures contained all things necessary for salvation, and that it was impious to place apostolic tradition on a level with Scripture."

They Condemned: II—"That certain books accepted as canonical in the Vulgate were apocryphal and not canonical."

They Condemned: III—"That Scripture must be studied in the original languages, and that there were errors in the Vulgate."

They Condemned: IV—"That the meaning of Scripture is plain, and that it can be understood without commentary with the help of Christ's Spirit." [6]

For eighteen long years the Council deliberated. The papal scholars determined what was the Catholic faith. During these eighteen years, the Papacy gathered up to itself what survived of Catholic territory. The Church

---

[6] Froude, The Council of Trent, pp. 174, 175.

of Rome consolidated her remaining forces and took her stand solidly on the grounds that tradition was of equal value with the Scriptures; that the seven apocryphal books of the Vulgate were as much Scripture as the other books; that those readings of the Vulgate in the accepted books, which differed from the Greek, were not errors, as Luther and the Reformers had said, but were authentic; and finally, that lay members of the church had no right to interpret the Scriptures apart from the clergy.

THE JESUIT BIBLE OF 1582

The opening decrees of the Council of Trent had set the pace for centuries to come. They pointed out the line of battle which the Catholic reaction would wage against the Reformation. First undermine the Bible, then destroy the Protestant teaching and doctrine.

If we include the time spent in studying these questions before the opening session of the Council in 1545 until the Jesuit Bible made its first appearance in 1582, fully forty years were passed in the preparation of Jesuit students who were being drilled in these departments of learning. The first attack on the position of the Reformers regarding the Bible must soon come. It was clearly seen then, as it is now, that if confusion on the origin and authenticity of the Scriptures could be spread abroad in the world, the amazing certainty of the Reformers on these points, which had astonished and confounded the Papacy, could be broken down. In time the Reformation would be splintered to pieces, and driven as the chaff before the wind. The leadership in the battle for the Reformation was passing over from Germany to England.[7] Here it advanced mightily, helped greatly by the new version of Tyndale.

Therefore, Jesuitical scholarship, with at least forty years of training, must bring forth in English a Jesuit Version capable of superseding the Bible of Tyndale. Could it be done?

---

[7] A. T. Innes, Church and State, p. 156.

Sixty years elapsed from the close of the Council of Trent (1563), to the landing of the Pilgrims in America. During those sixty years, England had been changing from a Catholic nation to a Bible-loving people. Since 1525, when Tyndale's Bible appeared, the Scriptures had obtained a wide circulation. As Tyndale foresaw, the influence of the divine Word had weaned the people away from pomp and ceremony in religion. But this result had not been obtained without years of struggle. Spain, at that time, was not only the greatest nation in the world, but also was fanatically Catholic. All the new world belonged to Spain; she ruled the seas and dominated Europe. The Spanish sovereign and the Papacy united in their efforts to send into England bands of highly trained Jesuits. By these, plot after plot was hatched to place a Catholic ruler on England's throne.

At the same time, the Jesuits were acting to turn the English people from the Bible, back to Romanism. As a means to this end, they brought forth in English a Bible of their own. Let it always be borne in mind that the Bible adopted by Constantine was in Greek; that Jerome's Bible was in Latin; but that the Jesuit Bible was in English. If England could be retained in the Catholic column, Spain and England together would see to it that all America, north and south, would be Catholic. In fact, wherever the influence of the English speaking race extended, Catholicism would reign. If this result were to be thwarted, it was necessary to meet the danger brought about by the Jesuit Version.

THE GREAT STIR OVER THE JESUIT BIBLE OF 1582

So powerful was the swing toward Protestantism during the reign of Queen Elizabeth, and so strong the love for Tyndale's Version, that there was neither place nor Catholic scholarship enough in England to bring forth a Catholic Bible in strength. Priests were in prison for their plotting, and many had fled to the Continent. There they founded schools to train English youth and send them back to England as priests. Two of these colleges alone sent over, in a few years, not less than three hundred priests.

The most prominent of these colleges, called seminaries, was at Rheims, France. Here the Jesuits assembled a company of learned scholars. From here they kept the Pope informed of the changes of the situation in England, and from here they directed the movements of Philip II of Spain as he prepared a great fleet to crush England and bring it back to the feet of the Pope.

The burning desire to give the common people the Holy Word of God, was the reason why Tyndale had translated it into English. No such reason impelled the Jesuits at Rheims. In the preface of their Rheims New Testament, they state that it was not translated into English because it was necessary that the Bible should be in the mother tongue, or that God had appointed the Scriptures to be read by all; but from the special consideration of the state of their mother country. This translation was intended to do on the inside of England, what the great navy of Philip II was to do on the outside. One was to be used as a moral attack, the other as a physical attack; both to reclaim England. The preface especially urged that those portions be committed to memory "which made most against heretics."

"The principal object of the Rhemish translators was not only to circulate their doctrines through the country, but also to depreciate as much as possible the English translations." [8]

The appearance of the Jesuit New Testament of 1582 produced consternation in England. It was understood at once to be a menace against the new English unity. It was to serve as a wedge between Protestants and Catholics. It was the product of unusual ability and years of learning. Immediately, the scholarship of England was astir. Queen Elizabeth sent forth the call for a David to meet this Goliath. Finding no one in her

---

[8] Brooke's Cartwright, p. 256.

kingdom satisfactory to her, she sent to Geneva, where Calvin was building up his great work, and besought Beza, the co-worker of Calvin, to undertake the task of answering the objectionable matter contained in this Jesuit Version. In this department of learning, Beza was easily recognized as chief. To the astonishment of the Queen, Beza modestly replied that her majesty had within her own realm, a scholar more able to undertake the task than he. He referred to Thomas Cartwright, the great Puritan divine. Beza said, "The sun does not shine on a greater scholar than Cartwright."

Cartwright was a Puritan, and Elizabeth disliked the Puritans as much as she did the Catholics. She wanted an Episcopalian or a Presbyterian to undertake the answer. Cartwright was ignored. But time was passing and English Protestantism wanted Cartwright. The universities of Cambridge and Oxford, Episcopalian though they were, sent to Cartwright a request signed by their outstanding scholars.[9] Cartwright decided to undertake it. He reached out one arm and grasped all the power of the Latin manuscripts and testimony. He reached out his other arm and in it he embraced all the vast stores of Greek and Hebrew literature. With inescapable logic, he marshaled the facts of his vast learning and leveled blow after blow against this latest and most dangerous product of Catholic theology.[10]

Meanwhile, 136 great Spanish galleons, some armed with 50 cannons were slowly sailing up the English Channel to make England Catholic. England had no ships. Elizabeth asked Parliament for 15 men-of-war,— they voted 30. With these, assisted by harbor tugs under Drake, England sailed forth to meet the greatest fleet the world had ever seen. All England teemed with excitement. God helped: the Armada was crushed, and England became a great sea power.

---

[9] Brooke's Cartwright, p. 260.
[10] English Hexapla, pp. 98, 99; F. J. Firth, The Holy Gospel, pp. 17, 18.

AFTER THE EXPOSURE BY CARTWRIGHT AND FULKE, THE
CATHOLICS DOCTORED AND REDOCTORED THE JESUIT
BIBLE OF 1582, UNTIL TODAY THE NAME DOUAY
IS A MISNOMER

The Rheims-Douay and the King James Version were published less than thirty years apart. Since then the King James has steadily held its own. The Rheims-Douay has been repeatedly changed to approximate the King James. So that the Douay of 1600 and that of 1900 are not the same in many ways.

"The New Testament was published at Rheims in 1582. The university was moved back to Douai in 1593, where the Old Testament was published in 1609-1610. This completed what is known as the original Douay Bible. There are said to have been two revisions of the Douay Old Testament and eight of the Douay New Testament, representing such an extent of verbal alterations, and modernized spelling that a Roman Catholic authority says, 'The version now in use has been so seriously altered that it can be scarcely considered identical with that which first went by the name of the Douay Bible,' and further that 'it never had any episcopal imprimatur, much less any papal approbation.'

"Although the Bibles in use at the present day by the Catholics of England and Ireland are popularly styled the Douay Version, they are most improperly so called; they are founded, with more or less alteration, on a series of revisions undertaken by Bishop Challoner in 1749-52. His object was to meet the practical want felt by the Catholics of his day of a Bible moderate in size and price, in readable English, and with notes more suitable to the time. . . . The changes introduced by him were so considerable that, according to Cardinal Newman, they 'almost amounted to a new translation.' So also, Cardinal Wiseman wrote, 'To call it any longer the Douay or Rhemish Version is an abuse of terms. It has been altered and modified until scarcely any verse remains as it was originally published. In nearly every case, Challoner's changes took the form approximating to the Authorized Version.' " [11]

---

[11] The Catholic Encyclopedia, Art., "Douay Bible."

Note the above quotations. Because if you seek to compare the Douay with the American Revised Version, you will find that the older, or first Douay of 1582, is more like it in Catholic readings than those editions of today, inasmuch as the 1582 Version had been doctored and redoctored. Yet, even in the later editions, you will find many of those corruptions which the Reformers denounced and which reappear in the American Revised Version.

THE NEW PLAN OF THE JESUITS TO DESTROY PROTESTANTISM

A thousand years had passed before time permitted the trial of strength between the Greek Bible and the Latin. They had fairly met in the struggles of 1582 and the thirty years following in their respective English translations. The Vulgate yielded before the Received Text. The Latin was vanquished before the Greek; the mutilated version before the pure Word. The Jesuits were obliged to shift their line of battle. They saw, that armed only with the Latin, they could fight no longer. They therefore resolved to enter the field of the Greek and become superb masters of the Greek; only that they might meet the influence of the Greek. They knew that manuscripts in Greek, of the type from which the Bible adopted by Constantine had been taken, were awaiting them,—manuscripts, moreover, which involved the Old Testament as well as the New. To use them to overthrow the Received Text would demand great training and almost Herculean labors; for the Received Text was apparently invincible.

But still more. Before they could get under way, the champions of the Greek had moved up and consolidated their gains. Flushed with their glorious victory over the Jesuit Bible of 1582, and over the Spanish Armada of 1588, every energy pulsating with certainty and hope, English Protestantism brought forth a perfect masterpiece. They gave to the world what has been considered

by hosts of scholars, the greatest version ever produced
in any language,—the King James Bible, called "The
Miracle of English Prose." This was not taken from the
Latin in either the Old or the New Testament, but from
the languages in which God originally wrote His Word,
namely, from the Hebrew in the Old Testament and from
the Greek in the New. The Jesuits had therefore before
them a double task,—both to supplant the authority of
the Greek of the Received Text by another Greek New
Testament, and then upon this mutilated foundation, to
bring forth a new English version which might retire
into the background, the King James. In other words,
they must, before they could again give standing to the
Vulgate, bring Protestantism to accept a mutilated Greek
text and an English version based upon it.

The manuscripts from which the New Version must be
taken, would be like the Greek manuscripts which Jerome
used in producing the Vulgate. The opponents of the
King James Version would even do more. They would
enter the field of the Old Testament, namely, the Hebrew,
and, from the many translations of it into Greek in the
early centuries, seize whatever advantages they could.

In other words, the Jesuits had put forth one Bible in
English, that of 1582, as we have seen; of course they
could get out another.

CHAPTER V

The King James Bible Born Amid the Great Struggles Over the Jesuit Version

THE hour had arrived, and from the human point of view, conditions were perfect, for God to bring forth a translation of the Bible which would sum up in itself the best of the ages. The heavenly Father foresaw the opportunity of giving His Word to the inhabitants of earth by the coming of the British Empire with its dominions scattered throughout the world, and by the great American Republic, both speaking the English language. Not only was the English language by 1611 in a more opportune condition than it had ever been before or ever would be again, but the Hebrew and the Greek likewise had been brought up with the accumulated treasures of their materials to a splendid working point. The age was not distracted by the rush of mechanical and industrial achievements. Moreover linguistic scholarship was at its peak. Men of giant minds, supported by excellent physical health, had possessed in a splendid state of perfection a knowledge of the languages and literature necessary for the ripest Biblical scholarship.

One hundred and fifty years of printing had permitted the Jewish rabbis to place at the disposal of scholars all the treasures in the Hebrew tongue which they had been accumulating for over two thousand years. In the words of the learned Professor E. C. Bissell:

"There ought to be no doubt that in the text which we inherit from the Massoretes, and they from the Talmudists, and they in turn from a period when versions and paraphases of the Scriptures in other languages now accessible to us were in common use—the same text being transmitted to this period from the time of Ezra under the peculiarly sacred seal of the Jewish canon—we have a substantially correct copy of the original documents, and one worthy of all confidence." [1]

We are told that the revival of Massoretic studies in more recent times was the result of the vast learning and energy of Buxtorf, of Basle. [2] He had given the benefits of his Hebrew accomplishments in time to be used by the translators of the King James Version. And we have the word of a leading Revisionist, highly recommended by Bishop Ellicott, that it is not to the credit of Christian scholarship that so little has been done in Hebrew researches during the past 300 years. [3]

What is true of the Hebrew is equally true of the Greek. The Unitarian scholar who sat on the English New Testament Revision Committee, acknowledged that the Greek New Testament of Erasmus (1516) is as good as any. [4] It should here be pointed out that Stephens (A.D. 1550), then Beza (1598), and Elzevir (1624), all, subsequently printed editions of the same Greek New Testament. Since the days of Elzevir it has been called the Received Text, or from the Latin, Textus Receptus. Of it Dr. A. T. Robertson also says:

"It should be stated at once that the Textus Receptus is not a bad text. It is not an heretical text. It is substantially correct." [5]

Again: "Erasmus seemed to feel that he had published the original Greek New Testament as it was written. . . . The third edition of Erasmus (1522) became the foundation of the Textus Receptus for Britain since it was followed by Stephens. There were 3300 copies of the first two editions of the Greek New Testament of Erasmus circulated. His work became the standard for three hundred years." [6]

This text is and has been for 300 years the best known and most widely used. It has behind it all the Protes-

---

[1] Chambers, Comp. to Revised O. T., pp. 63, 64.
[2] A New Commentary by Bishop Gore and Others, Part 1, p. 651.
[3] Chambers, Comp. to Revised, p. 66.
[4] Rev. G. Vance Smith, *Nineteeth Century*, July, 1881.
[5] Robertson, Introduction, p. 21.   [6] Idem, pp. 18, 19.

tant scholarship of nearly three centuries. It ought to be pointed out that those who seem eager to attack the King James and the Greek behind it, when the enormous difficulties of the Revised Greek Testament are pointed out, will claim the Revised Text is all right because it is like the Greek New Testament from which the King James was translated: on the other hand, when they are not called to account, they will say belittling things about the Received Text and the scholars who translated the King James Bible.

BETTER CONDITION OF ENGLISH LANGUAGE IN 1611

We now come, however, to a very striking situation which is little observed and rarely mentioned by those who discuss the merits of the King James Bible. The English language in 1611 was in the very best condition to receive into its bosom the Old and New Testaments. Each word was broad, simple, and generic. That is to say, words were capable of containing in themselves not only their central thoughts, but also all the different shades of meaning which were attached to that central thought. Since then, words have lost that living, pliable breadth. Vast additions have been made to the English vocabulary during the past 300 years, so that several words are now necessary to convey the same meaning which formerly was conveyed by one. It will then be readily seen that while the English vocabulary has increased in quantity, nevertheless, single words have lost their many shades, combinations of words have become fixed, capable of only one meaning, and therefore less adaptable to receiving into English the thoughts of the Hebrew which likewise is a simple, broad, generic language. New Testament Greek, is, in this respect, like the Hebrew. When our English Bible was revised, the Revisers labored under the impression that the sacred writers of the Greek New Testament did not write in the everyday language of the common people. Since then the accumulated stores of archæological findings have demonstrated that the language of the Greek New Testament was the language of the simple, ordinary people, rather than the language of scholars; and is flexible, broad, generic, like the English of 1611. Or in the words of another:

"It is sometimes regretted that our modern English has lost, or very nearly lost, its power of inflection; but whatever may have been thus lost to the ear has been more than compensated to the sense, by our wealth of finely shaded auxiliary words. There is no differentiation of wish, will, condition, supposition, potentiality, or possibility representable in syllables of human speech, or conceivable to the mind of man, which cannot be precisely put in some form of our English verb. But here, again, our power of precision has been purchased at a certain cost. For every form of our verbal combinations has now come to have its own peculiar and appropriate sense, and no other; so that, when we use any one of those forms, it is understood by the hearer or reader that we intend the special sense of that form, and of that alone. In this respect, as in the specific values of our synonyms, we encounter a self-evident difficulty in the literal translation of the Scriptures into modern English. For there is no such refinement of tense and mood in the Hebrew language; and, although the classical Greek was undoubtedly perfect in its inflections, the writers of the New Testament were either ignorant of its powers, or were not capable of using them correctly."[1]

The above writer then points out that the authors of the New Testament did not always use that tense of the Greek verb, called the aorist, in the same rigid, specific sense, in which the Revisers claimed they had done. Undoubtedly, in a general way, the sacred writers understood the meaning of the aorist as distinguished from the perfect and imperfect; but they did not always use it so specifically as the Revisers claim. I continue from the same writer:

---

[1] John Fulton, *Forum*, June, 1887.

"The self-imposed rule of the Revisers required them invariably to translate the aoristic forms by their closest English equivalents; but the vast number of cases in which they have forsaken their own rule shows that it could not be followed without in effect changing the meaning of the original; and we may add that to whatever extent that rule has been slavishly followed, to that extent the broad sense of the original has been marred. The sacred writers wrote with a broad brush; the pen of the Revisers was a finely pointed stylus. The living pictures of the former furnish a grand panorama of providential history; the drawing of the latter is the cunning work of fine engravers, wrought in hair lines, and on polished plates of steel. The Westminster Version is not, and, as its purpose was conceived by the Revisers, could not be made, anything like a photograph of the originals. The best of photographs lacks life and color, but it does produce the broad effects of light and shade. It has no resemblance to the portrait of the Chinese artist, who measures each several feature with the compass, and then draws it by the scale. The work of the Revisers is a purely Chinese work of art, in which the scale and compass are applied to microscopic niceties, with no regard whatever to light and shade, or to the life and color of their subject. It follows that the more conscientiously their plan was followed, the more certainly must they fail to produce a lifelike rendering of the living word of the original." [8]

ORIGIN OF THE KING JAMES VERSION

After the life and death struggles with Spain, and the hard fought battle to save the English people from the Jesuit Bible of 1582, victorious Protestantism took stock of its situation and organized for the new era which had evidently dawned. A thousand ministers, it is said, sent in a petition, called the Millenary Petition, to King James who had now succeeded Elizabeth as sovereign. One author describes the petition as follows:

"The petition craved reformation of sundry abuses in the worship, ministry, revenues, and discipline of the

[8] Idem.

national Church . . . . Among other of their demands, Dr. Reynolds, who was the chief speaker in their behalf, requested that there might be a new translation of the Bible, without note or comment." [9]

The strictest element of Protestantism, the Puritan, we conclude, was at the bottom of this request for a new and accurate translation, and the Puritan element on the committee appointed was strong.[10]

The language of the Jesuit Bible had stung the sensibilities and the scholarship of Protestants. In the preface of that book it had criticized and belittled the Bible of the Protestants. The Puritans felt that the corrupted version of the Rheimists was spreading poison among the people, even as formerly by withholding the Bible, Rome had starved the people.[11]

THE UNRIVALED SCHOLARSHIP OF THE REFORMERS

The first three hundred years of the Reformation produced a grand array of scholars, who have never since been surpassed, if indeed they have been equaled. Melanchthon, the coworker of Luther, was of so great scholarship that Erasmus expressed admiration for his attainments. By his organization of schools throughout Germany and by his valuable textbooks, he exercised for many years a more powerful influence than any other teacher. Hallam said that far above all others he was the founder of general learning throughout Europe. His Latin grammar was "almost universally adopted in Europe, running through fifty-one editions and continuing until 1734," that is, for two hundred years it continued to be the textbook even in the Roman Catholic schools of Saxony. Here the names might be added of Beza, the great scholar and coworker with Calvin, of Bucer, of Cartwright, of the Swiss scholars of the Reformation, of a host of others who were unsurpassed in learning in their day and have never been surpassed since.

---

[9] McClure, The Translators Revived, pp. 57, 58.
[10] Idem, pp. 130, 131.   [11] Brooke's Cartwright, p. 274.

It was said of one of the translators of the King James that "such was his skill in all languages, especially the Oriental, that had he been present at the confusion of tongues at Babel, he might have served as Interpreter-General." [12]   In view of the vast stores of material which were available to verify the certainty of the Bible at the time of the Reformation, and the prodigious labors of the Reformers in this material for a century, it is very erroneous to think that they had not been sufficiently overhauled by 1611.

It is an exaggerated idea, much exploited by those who are attacking the Received Text, that we of the present have greater sources of information, as well as more valuable, than had the translators of 1611.   The Reformers themselves considered their sources of information perfect. Doctor Fulke says:

"But as for the Hebrew and Greek that now is, (it) may easily be proved to be the same that always hath been; neither is there any diversity in sentence, howsoever some copies, either through negligence of the writer, or by any other occasion, do vary from that which is commonly and most generally received in some letters, syllables, or words." [13]

We cannot censure the Reformers for considering their sources of information sufficient and authentic enough to settle in their minds the infallible inspiration of the Holy Scriptures, since we have a scholar of repute to-day rating their material as high as the material of the present.   Doctor Jacobus thus indicates the relative value of information available to Jerome, to the translators of the King James, and to the Revisers of 1900:

"On the whole, the differences in the matter of the sources available in 390, 1590, and 1890 are not very serious." [14]

ALEXANDRINUS, VATICANUS, AND SINAITICUS

So much has been said about the Alexandrinus, Vaticanus, and Sinaitic Manuscripts being made available

---

[12] McClure, p. 87.   [13] Fulke's Defense, 1583, p. 73.
[14] Jacobus, Cath. and Prot. Bibles, p. 41.

since 1611, that a candid examination ought to be given to see if it is all really as we have repeatedly been told.

The Alexandrinus Manuscript arrived in London in 1627, we are informed, just sixteen years too late for use by the translators of the King James. We would humbly inquire if a manuscript must dwell in the home town of scholars in order for them to have the use of its information? If so, then the Revisers of 1881 and 1901 were in a bad way. Who donated the Alexandrinus Manuscript to the British Government? It was Cyril Lucar, the head of the Greek Catholic Church. Why did he do it? What was the history of the document before he did it? An answer to these inquiries opens up a very interesting chapter of history.

Cyril Lucar (1568-1638) born in the east, early embraced the principles of the Reformation, and for it, was pursued all his life by the Jesuits. He spent some time at Geneva with Beza and Calvin. When holding an important position in Lithuania, he opposed the union of the Greek Church there and in Poland with Rome. In 1602 he was elected Patriarch of Alexandria, Egypt, where the Alexandrinus MS. had been kept for years. It seems almost certain that this great Biblical scholar would have been acquainted with it. Thus he was in touch with this manuscript before the King James translators began work. Later he was elected the head of the Greek Catholic Church. He wrote a confession of faith which distinguished between the canonical and apocryphal books. He was thoroughly awake to the issues of textual criticism. These had been discussed repeatedly and to the smallest details at Geneva, where Cyril Lucar had passed some time. Of him one encyclopedia states:

"In 1602 Cyril succeeded Meletius as patriarch of Alexandria. While holding this position he carried on an active correspondence with David le Leu, de Wilelm, and the Romonstrant Uytenbogaert of Holland, Abbot, archbishop of Canterbury, Leger, professor of Geneva, the republic of Venice, the Swedish King, Gustavus Adolphus, and his chancellor, Axel Oxenstierna. Many of these letters, written in different languages, are still extant. They show that Cyril was an earnest opponent of Rome, and a great admirer of the Protestant Reformation. He sent for all the important works, Protestant and Roman Catholic, published in the Western countries, and sent several young men to England to get a thorough theological education. The friends of Cyril in Constantinople, and among them the English, Dutch, and Swedish ambassadors, endeavored to elevate Cyril to the patriarchal see of Constantinople. . . .

"The Jesuits, in union with the agents of France, several times procured his banishment, while his friends, supported by the ambassadors of the Protestant powers in Constantinople, obtained, by means of large sums of money, his recall. During all these troubles, Cyril, with remarkable energy, pursued the great task of his life. In 1627 he obtained a printing press from England, and at once began to print his Confession of Faith and several catechisms. But, before these documents were ready for publication, the printing establishment was destroyed by the Turkish Government at the instigation of the Jesuits. Cyril then sent his Confession of Faith to Geneva, where it appeared, in 1629, in the Latin language, under the true name of the author, and with a dedication to Cornelius de Haga. It created throughout Europe a profound sensation."[15]

We think enough has been given to show that the scholars of Europe and England, in particular, had ample opportunity to become fully acquainted by 1611 with the problems involved in the Alexandrinus Manuscript.

Let us pursue the matter a little further. The Catholic Encyclopaedia does not omit to tell us that the New Testament from Acts on, in Codex A (the Alexandrinus), agrees with the Vatican Manuscript. If the problems presented by the Alexandrinus Manuscript, and consequently by the Vaticanus, were so serious, why were we obliged to wait till 1881-1901 to learn of the glaring mistakes of the translators of the King James, when the

---

[15] McClintock and Strong, Encyl., Vol. II, p. 685.

manuscript arrived in England in 1627? The *Forum* informs us that 250 different versions of the Bible were tried in England between 1611 and now, but they all fell flat before the majesty of the King James. Were not the Alexandrinus and the Vaticanus able to aid these 250 versions, and overthrow the other Bible, resting, as the critics explain, on an insecure foundation?

The case with the Vaticanus and the Sinaiticus is no better. The problems presented by these two manuscripts were well known, not only to the translators of the King James, but also to Erasmus. We are told that the Old Testament portion of the Vaticanus has been printed since 1587.

"The third great edition is that commonly known as the 'Sixtine,' published at Rome in 1587 under Pope Sixtus V. . . . Substantially, the 'Sixtine' edition gives the text of B. . . . The 'Sixtine' served as the basis for most of the ordinary editions of the LXX for just three centuries." [16]

We are informed by another author that, if Erasmus had desired, he could have secured a transcript of this manuscript.[17] There was no necessity, however, for Erasmus to obtain a transcript because he was in correspondence with Professor Paulus Bombasius at Rome, who sent him such variant readings as he wished.[18]

"A correspondent of Erasmus in 1533 sent that scholar a number of selected readings from it (Codex B), as proof of its superiority to the Received Greek Text." [19]

Erasmus, however, rejected these varying readings of the Vatican MS. because he considered from the massive evidence of his day that the Received Text was correct.

The story of the finding of the Sinaitic MS. by Tischendorf in a monastery at the foot of Mt. Sinai, illustrates the history of some of these later manuscripts. Tis-

[16] Ottley, Handbook of the Septuagint, p. 64.
[17] Bissell, Historic Origin of Bible, p. 84.
[18] S. P. Tregelles, On the printed Text of the Greek Test., p. 22.
[19] Kenyon, Our Bible, p. 133.

chendorf was visiting this monastery in 1844 to look for these documents. He discovered in a basket, over forty pages of a Greek MS. of the Bible. He was told that two other basket loads had been used for kindling. Later, in 1859, he again visited this monastery to search for other MSS. He was about to give up in despair and depart when he was told of a bundle of additional leaves of a Greek MS. When he examined the contents of this bundle, he saw them to be a reproduction of part of the Bible in Greek. He could not sleep that night. Great was the joy of those who were agitating for a revision of the Bible when they learned that the new find was similar to the Vaticanus, but differed greatly from the King James. Dr. Riddle informs us that the discovery of the Sinaiticus settled in its favor the agitation for revision.

Just a word on the two styles of manuscripts before we go further. Manuscripts are of two kinds—uncial and cursive. Uncials are written in large square letters much like our capital letters; cursives are of a free running hand.

We have already given authorities to show that the Sinaitic MS. is a brother of the Vaticanus. Practically all of the problems of any serious nature which are presented by the Sinaitic, are the problems of the Vaticanus. Therefore the translators of 1611 had available all the variant readings of these manuscripts and rejected them.

The following words from Dr. Kenrick, Catholic Bishop of Philadelphia, will support the conclusion that the translators of the King James knew the readings of Codices ℵ, A, B, C, D, where they differed from the Received Text and denounced them. Bishop Kenrick published an English translation of the Catholic Bible in 1849. I quote from the preface:

"Since the famous manuscripts of Rome, Alexandria, Cambridge, Paris, and Dublin, were examined . . . a verdict has been obtained in favor of the Vulgate.

"At the Reformation, the Greek text, as it then stood, was taken as a standard, in conformity to which the versions of the Reformers were generally made; whilst the Latin Vulgate was depreciated, or despised, as a mere version." [20]

In other words, the readings of these much boasted manuscripts, recently made available are those of the Vulgate. The Reformers knew of these readings and rejected them, as well as the Vulgate.

Men of 1611 Had all the Material Necessary

Let us suppose, for the sake of argument, that the translators of 1611 did not have access to the problems of the Alexandrinus, the Sinaiticus, and the Vaticanus by direct contact with these uncials. It mattered little. They had other manuscripts accessible which presented all the same problems. We are indebted for the following information to Dr. F. C. Cook, editor of the "Speaker's Commentary," chaplain to the Queen of England, who was invited to sit on the Revision Committee, but refused:

"That Textus Receptus was taken in the first instance, from late cursive manuscripts; but its readings are maintained only so far as they agree with the best ancient versions, with the earliest and best Greek and Latin Fathers, and with the vast majority of unical and cursive manuscripts." [21]

It is then clear that among the great body of cursive and uncial manuscripts which the Reformers possessed, the majority agreed with the Received Text; there were a few, however, among these documents which belonged to the counterfeit family. These dissenting few presented all the problems which can be found in the Alexandrinus, the Vaticanus, and the Sinaiticus. In other words, the translators of the King James came to a diametrically opposite conclusion from that arrived at by the Revisers of 1881, although the men of 1611, as well as those

---

[20] Quoted in Rheims and Douay, by Dr. H. Cotton, p. 155.
[21] F. C. Cook, Revised Version of the First Three Gospels, p. 226.

of 1881, had before them the same problems and the same evidence. We shall present testimony on this from another authority:

"The popular notion seems to be, that we are indebted for our knowledge of the true texts of Scripture to the existing uncials entirely; and that the essence of the secret dwells exclusively with the four or five oldest of those uncials. By consequence, it is popularly supposed that since we are possessed of such uncial copies, we could afford to dispense with the testimony of the cursives altogether. A more complete misconception of the facts of the case can hardly be imagined. For the plain truth is THAT ALL THE PHENOMENA EXHIBITED BY THE UNCIAL MANUSCRIPTS are reproduced by the cursive copies." [22] (Caps. Mine)

We give a further testimony from another eminent authority:

"Our experience among the Greek cursives proves to us that transmission has not been careless, and they do represent a wholesome traditional text in the passages involving doctrine and so forth." [23]

As to the large number of manuscripts in existence, we have every reason to believe that the Reformers were far better acquainted with them than later scholars. Doctor Jacobus in speaking of textual critics of 1582, says:

"The present writer has been struck with the critical acumen shown at that date (1582), and the grasp of the relative value of the common Greek manuscripts and the Latin version." [24]

On the other hand, if more manuscripts have been made accessible since 1611, little use has been made of what we had before and of the majority of those made available since. The Revisers systematically ignored the whole world of manuscripts and relied practically on only three or four. As Dean Burgon says, "But nineteen-

---

[22] Burgon and Miller, The Traditional Text., p. 202.
[23] Dr. H. C. Hoskier, Concerning the Genesis of the Versions, p. 416.
[24] Dr. Jacobus, Cath. and Prot. Bibles, p. 212.

twentieths of those documents, for any use which has been made of them, might just as well be still lying in the monastic libraries from which they were obtained." We feel, therefore, that a mistaken picture of the case has been presented with reference to the material at the disposition of the translators of 1611 and concerning their ability to use that material.

PLANS OF WORK FOLLOWED BY THE KING JAMES TRANSLATORS

The forty-seven learned men appointed by King James to accomplish this important task were divided first into three companies: one worked at Cambridge, another at Oxford, and the third at Westminster. Each of these companies again split up into two. Thus, there were six companies working on six allotted portions of the Hebrew and Greek Bibles. Each member of each company worked individually on his task, then brought to each member of his committee the work he had accomplished. The committee all together went over that portion of the work translated. Thus, when one company had come together, and had agreed on what should stand, after having compared their work, as soon as they had completed any one of the sacred books, they sent it to each of the other companies to be critically reviewed. If a later company, upon reviewing the book, found anything doubtful or unsatisfactory, they noted such places, with their reasons, and sent it back to the company whence it came. If there should be a disagreement, the matter was finally arranged at a general meeting of the chief persons of all the companies at the end of the work. It can be seen by this method that each part of the work was carefully gone over at least fourteen times. It was further understood that if there was any special difficulty or obscurity, all the learned men of the land could be called upon by letter for their judgment. And finally each bishop kept the clergy of his diocese notified concerning the progress of the work, so that if any one felt constrained to send any particular observations, he was notified to do so.

How astonishingly different is this from the method employed by the Revisers of 1881! The Old Testament Committee met together and sat as one body secretly for ten years. The New Testament Committee did the same. This arrangement left the committee at the mercy of a determined triumvirate to lead the weak and to dominate the rest. All reports indicate that an iron rule of silence was imposed upon these Revisers during the ten years. The public was kept in suspense all the long, weary ten years. And only after elaborate plans had been laid to throw the Revised Version all at once upon the market to effect a tremendous sale, did the world know what had gone on.

The Giants of Learning

No one can study the lives of those men who gave us the King James Bible without being impressed with their profound and varied learning.

"It is confidently expected," says McClure, "that the reader of these pages will yield to the conviction that all the colleges of Great Britain and America, even in this proud day of boastings, could not bring together the same number of divines equally qualified by learning and piety for the great undertaking. Few indeed are the living names worthy to be enrolled with those mighty men. It would be impossible to convene out of any one Christian denomination, or out of all, a body of translators, on whom the whole Christian community would bestow such confidence as is reposed upon that illustrious company, or who would prove themselves as deserving of such confidence. Very many self-styled 'improved versions' of the Bible, or of parts of it, have been paraded before the world, but the religious public has doomed them all, without exception, to utter neglect." [25]

The translators of the King James, moreover, had something beyond great scholarship and unusual skill. They had gone through a period of great suffering. They

---

[25] McClure, p. 64.

had offered their lives that the truths which they loved might live. As the biographer of William Tyndale has aptly said,—

"So Tyndale thought; but God had ordained that not in the learned leisure of a palace, but amid the dangers and privations of exile should the English Bible be produced. Other qualifications were necessary to make him a worthy translator of Holy Scripture than mere grammatical scholarship. . . . At the time he bitterly felt what seemed to be the total disappointment of all his hopes; but he afterwards learned to trace in what appeared a misfortune the fatherly guidance of God; and this very disappointment, which compelled him to seek his whole comfort in the Word of God, tended to qualify him for the worthy performance of his great work." [26]

Doctor Cheyne in giving his history of the founders of higher criticism, while extolling highly the mental brilliancy of the celebrated Hebrew scholar, Gesenius, expresses his regrets for the frivolity of that scholar.[27] No such weakness was manifested in the scholarship of the Reformers.

"Reverence," says Doctor Chambers, "it is this more than any other one trait that gave to Luther and Tyndale, their matchless skill and enduring preëminence as translators of the Bible." [28]

It is difficult for us in this present prosperous age to understand how deeply the heroes of Protestantism in those days were forced to lean upon the arm of God. We find them speaking and exhorting one another by the promises of the Lord, that He would appear in judgment against their enemies. For that reason they gave full credit to the doctrine of the Second Coming of Christ as taught in the Holy Scriptures. Passages of notable value which refer to this glorious hope were not wrenched from their forceful setting as we find them in the Revised

---

[26] Demaus, William Tyndale, pp. 84, 85.
[27] Dr. Cheyne, Founders of O. T. Criticism, pp. 58, 59.
[28] Chambers, Companion, p. 53.

Versions and some modern Bibles, but were set forth with a fullness of clearness and hope.

THE KING JAMES BIBLE A MASTERPIECE

The birth of the King James Bible was a death stroke to the supremacy of Roman Catholicism. The translators little foresaw the wide extent of circulation and the tremendous influence to be won by their book. They little dreamed that for three hundred years it would form the bond of English Protestantism in all parts of the world. One of the brilliant minds of the last generation, Faber, who as a clergyman in the Church of England, labored to Romanize that body, and finally abandoned it for the Church of Rome, cried out,—

"Who will say that the uncommon beauty and marvelous English of the Protestant Bible is not one of the great strongholds of heresy in this country?" [29]

Yes, more, it has not only been the stronghold of Protestantism in Great Britain, but it has built a gigantic wall as a barrier against the spread of Romanism.

"The printing of the English Bible has proved to be by far the mightiest barrier ever reared to repel the advance of Popery, and to damage all the resources of the Papacy." [30]

Small wonder then that for three hundred years incessant warfare has been waged upon this instrument created by God to mold all constitutions and laws of the British Empire, and of the great American Republic, while at the same time comforting, blessing, and instructing the lives of the millions who inhabit these territories.

Behold what it has given to the world! The machinery of the Catholic Church can never begin to compare with the splendid machinery of Protestantism. The Sabbath School, the Bible printing houses, the foreign missionary societies, the Y. M. C. A., the Y. W. C. A., the Woman's Christian Temperance Union, the Protestant

---

[29] Eadie, The English Bible, Vol. II, p. 158.   [30] McClure, p. 71.

denominational organizations,—these all were the off-spring of Protestantism. Their benefits have gone to all lands and been adopted by practically all nations. Shall we throw away the Bible from which such splendid organizations have sprung?

Something other than an acquaintanceship, more or less, with a crushing mass of intricate details in the Hebrew and the Greek, is necessary to be a successful translator of God's Holy Word. God's Holy Spirit must assist. There must exist that which enables the workman at this task to have not only a conception of the whole but also a balanced conception, so that there will be no conflicts created through lack of skill on the part of the translator. That the giants of 1611 produced this effect and injured no doctrine of the Lord by their labors, may be seen in these few words from Sir Edmund Beckett, as, according to Gladstone, [31] he convincingly reveals the failure of the Revised Version:

"Not their least service, is their showing us how very seldom the Authorized Version is materially wrong, and that no doctrine has been misrepresented there." [32]

To show the unrivaled English language of the King James Bible, I quote from Doctor William Lyon Phelps, Professor of English Literature in Yale University:

"Priests, atheists, skeptics, devotees, agnostics, and evangelists, are generally agreed that the Authorized Version of the English Bible is the best example of English literature that the world has ever seen. . . .

"Every one who has a thorough knowledge of the Bible may truly be called educated; and no other learning or culture, no matter how extensive or elegant, can, among Europeans and Americans, form a proper substitute. Western civilization is founded upon the Bible. . . . I thoroughly believe in a university education for both men and women; but I believe a knowledge of the Bible without a college course is more valuable than a college course without the Bible. . . .

---

[31] Lathbury, Ecclesiastical and Religious Correspondence of Gladstone, Vol. II, p. 320.
[32] Sir Edmund Beckett, Revised New Testament, p. 16.

"The Elizabethan period—a term loosely applied to the years between 1558 and 1642—is generally regarded as the most important era in English literature. Shakespeare and his mighty contemporaries brought the drama to the highest point in the world's history; lyrical poetry found supreme expression; Spencer's Faerie Queene was an unique performance; Bacon's Essays have never been surpassed. But the crowning achievement of those spacious days was the Authorized Translation of the Bible, which appeared in 1611. Three centuries of English literature followed; but, although they have been crowded with poets and novelists and essayists, and although the teaching of the English language and literature now gives employment to many earnest men and women, the art of English composition reached its climax in the pages of the Bible. . . .

"Now, as the English speaking people have the best Bible in the world, and as it is the most beautiful monument erected with the English alphabet, we ought to make the most of it, for it is an incomparably rich inheritance, free to all who can read. This means that we ought invariably in the church and on public occasions to use the Authorized Version; all others are inferior." [33]

This statement was made twenty years after the American Revised Version appeared.

---

[33] Ladies Home Journal, Nov., 1921.

CHAPTER VI

Comparisons to Show How the Jesuit Bible Reappears in the American Revised Version

"I have been surprised, in comparing the Revised Testament with other versions, to find how many of the changes, which are important and valuable, have been anticipated by the Rhemish translation, which now forms a part of what is known as the Douay Bible. . . . And yet a careful comparison of these new translations with the Rhemish Testament, shows them, in many instances, to be simply a return to this old version, and leads us to think that possibly there were as finished scholars three hundred years ago as now, and nearly as good apparatus for the proper rendering of the original text." [1]

T HE modern Bible we have selected to compare with the Jesuit Bible of 1582, is the Revised Version. It led the way and laid the basis for all Modern Speech Bibles to secure a large place. On the following passages from the Scriptures, we have examined The Twentieth Century, Fenton, Goodspeed, Moffatt, Moulton, Noyes, Rotherham, Weymouth, and Douay. With two exceptions, these all in the main agree with the change of thought in the Revised; and the other two agree to a considerable extent. They all, with other modern Bibles not mentioned, represent a family largely built on the Revised Greek New Testament, or one greatly similar, or were the products of a common influence. Therefore, marshaling together a number of recent New Testaments by different editors to support a changed passage in the Revised, proves nothing: perhaps they all have followed the same Greek New Testament reading.

I. *Matthew 6:13*

(1) KING JAMES BIBLE OF 1611. "And lead us not into temptation, but deliver us from evil: *For thine is the kingdom,*

---

[1] Dr. B. Warfield's Collection of Opinions, Vol. II, pp. 52, 53.

and the power, and the glory, for ever. Amen."
  (2) JESUIT VERSION OF 1582. "And lead us not into temptation.
     But deliver us from evil. Amen."
  (3) AMERICAN REVISED VERSION OF 1901. "And bring us not
     into temptation, but deliver us from the evil one."

The Reformers protested against this mutilation of
the Lord's prayer. The Jesuits and Revisers accepted the
mutilation.

II. *Matthew 5:44*

  (1) KING JAMES BIBLE. "But I say unto you, Love your ene-
     mies, bless them that curse you, do good to them that hate
     you, and pray for them which despitefully use you, and
     persecute you."
  (2) JESUIT VERSION. "But I say to you, love your enemies, do
     good to them that hate you: and pray for them that perse-
     cute and abuse you."
  (3) AMERICAN REVISED. "But I say unto you, Love your ene-
     mies, and pray for them that persecute you."

The phrase "bless them that curse you" is omitted
from both the Revised and the Jesuit. On this Canon
Cook says, "Yet this enormous omission rests on the sole
authority of ℵ and B." [2]   (That is, on the Vatican Manuscript and the one found in 1859 in a Catholic monastery.)   Thus we see that the Revised Version is not a
revision in any sense whatever, but a new Bible based on
different manuscripts from the King James, on Catholic
manuscripts in fact.

III. *Luke 2:33*

  (1) KING JAMES BIBLE. "And *Joseph* and His mother mar-
     velled at those things which were spoken of Him."
  (2) JESUIT VERSION. "And *His father* and mother were mar-
     velling upon those things which were spoken concerning
     Him."
  (3) AMERICAN REVISED: "And *His father* and His mother were
     marvelling at the things which were spoken concerning
     Him."

Note that the Jesuit and American Revised Versions
give Jesus a human father, or at least failed to make the
distinction.   Helvidius, the devout scholar of northern
Italy (400 A.D.), who had the pure manuscripts, accused

---

    [2] Cook, Revised Version, p. 51.

Jerome of using corrupt manuscripts on this text.³ These corrupt manuscripts are represented in the Jesuit Version of 1582 and are followed by the Revised Version of 1901.

IV. *Luke 4:8*

(1) KING JAMES BIBLE. "And Jesus answered and said unto him, *Get thee behind me, Satan;* for it is written, Thou shalt worship the Lord thy God, and Him only shalt thou serve."

(2) JESUIT VERSION. "And Jesus answering, said to him, It is written, Thou shalt adore the Lord thy God and Him only shalt thou serve."

(3) AMERICAN REVISED. "And Jesus answered and said unto him, It is written, Thou shalt worship the Lord thy God, and Him only shalt thou serve."

The expression, "get thee behind me, Satan," was early omitted because Jesus used the same expression later to Peter (in Matt. 16:23) to rebuke the apostle. The papal corrupters of the manuscripts did not wish Peter and Satan to stand on the same basis. Note again the fatal parallel between the Jesuit and Revised Versions. We were revised backwards.

V. *Luke 11:2-4*

(1) KING JAMES BIBLE. "And He said unto them, When ye pray, say, Our Father *which art in heaven,* Hallowed be Thy name. Thy kingdom come. *Thy will be done, as in heaven, so in earth.* Give us day by day our daily bread. And forgive us our sins; for we also forgive every one that is indebted to us. And lead us not into temptation; *but deliver us from evil.*"

(2) JESUIT VERSION. "And He said to them, When you pray, say, Father, sanctified be Thy name. Thy kingdom come. Our daily bread give us this day. And forgive us our sins, for because ourselves also do forgive every one that is in debt to us, And lead us not into temptation."

(3) AMERICAN REVISED. "And He said unto them, When ye pray, say, Father, Hallowed be Thy name. Thy kingdom come. Give us day by day our daily bread. And forgive us our sins; for we ourselves also forgive every one that is indebted to us. And bring us not into temptation."

This mutilation of the secondary account of the Lord's

---

³ Nicene and Post-Nicene Fathers (Christian Lit. Ed.), Vol. VI, p. 338.

prayer needs no comment, except to say again that the
Jesuit Version and the American Revised agree.

VI.   *Acts 13:42*

(1) KING JAMES BIBLE.   "And when *the Jews* were gone out of
the synagogue, *the Gentiles* besought that these words might
be preached to them the next Sabbath."

(2) JESUIT VERSION.   "And as they were going forth, they desired them that the Sabbath following they would speak
unto them these words."

(3) AMERICAN REVISED.   "And as they went out, they besought
that these words might be spoken to them the next Sabbath."

From the King James, it is clear that the Sabbath was
the day on which the Jews worshiped.

VII.   *Acts 15:23*

(1) KING JAMES BIBLE.   "And they wrote letters by them after
this manner: The apostles and elders and brethren send
greeting unto the brethren which are of the Gentiles in
Antioch and Syria and Cilicia."

(2) JESUIT VERSION.   "Writing by their hands.   The Apostles
and Ancients, brethren, to the brethren of the Gentiles that
are at Antioch and in Syria and Cilicia, greeting."

(3) AMERICAN REVISED.   "And they wrote thus by them, The
apostles and the elders, brethren, unto the brethren who
are of the Gentiles in Antioch and Syria and Cilicia, greeting."

Notice in the Jesuit Bible and Revised how the clergy
is set off from the laity.   Not so in the King James.

VIII.   *Acts 16:7*

(1) KING JAMES BIBLE.   "After they were come to Mysia, they
assayed to go into Bithynia: but the Spirit suffered them
not."

(2) JESUIT VERSION.   "And when they were come into Mysia,
they attempted to go into Bithynia: and the Spirit of Jesus
suffered them not."

(3) AMERICAN REVISED.   "And when they were come over
against Mysia, they assayed to go into Bithynia; and the
Spirit of Jesus suffered them not."

Milligan, who echoed the theology of the Revisers, says:
"Acts 16:7, where the striking reading 'the Spirit of
Jesus' (not simply, as in the Authorized Version, "the
Spirit") implies that the Holy Spirit had so taken posses-

sion of the Person of the Exalted Jesus that He could be spoken of as 'the Spirit of Jesus.' " [4]

IX. *Romans 5:1*

(1) KING JAMES BIBLE. "Therefore being justified by faith, we have peace with God through our Lord Jesus Christ."

(2) JESUIT VERSION. "Being justified therefore by faith, let us have peace toward God by our Lord Jesus Christ."

(3) AMERICAN REVISED. "Being therefore justified by faith, let us (margin) have peace with God through our Lord Jesus Christ."

" 'Beginning in the Spirit' is another way of saying 'being justified by faith.' " [5]

If, therefore, the phrase, "Being justified by faith," is simply a beginning, as the Catholics think, they feel justified in finishing with "let us have peace." The Reformers saw that "let us have peace" is a serious error of doctrine, so Dr. Robinson testifies.[6]

X. *I Cor. 5:7*

(1) KING JAMES BIBLE. "Purge out therefore the old leaven, that ye may be a new lump, as ye are unleavened. For even Christ our passover is sacrificed for us."

(2) JESUIT VERSION. "Purge the old leaven that you may be a new paste, as you are azymas. For our Pasch, Christ is immolated."

(3) AMERICAN REVISED. "Purge out the old leaven, that ye may be a new lump, even as ye are unleavened. For our passover also hath been sacrificed, even Christ."

By leaving out "for us," the Jesuit Bible and Revised Version strike at the doctrine of the atonement. People are sometimes sacrificed for naught; sacrificed "for us," which is omitted in the Revised, is the center of the whole gospel.

XI. *I Cor. 15:47*

(1) KING JAMES BIBLE. "The first man is of the earth, earthy: the second man is *the Lord* from heaven."

(2) JESUIT VERSION. "The first man of earth, earthly; the second man from heaven, heavenly."

(3) AMERICAN REVISED. "The first man is of the earth, earthy: the second man is of heaven."

---

[4] George Milligan, The Expository Value of Revised Version, p. 99.
[5] Benjamin Jowett, Interpretation of the Scriptures, p. 451.
[6] Dr. G. L. Robinson, Where Did We Get Our Bible? p. 182.

The word "Lord" is omitted in the Jesuit and Revised Versions. The Authorized tells specifically who is that Man from heaven.

XII.　*Ephesians 3:9*

(1) KING JAMES BIBLE. "And to make all men see what is the fellowship of the mystery, which from the beginning of the world hath been hid in God, *who created all things by Jesus Christ.*"

(2) JESUIT VERSION. "And to illuminate all men what is the dispensation of the Sacrament hidden from worlds in God, who created all things."

(3) AMERICAN REVISED. "And to make all men see what is the dispensation of the mystery which for ages hath been hid in God who created all things."

The great truth that Jesus is Creator is omitted in both the Jesuit and the Revised.

XIII.　*Col. 1:14*

(1) KING JAMES BIBLE. "In whom we have redemption through His blood, even the forgiveness of sins."

(2) JESUIT VERSION. "In whom we have redemption the remission of sins."

(3) AMERICAN REVISED. "In whom we have our redemption, the forgiveness of our sins."

The phrase "through His blood" is not found in either the Jesuit or American Revised Versions; its omission can be traced to Origen (200 A.D.), who expressly denies that either the body or soul of our Lord was offered as the price of our redemption.

Eusebius was a devoted follower of Origen; and Eusebius edited the Vatican Manuscript. The omission is in that MS. and hence in the American Revised Version. Moreover, Jerome was a devoted follower of both Origen and Eusebius. The phrase "through His blood" is not in the Vulgate and hence not in the Jesuit Bible.

Here is the fatal parallel between the Jesuit Version and the American Revised Version. This omission of the atonement through blood is in full accord with modern liberalism, and strikes at the very heart of the gospel.

XIV. *I Timothy 3:16*

(1) KING JAMES BIBLE. "And without controversy great is the mystery of godliness: God was manifest in the flesh, justified in the Spirit, seen of angels, preached unto the Gentiles, believed on in the world, received up into glory."

(2) JESUIT VERSION. "And manifestly it is a great Sacrament of piety, which was manifested in flesh, was justified in spirit, appeared to Angels, hath been preached to Gentiles, is believed in the world, is assumpted in glory."

(3) AMERICAN REVISED. "And without controversy great is the mystery of godliness;
He who was manifested in the flesh,
Justified in the spirit,
Seen of angels,
Preached among the nations,
Believed on in the world,
Received up in glory."

What a piece of revision this is! The teaching of the divinity of our Lord Jesus Christ upheld by the King James Bible in this text is destroyed in both the other versions. The King James says, "God" was manifest in the flesh; the Revised says, "He who." "He who" might have been an angel or even a good man like Elijah. It would not have been a great mystery for a man to be manifest in the flesh.

XV. *2 Timothy 4:1*

(1) KING JAMES BIBLE. "I charge thee therefore before God, and the Lord Jesus Christ, who shall judge the quick and the dead at His appearing and His Kingdom."

(2) JESUIT VERSION. "I testify before God and Jesus Christ who shall judge the living and the dead, and by His advent and His kingdom."

(3) AMERICAN REVISED. "I charge thee in the sight of God, and of Christ Jesus, who shall judge the living and the dead, and by His appearing and His kingdom."

The King James in this text, fixes the great day of judgment as occurring at the time of His appearing, and His kingdom. The Jesuit and Revised place it in the indefinite future.

XVI. *Hebrews 7:21*

(1) KING JAMES BIBLE. "(For those priests were made without an oath; but this with an oath by him that said unto him, The Lord sware and will not repent, Thou art a priest for ever *after the order of Melchisedec*)."

(2) JESUIT VERSION. "But this with an oath, by him that said unto him: Our Lord hath sworn, and it shall not repent Him: Thou art a Priest forever."

(3) AMERICAN REVISED. "(For they indeed have been made priests without an oath; but he with an oath by him that saith of him,
The Lord sware and will not repent Himself,
Thou art a priest forever)."

The phrase "after the order of Melchisedec" found in the King James Bible is omitted in the other two versions.

XVII. *Rev. 22:14*

(1) KING JAMES BIBLE. "Blessed are they that do His commandments, that they may have right to the tree of life, and may enter in through the gates into the city."

(2) JESUIT VERSION. "Blessed are they that wash their stoles: that their power may be in the tree of life, and they may enter by the gates into the city."

(3) AMERICAN REVISED. "Blessed are they that wash their robes, that they may have the right to come to the tree of life, and may enter in by the gates into the city."

This passage, in the King James, gives us the right to the tree of life by keeping the commandments. The passage was changed in the Rheims New Testament. It was restored by the Authorized, and changed back to the Rheims (Jesuit Bible) by the Revised.

We might continue these comparisons by using other passages not here given. We prefer to invite the reader to notice other instances as they present themselves in later chapters.

NOTE—The heat of the fierce battle over the Jesuit Bible in 1582 had not yet died down when thirty years later the King James of 1611 appeared. Both versions were in English. This latter volume was beneficiary of the long and minute searchings which the truth of the day underwent.

Any thought that Catholicism had any influence over the King James Bible must be banished not only upon remembering the circumstances of its birth but also by the plea from its translators to King James for protection from a papish retaliation.

We find in the Preface to the King James Bible the following words:

"So that if, on the one side, we shall be traduced by Popish Persons at home or abroad, who therefore will malign us, . . . we may rest secure, . . . sustained without by the powerful protection of Your Majesty's grace and favor."

CHAPTER VII

Three Hundred Years of Attack Upon the King James Bible

"Wherever the so-called Counter-Reformation, started by the Jesuits, gained hold of the people, the vernacular was suppressed and the Bible kept from the laity. So eager were the Jesuits to destroy the authority of the Bible—the paper pope of the Protestants, as they contemptuously called it—that they even did not refrain from criticizing its genuineness and historical value." [1]

THE opponents of the noble work of 1611 like to tell the story of how the great printing plants which publish the King James Bible have been obliged to go over it repeatedly to eliminate flaws of printing, to eliminate words which in time have changed in their meaning, or errors which have crept in through the years because of careless editing by different printing houses. They offer this as an evidence of the fallibility of the Authorized Version. They seem to overlook the fact that this labor of necessity is an argument for, rather than against the dependability of the translations. Had each word of the Bible been set in a cement cast, incapable of the slightest flexibility and been kept so throughout the ages, there could have been no adaptability to the ever-changing structure of human language. The artificiality of such a plan would have eliminated the living action of the Holy Spirit and would accuse both man and the Holy Spirit of being without an intelligent care for the divine treasure.

On this point the scholars of the Reformation made their position clear under three different aspects. First, they claimed that the Holy Scriptures had come down to them unimpaired throughout the centuries.[2] Second,

---

[1] Von Dobschutz, The Influence of the Bible, p. 136.
[2] McClintock and Strong, Encycl. Art., "Semler."

they recognized that to reform any manifest oversight was not placing human hands on a divine work and was not contrary to the mind of the Lord. Dr. Fulke says:

"Nevertheless, whereinsoever Luther, Beza, or the English translators, have reformed any of their former oversights, the matter is not so great, that it can make an heresy." [3]

And lastly, they contended that the Received Text, both in Hebrew and in Greek, as they had it in their day would so continue unto the end of time. [4]

In fact, a testimony no less can be drawn from the opponents of the Received Text. The higher critics, who have constructed such elaborate scaffolding, and who have built such great engines of war as their *apparatus criticus*, are obliged to describe the greatness and strength of the walls they are attacking in order to justify their war machine. On the Hebrew Old Testament, one of a group of the latest and most radical critics says:

"DeLagarde would trace all manuscripts back to a single archetype which he attributed to Rabbi Aquiba, who died in A.D. 135. Whether this hypothesis is a true one or not will probably never be known; it certainly represents the fact that from about his day variations of the consonantal text ceased almost entirely." [5]

While of the Greek New Testament, Dr. Hort, who was an opponent of the Received Text and who dominated the English New Testament Revision Committee, says:

"An overwhelming proportion of the text in all known cursive manuscripts except a few is, as a matter of fact, identical." [6]

Thus strong testimonies can be given not only to the Received Text, but also to the phenomenal ability of the manuscript scribes writing in different countries and in different ages to preserve an identical Bible in the overwhelming mass of manuscripts.

---

[3] Fulke's Defense, p. 60.   [4] Brooke's Cartwright, pp. 274, 275.
[5] Gore, A New Commentary, Part I, p. 647.   [6] Hort's Introduction, p. 143.

The large number of conflicting readings which higher critics have gathered must come from only a few manuscripts, since the overwhelming mass of manuscripts is identical.

The phenomenon presented by this situation is so striking that we are pressed in spirit to inquire, Who are these who are so interested in urging on the world the finds of their criticism? All lawyers understand how necessary for a lawsuit it is to find some one "to press the case." Thousands of wills bequeath property which is distributed in a way different from the wishes of the testator because there are none interested enough to "press the case." The King James Bible had hardly begun its career before enemies commenced to fall upon it. Though it has been with us for three hundred years in splendid leadership—a striking phenomenon—nevertheless, as the years increase, the attacks become more furious. If the book were a dangerous document, a source of corrupting influence and a nuisance, we would wonder why it has been necessary to assail it since it would naturally die of its own weakness. But when it is a divine blessing of great worth, a faultless power of transforming influence, who can it be who are so stirred up as to deliver against it one assault after another? Great theological seminaries, in many lands, led by accepted teachers of learning, are laboring constantly to tear it to pieces. Point us out anywhere, any situation similar concerning the sacred books of any other religion, or even of Shakespeare, or of any other work of literature. Especially since 1814 when the Jesuits were restored by the order of the Pope—if they needed restoration—have the attacks by Catholic scholars on the Bible, and by other scholars who are Protestants in name, become bitter.

"For it must be said that the Roman Catholic or the Jesuitical system of argument—the work of the Jesuits from the sixteenth century to the present day—evinces an amount of learning and dexterity, a subtility of reasoning, a sophistry, a plausibility combined, of which ordinary Christians have but little idea. . . . Those who do so (take the trouble to investigate) find that, if tried by the rules of right reasoning, the argument is defective, assuming points which should be proved; that it is logically false, being grounded in sophisms; that it rests in many cases on quotations which are not genuine. . . on passages which, when collated with the original, are proved to be wholly inefficacious as proofs." [7]

As time went on, this wave of higher criticism mounted higher and higher until it became an ocean surge inundating France, Germany, England, Scotland, the Scandinavian nations, and even Russia. When the Privy Council of England handed down in 1864 its decision, breathlessly awaited everywhere, permitting those seven Church of England clergymen to retain their positions, who had ruthlessly attacked the inspiration of the Bible, a cry of horror went up from Protestant England; but "the whole Catholic Church," said Dean Stanley, "is, as we have seen, with the Privy Council and against the modern dogmatists." [8] By modern dogmatists, he meant those who believe "the Bible, and the Bible only."

The tide of higher criticism was soon seen to change its appearance and to menace the whole framework of fundamentalist thinking. The demand for revision became the order of the day. The crest was seen about 1870 in France, Germany, England, and the Scandinavian countries.[9] Time-honored Bibles in these countries were radically overhauled and a new meaning was read into words of Inspiration.

Three lines of results are strongly discernible as features of the movement. First, "collation" became the watchword. Manuscripts were laid alongside of manuscripts to detect various readings and to justify that reading which the critic chose as the right one. With the majority of workers, especially those whose ideas have stamped the revision, it was astonishing to see how

---

[7] Wm. Palmer, Narrative of Events on the Tracts, p. 23.
[8] Stanley, Essays, p. 140.   [9] Chambers, Companion to Revised, pp. 13, 14.

they turned away from the overwhelming mass of MSS.
and invested with tyrannical superiority a certain few
documents, some of them of a questionable character.
Second, this wave of revision was soon seen to be hostile to the Reformation. There is something startlingly
in common to be found in the modernist who denies the
element of the miraculous in the Scriptures, and the Catholic Church which invests tradition with an inspiration
equal to the Bible. As a result, it seems a desperately
hard task to get justice done to the Reformers or their
product. As Dr. Demaus says:

"For many of the facts of Tyndale's life have been disputed or distorted, through carelessness, through prejudice, and through the malice of that school of writers in
whose eyes the Reformation was a mistake, if not a
crime, and who conceive it to be their mission to revive
all the old calumnies that have ever been circulated
against the Reformers, supplementing them by new ac-
cusations of their own invention." [10]

A third result of this tide of revision is that when our
time-honored Bibles are revised, the changes are generally in favor of Rome. We are told that Bible revision
is a step forward; that new MSS. have been made available and advance has been made in archaeology, phil-
ology, geography, and the apparatus of criticism. How
does it come then that we have been revised back into
the arms of Rome? If my conclusion is true, this so-
called Bible revision has become one of the deadliest of
weapons in the hands of those who glorify the Dark
Ages and who seek to bring western nations back to the
theological thinking which prevailed before the Reformation.

THE FOUNDERS OF TEXTUAL CRITICISM

The founders of this critical movement were Catholics.
One authority pointing out two Catholic scholars, says:

"Meanwhile two great contributions to criticism and
knowledge were made in France: Richard Simon, the

---

[10] Demaus, William Tyndale, p. 13.

Oratorian, published between 1689 and 1695 a series of four books on the text, the versions, and the principal commentators of the New Testament, which may be said to have laid the foundation of modern critical inquiry: Pierre Sabatier, the Benedictine, collected the whole of the pre-Vulgate Latin evidence for the text of the Bible." [11]

So says a modernist of the latest type and held in high repute as a scholar.

Dr. Hort tells us that the writings of Simon had a large share in the movement to discredit the Textus Receptus class of MSS. and Bibles. While of him and other outstanding Catholic scholars in this field, the Catholic Encyclopedia says:

"A French priest, Richard Simon (1638-1712), was the first who subjected the general questions concerning the Bible to a treatment which was at once comprehensive in scope and scientific in method. Simon is the forerunner of modern Biblical criticism. . . . The use of internal evidence by which Simon arrived at it entitles him to be called the father of Biblical criticism." [12]

"In 1753 Jean Astruc, a French Catholic physician of considerable note, published a little book, 'Conjectures sur les memoires originaux dont il parait que Moise s'est servi pour composer le livre de la Genese,' in which he conjectured, from the alternating use of two names of God in the Hebrew Genesis, that Moses had incorporated therein two pre-existing documents, one of which employed *Elohim* and the other *Jehovah*. The idea attracted little attention till it was taken up by a German scholar, who, however, claims to have made the discovery independently. This was Johann Gottfried Eichhorn. . . . Eichhorn greatly developed Astruc's hypothesis." [13]

"Yet it was a Catholic priest of Scottish origin, Alexander Geddes (1737-1802), who broached a theory of the origin of the Five Books (to which he attached Josue) exceeding in boldness either Simon's or Eichhorn's. This was the well-known 'Fragment' hypothesis, which reduced the Pentateuch to a collection of fragmentary sec-

---

[11] Gore, New Commentary, Part III, p. 719.
[12] Catholic Encyclopedia, Vol. IV, p. 492.   [13] Idem, pp. 492, 493.

tions partly of Mosaic origin, but put together in the reign of Solomon. Geddes' opinion was introduced into Germany in 1805 by Vater." [14]

Some of the earliest critics in the field of collecting variant readings of the New Testament in Greek, were Mill and Bengel. We have Dr. Kenrick, Catholic Bishop of Philadelphia in 1849, as authority that they and others had examined these manuscripts recently exalted as superior, such as the Vaticanus, Alexandrinus, Beza, and Ephraem, and had pronounced in favor of the Vulgate, the Catholic Bible. [15]

Simon, Astruc, and Geddes, with those German critics, Eichhorn, Semler, and DeWitte, who carried their work on further and deeper, stand forth as leaders and representatives in the period which stretches from the date of the King James (1611) to the outbreak of the French Revolution (1789). Simon and Eichhorn were co-authors of a Hebrew Dictionary. [16] These outstanding six, —two French, one Scotch, and three German,—with others of perhaps not equal prominence, began the work of discrediting the Received Text, both in the Hebrew and in the Greek, and of calling in question the generally accepted beliefs respecting the Bible which had prevailed in Protestant countries since the birth of the Reformation. There was not much to do in France, since it was not a Protestant country and the majority had not far to go to change their belief; there was not much done in England or Scotland because there a contrary mentality prevailed. The greatest inroads were made in Germany. Thus matters stood when in 1773, European nations arose and demanded that the Pope suppress the order of the Jesuits. It was too late, however, to smother the fury which sixteen years later broke forth in the French Revolution.

The upheaval which followed engaged the attention of all mankind for a quarter of a century. It was the period of indignation foreseen by the prophet Daniel. As the armies of the Revolution and of Napoleon marched and counter-marched over the territories of Continental Europe, the foundations of the ancient regime were broken up. Even from the Vatican the cry arose, "Religion is destroyed." And when in 1812 Napoleon was taken prisoner, and the deluge had passed, men looked out upon a changed Europe. England had escaped invasion, although she had taken a leading part in the overthrow of Napoleon. France restored her Catholic monarchs,—the Bourbons who "never learned anything and never forgot anything." In 1814 the Pope promptly restored the Jesuits.

Then followed in the Protestant world two outstanding currents of thought: first, on the part of many, a stronger expression of faith in the Holy Scriptures, especially in the great prophecies which seemed to be on the eve of fulfillment where they predict the coming of a new dispensation. The other current took the form of a reaction, a growing disbelief in the leadership of accepted Bible doctrines whose uselessness seemed proved by their apparent impotence in not preventing the French Revolution. And, as in the days before that outbreak, Germany, which had suffered the most, seemed to be fertile soil for a strong and rapid growth of higher criticism.

GRIESBACH AND MÖHLER

Among the foremost of those who tore the Received Text to pieces in the Old Testament stand the Hollander, Kuehnen, and the German scholars, Ewald and Wellhausen. Their findings, however, were confined to scholarly circles. The public were not moved by them, as their work appeared to be only negative. The two German critics who brought the hour of revision much nearer were the Protestant Griesbach, and the Catholic Möhler. Möhler (1796-1838) did not spend his efforts on the text as did Griesbach, but he handled the points of difference in doctrine between the Protestants and the Catholics in

such a way as to win over the Catholic mind to higher
criticism and to throw open the door for Protestants who
either loved higher criticism, or who, being disturbed by
it, found in Catholicism, a haven of refuge. Of him
Hagenbach says:

"Whatever vigorous vitality is possessed by the most
recent Catholic theological science is due to the labors
of this man." [17]

While Kurtz says:

"He sent rays of his spirit deep into the hearts and
minds of hundreds of his enthusiastic pupils by his writings, addresses, and by his intercourses with them; and
what the Roman Catholic Church of the present possesses
of living scientific impulse and feeling was implanted, or
at least revived and excited by him. . . . In fact, long as
was the opposition which existed between both churches,
no work from the camp of the Roman Catholics produced as much agitation and excitement in the camp of
the Protestants as this." [18]

Or, as Maurice writes concerning Ward, one of the
powerful leaders of the Oxford Movement:

"Ward's notion of Lutheranism is taken, I feel pretty
sure, from Möhler's very gross misrepresentations." [19]

Griesbach (1745-1812) attacked the Received Text of
the New Testament in a new way. He did not stop at
bringing to light and emphasizing the variant readings
of the Greek manuscripts; he classified readings into
three groups, and put all manuscripts under these group-
ings, giving them the names of "Constantinopolitan," or
those of the Received Text, the "Alexandrian," and the
"Western." While Griesbach used the Received Text as
his measuring rod, nevertheless, the new Greek New Testament he brought forth by this measuring rod followed
the Alexandrian manuscripts or,—Origen. His classification of the manuscripts was so novel and the result

---

[17] Hagenbach, Church History, Vol. II, p. 446.
[18] Kurtz, History of the Reformation, Vol. II, p. 391.
[19] Life of T. D. Maurice by his Son, Vol. 1, p. 362.

of such prodigious labors, that critics everywhere hailed his Greek New Testament as the final word. It was not long, however, before other scholars took Griesbach's own theory of classification and proved him wrong.

ROMANTICISM AND SIR WALTER SCOTT

The effective manner in which other currents appeared during this period, which, working together, contributed toward one central point, may be seen in the unusual factors which arose to call the thoughts of men back to the Middle Ages. All that contributed to the glamour and the romanticism of the ages of chivalry seemed to start forth with a new freshness of life. The Gothic architecture, which may be seen in the cathedrals erected while St. Louis of France and Thomas A. Beckett of England were medieval heroes, again became the fashion. Religious works appeared whose authors glorified the saints and the princes of the days of the crusades. Sir Walter Scott is generally esteemed by everyone as being the outstanding force which led the minds of fiction readers to the highest enthusiasm over the exploits of Catholic heroes and papal armies.[20]

Many forces were at work, mysterious in the unexpected way they appeared and arousing public interest in the years which preceded the Reformation. Painters of England, France, and Germany, there were, who gave to Medieval scenes a romance, and so aroused in them new interest.

WINER

Winer (1789-1858), a brilliant student in theology, but especially in Biblical Greek, was destined to transmit through modern rules affecting New Testament Greek, the results of the research and speculations produced by the higher critics and German theologians who had gone before him and were working contemporaneously with him. Dean Farrar calls Winer, "The highest authority in Hellenistic Grammar." Griesbach had blazed a new

---

[20] Cadman, Three Religious Leaders, pp. 476-478.

trail, when by his classification of manuscripts, he cast
reflection upon the authority of the Received Text. Möhler and Görres had so revivified and exalted Catholic
theology that the world of scholars was prepared to receive some new devices which they called rules, in handling the grammatical elements of the New Testament
Greek. These rules differed greatly in viewpoint from
those of the scholars of the Reformation. Winer was
that man who provided such rules.

In order to understand what Winer did, we must ask
ourselves the question: In the Bible, is the Greek New
Testament joined to a Hebrew Old Testament, or to a
group of Greek writings? Or in other words: Will the
language of the Greek New Testament be influenced by
the molds of pagan thought coming from the Greek
world into the books of the New Testament, or will it be
molded by the Hebrew idioms and phrases of the Old
Testament directly inspired of God? The Reformers
said that the Greek of the New Testament was cast in
Hebrew forms of thought, and translated freely; the Revisers literally. The Revisers followed Winer. We see
the results of their decision in the Revised New Testament.

To understand this a little more clearly, we need to remember that the Hebrew language was either deficient
in adjectives, or dearly liked to make a noun serve in
place of an adjective. The Hebrews often did not say a
"strong man;" they said a "man of strength." They did
not always say an "old woman;" they said a "woman of
age." In English we would use the latter expression
only about once where we would use the former many
times. Finding these Hebrew methods of handling New
Testament Greek, the Reformers translated them into the
idiom of the English language, understanding that that
was what the Lord intended. Those who differed from
the Reformers claimed that these expressions should be
carried over literally, or what is known as translitera-
tion. Therefore the Revisers did not translate; they

transliterated and gloried in their extreme literalism. Let us illustrate the results of this new method.

HEBRAISMS

King James (Reformers)	Revised (Winer)
Matt. 5:22 "hell fire"	"hell of fire"
Titus 2:13 "the glorious appearing"	"the appearing of the glory"
Phil. 3:21 "His glorious body"	"the body of His glory"

The first means Christ's glorified body, the second might mean good deeds.

Dr. Vance Smith, Unitarian scholar on the Revision Committee, said that "hell of fire" opened the way for the other hells of pagan mythology.

THE ARTICLE (ITS NEW RULES)

Matt. 11:2 "Christ"	"the Christ"
Heb. 9:27 "the judgment"	"judgment"

Dean Farrar in his defense of the Revised Version says that, in omitting the article in Hebrews 9:27, the Revisers changed the meaning from the great and final judgment, to judgments in the intermediate state (such as purgatory, limbo, etc.), thus proving the intermediate state. From the growing favor in which the doctrine of purgatory is held, we believe the learned Dean had this in mind. Pages of other examples could be given of how the new rules can be used as a weapon against the King James.

So the modern rules which they apparently followed when it suited their theology, on the "article," the "tenses,"—aorists and perfect,—the "pronoun," the "preposition," the "intensive," "Hebraisms," and "parallelisms," pave the way for new and anti-Protestant doctrines concerning the "Person of Christ," "Satan," "Inspiration of the Bible," "The Second Coming of Christ," and other topics dealt with later.

On this point the *Edinburgh Review*, July, 1881, says:

"Our Revisers have subjected their original to the most exhaustive grammatical analysis, every chapter testifies to the fear of Winer that was before their eyes, and their familiarity with the intricacies of modern verbal criticisms."

THE MOULTON FAMILY

Let me now introduce Professor W. F. Moulton, of Cambridge, England; his brother, Professor R. G. Moulton, of Chicago University; and his son, Dr. J. H. Moulton of several colleges and universities.

Professor W. F. Moulton of Leys College, Cambridge, England, was a member of the English New Testament Revision Committee. To him we owe, because of his great admiration for it, the translation into English of Winer's Grammar of New Testament Greek. It went through a number of editions, had a wide circulation, and exercised a dominant influence upon the thinking of modern Greek scholars.

Professor W. F. Moulton had a very strong part in the selecting of the members who should serve on the English New Testament Revision Committee. Of this, his son, Professor James H. Moulton, says regarding Bishop Ellicott, leading promoter of revision, and chairman of the New Testament Revision Committee:

"Doctor Ellicott had been in correspondence on Biblical matters with the young Assistant Tutor. . . . His estimate of his powers was shown first by the proposal as to Winer, and not long after by the Bishop's large use of my father's advice in selecting new members of the Revision Company. Mr. Moulton took his place in the Jerusalem Chamber in 1870, the youngest member of the Company; and in the same year his edition of Winer appeared." [21]

Of Professor Moulton's work, Bishop Ellicott writes:

"Their (the Revisers') knowledge of New Testament Greek was distinctly influenced by the grammatical views of Professor Winer, of whose valuable grammar of the Greek Testament one of our company . . . had been a well-known and successful translator." [22]

---

[21] J. H. Moulton, A Grammar of the Greek N. T., p. viii.
[22] Bishop C. J. Ellicott, Addresses on the Revised Version, pp. 106, 107.

Professor W. F. Moulton, a Revisionist, also wrote a book on the "History of the Bible." In this book he glorifies the Jesuit Bible of 1582 as agreeing "with the best critical editions of the present day." "Hence," he says, "we may expect to find that the Rhemish New Testament (Jesuit Bible of 1582) frequently anticipates the judgment of later scholars as to the presence or absence of certain words, clauses, or even verses." And again, "On the whole, the influence of the use of the Vulgate would, in the New Testament, be more frequently for good than for harm in respect of *text*." [23] With respect to the use of the article, he says, "As the Latin language has no definite article, it might well be supposed that of all English versions, the Rhemish would be least accurate in this point of translation. The very reverse is actually the case. There are many instances (a comparatively hasty search has discovered more than forty) in which, of all versions, from Tyndale's to the Authorized inclusive, this alone is correct in regard to the article." [24] All this tended to belittle the King James and create a demand for a different English Bible.

You will be interested to know that his brother, Professor R. G. Moulton, believes the book of Job to be a drama. He says:

"But the great majority of readers will take these chapters to be part of the parable into which the history of Job has been worked up. The incidents in heaven, like the incidents of the prodigal son, they will understand to be spiritually imagined, not historically narrated." [25]

Since "Get thee behind me, Satan" has been struck out in the Revised in Luke 4:8, and the same phrase now applied only to Peter (Matt. 16:23), it is necessary, since Peter is called Satan by Christ, to use modern rules and exalt Satan.

[23] W. F. Moulton, The English Bible, pp. 184, 185.
[24] Idem, p. 188.
[25] R. G. Moulton, The Literary Study of the Bible, p. 37.

"Among the sons of God," R. G. Moulton further tells us, "it is said, comes 'the Satan.' It is best to use the article and speak of '*the* Satan'; or as the margin gives it, 'the Adversary': that is, the Adversary *of the Saints*. . . . Here (as in the similar passage of Zechariah) the Satan is an official of the Court of Heaven. . . . The Roman Church has exactly caught this conception in its 'Advocatus Diaboli': such an advocate may be in fact a pious and kindly ecclesiastic, but he has the function assigned him of searching out all possible evil that can be alleged against a candidate for canonization, lest the honours of the church might be given without due enquiry." [26]

From the study which you have had of Winer and the Moultons, I think it will be easy to see the trend of German higher criticism as it has been translated into English literature and into the revised edition of the Bible.

CARDINAL WISEMAN (1802-1865)

The new birth of Catholicism in the English world can be credited to no one more than to that English youth— later to become a cardinal—who pursued at Rome his Oriental studies. There under the trained eye of Cardinal Mai, the editor of the Vatican Manuscript, Wiseman early secured an influential leadership among higher critics by his researches and theories on the earliest texts. "Without this training," he said later, "I should not have thrown myself into the Puseyite controversy at a later period." [27] He was thrilled over the Catholic reaction taking place everywhere on the Continent, and, being English, he longed to have a share in bringing about the same in England. He was visited in Rome by Gladstone, by Archbishop Trench, a promoter of revision and later a member of the English New Testament Revision Committee; also by Newman, Froude, and Manning; [28] by the leaders of the Catholic reaction in Germany,—Bunsen, Görres, and Overbeck; and by the leaders of the same in France,—Montalembert, Lacordaire, and Lamennais.

---

[26] Idem, pp. 28, 29.
[27] Wilfred Ward, Life and Times of Cardinal Wiseman, Vol. 1, p. 65.
[28] Idem, p. 93.

Wiseman's theories on the Old Latin Manuscripts—
later to be disproved—gave a decided impetus to the
campaign against the Received Text. Scrivener, generally well-balanced, was affected by his conclusions.
"Even in our day such writers as Mr. Scrivener, Bishop
Westcott, and Tregelles, as well as German and Italian
scholars, have made liberal use of his arguments and
researches." [29] "Wiseman has made out a case," says
Scrivener, "which all who have followed him, Lachmann,
Tischendorf, Davidson, and Tregelles, accept as irresistible." [30] Some of the most distinguished men of Europe
attended his lectures upon the reconciliation of science
and religion. The story of how he was sent to England, founded the *Dublin Review,* and working on the
outside of Oxford with the remnants of Catholicism in
England and with the Catholics of the Continent, while
Newman on the inside of Oxford, as a Church of England clergyman, worked to Romanize that University
and that Church; of how Wiseman organized again the
Catholic hierarchy in Great Britain, a step which convulsed England from end to end, will be subjects for
later consideration. Suffice it now to say that Wiseman
lived long enough to exult openly [31] that the King James
Version had been thrust aside and the preëminence of
the Vulgate reëstablished by the influence of his attacks
and those of other textual critics.

The Gnosticism of German Theology Invades England

Coleridge, Thirwall, Stanley, Westcott

By 1833 the issue was becoming clearly defined. It
was Premillenarianism, that is, belief in the return of
Christ before the millennium, or Liberalism; it was with
regard to the Scriptures, literalism or allegorism. As
Cadman says of the Evangelicals of that day:

[29] Ward, Life of Wiseman, Vol. 1, p. 57.
[30] Scrivener, Introduction to the Criticism of the N. T., Vol. II, p. 44.
[31] Wiseman's Essays, Vol. 1, p. 104.

"Their fatalism inclined many of them to Premillenarianism as a refuge from the approaching catastrophes of the present dispensation. . . . Famous divines strengthened and adorned the wider ranks of Evangelicalism, but few such were found within the pale of the Establishment. Robert Hall, John Foster, William Jay of Bath, Edward Irving, the eccentric genius, and in Scotland, Thomas Chalmers, represented the vigor and fearlessness of an earlier day and maintained the excellence of Evangelical preaching." [32]

How deeply the conviction, that the great prophecies which predicted the approaching end of the age, had gripped the public mind can be seen in the great crowds which assembled to hear Edward Irving. They were so immense that he was constantly compelled to secure larger auditoriums. Even Carlyle could relate of his own father in 1832:

"I have heard him say in late years with an impressiveness which all his perceptions carried with them, that the lot of a poor man was growing worse and worse; that the world would not and could not last as it was; that mighty changes of which none saw the end were on the way. To him, as one about to take his departure, the whole was but of secondary moment. He was looking toward 'a city that had foundations.' " [33]

Here was a faith in the Second Coming of Christ, at once Protestant and evangelical, which would resist any effort so to revise the Scriptures as to render them colorless, giving to them nothing more than a literary endorsement of plans of betterment, merely social or political. This faith was soon to be called upon to face a theology of an entirely different spirit. German religious thinking at that moment was taking on an aggressive attitude. Schleiermacher had captured the imagination of the age and would soon mold the theology of Oxford and Cambridge. Though he openly confessed himself a Protestant, nevertheless, like Origen of old, he sat at the feet

---

[32] Cadman, Three Religious Leaders, pp. 416, 417.
[33] Froude, Carlyle's Reminiscences, p. 48.

of Clement, the old Alexandrian teacher of 190 A.D.

Clement's passion for allegorizing Scripture offered an easy escape from those obligations imposed upon the soul by a plain message of the Bible. Schleiermacher modernized Clement's philosophy and made it beautiful to the parlor philosophers of the day by imaginary analysis of the realm of spirit. It was the old Gnosticism revived, and would surely dissolve Protestantism wherever accepted and would introduce such terms into the Bible, if revision could be secured, as to rob the trumpet of a certain sound. The great prophecies of the Bible would become mere literary addresses to the people of bygone days, and unless counter-checked by the noble Scriptures of the Reformers, the result would be either atheism or papal infallibility.

If Schleiermacher did more to captivate and enthrall the religious thinking of the nineteenth century than any other one scholar, Coleridge, his contemporary, did as much to give aggressive motion to the thinking of England's youth of his day, who, hardly without exception, drank enthusiastically of his teachings. He had been to Germany and returned a fervent devotee of its theology and textual criticism. At Cambridge University he became the star around which grouped a constellation of leaders in thought. Thirwall, Westcott, Hort, Moulton, Milligan, who were all later members of the English Revision Committees and whose writings betray the voice of the master, felt the impact of his doctrines.

"His influence upon his own age, and especially upon its younger men of genius, was greater than that of any other Englishman. . . . Coleridgeans may be found now among every class of English divines, from the Broad Church to the highest Puseyites," says McClintock and Strong's Encyclopedia.

The same article speaks of Coleridge as "Unitarian," "Metaphysical," a "Theologian," "Pantheistic," and says that "he identifies reason with the divine Logos," and that he holds "views of inspiration as low as the rationalists," and also holds views of the Trinity "no better than a refined, Platonized Sabellianism."

LACHMANN, TISCHENDORF, AND TREGELLES

We have seen above how Lachmann, Tischendorf, and Tregelles fell under the influence of Cardinal Wiseman's theories. There are more recent scholars of textual criticism who pass over these three and leap from Griesbach to Westcott and Hort, claiming that the two latter simply carried out the beginnings of classification made by the former.[34] Nevertheless, since many writers bid us over and over again to look to Lachmann, Tischendorf, and Tregelles,—until we hear of them morning, noon, and night, —we would seek to give these laborious scholars all the praise justly due them, while we remember that there is a limit to all good things.

Lachmann's (1793-1851) bold determination to throw aside the Received Text and to construct a new Greek Testament from such manuscripts as he endorsed according to his own rules, has been the thing which endeared him to all who give no weight to the tremendous testimony of 1500 years of use of the Received Text. Yet Lachmann's canon of criticism has been deserted both by Bishop Ellicott, and by Dr. Hort. Ellicott says, "Lachmann's text is really one based on little more than four manuscripts, and so is really more of a critical recension than a critical text." [35] And again, "A text composed on the narrowest and most exclusive principles." [35] While Dr. Hort says:

"Not again, in dealing with so various and complex a body of documentary attestation, is there any real advantage in attempting, with Lachmann, to allow the distributions of a very small number of the most ancient existing documents to construct for themselves a provisional text." [36]

Tischendorf's (1815-1874) outstanding claim upon his-

---

[34] Gore, A New Commentary, Part III, p. 720.
[35] Ellicott, Considerations on Revision of the N. T., p. 46.
[36] Hort's Introduction, p. 288.

tory is his discovery of the Sinaitic Manuscript in the
convent at the foot of Mt. Sinai. Mankind is indebted
to this prodigious worker for having published manuscripts not accessible to the average reader. Nevertheless, his discovery of Codex Aleph (א) toppled over his
judgment. Previous to that he had brought out seven
different Greek New Testaments, declaring that the
seventh was perfect and could not be superseded. Then,
to the scandal of textual criticism, after he had found
the Sinaitic Manuscript, he brought out his eighth Greek
New Testament, which was different from his seventh in
3572 places.[37] Moreover, he demonstrated how textual
critics can artificially bring out Greek New Testaments
when, at the request of a French Publishing house, Fir-
min Didot, he edited an edition of the Greek Testament
for Catholics, conforming it to the Latin Vulgate.[38]

Tregelles (1813-1875) followed Lachmann's principles
by going back to what he considered the ancient manuscripts and, like him, he ignored the Received Text and
the great mass of cursive manuscripts.[39] Of him, Ellicott
says, "His critical principles, especially his general principles of estimating and regarding modern manuscripts,
are now, perhaps justly, called in question by many competent scholars," and that his text "is rigid and mechanical, and sometimes fails to disclose that critical instinct
and peculiar scholarly sagacity which is so much needed
in the great and responsible work of constructing a critical text of the Greek Testament." [40]

In his splendid work which convinced Gladstone that
the Revised Version was a failure, Sir Edmund Beckett
says of the principles which controlled such men as
Lachmann, Tischendorf, Tregelles, Westcott, and Hort in
their modern canons of criticism:

"If two, or two-thirds of two dozen men steeped in
Greek declare that they believe that he (John) ever

[37] Burgon and Miller, Traditional Text, p. 7.
[38] Ezra Abbott, Unitarian Review, March, 1875.
[39] Schaff, Companion to Greek Testament, p. 264.
[40] Ellicott, Considerations, pp. 47, 48.

wrote that he saw in a vision seven angels clothed in stone with golden girdles, which is the only honest translation of their Greek, and defend it with such arguments as these, I . . . distrust their judgment on the 'preponderance of evidence' for new readings altogether, and all their modern canons of criticism, which profess to settle the relative value of manuscripts, with such results as this and many others." [41]

Such were the antecedent conditions preparing the way to draw England into entangling alliances, to de-Protestantize her national church and to advocate at a dangerous hour the necessity of revising the King James Bible. The Earl of Shaftesbury, foreseeing the dark future of such an attempt, said in May, 1856:

"When you are confused or perplexed by a variety of versions, you would be obliged to go to some learned pundit in whom you reposed confidence, and ask him which version he recommended; and when you had taken his version, you must be bound by his opinion. I hold this to be the greatest danger that now threatens us. It is a danger pressed upon us from Germany, and pressed upon us by the neogolical spirit of the age. I hold it to be far more dangerous than Tractarianism or Popery, both of which I abhor from the bottom of my heart. This evil is tenfold more dangerous, tenfold more subtle than either of these, because you would be ten times more incapable of dealing with the gigantic mischief that would stand before you." [42]

THE POLYCHROME BIBLE AND THE SHORTER BIBLE

The results of this rising tide of higher criticism were the rejection of the Received Text and the mania for revision. It gave us, among other bizarre versions, the "Polychrome" and also the "Shorter Bible." The Polychome Bible is generally an edition of the separate books of the Scriptures, each book having every page colored many times to represent the different writers.

Any one who will take the pains to secure a copy of

---

[41] Beckett, The Revised N. T., pp. 181, 182.
[42] Bissell, Origin of the Bible, p. 355.

the "Shorter Bible" in the New Testament, will recognize that about four thousand of the nearly eight thousand verses in that Scripture have been entirely blotted out. We offer the following quotation from the *United Presbyterian* of December 22, 1921, as a description of the "Shorter Bible:"

"The preface further informs us that only about one-third of the Old Testament and two-thirds of the New Testament are possessed of this 'vital interest and practical value.' The Old Testament ritual and sacrificial system, with their deep lessons and their forward look to the atonement through the death of Christ are gone. As a result of this, the New Testament references to Christ as the fulfillment of the Old Testament sacrifices are omitted. Such verses as, 'Behold the Lamb of God which taketh away the sin of the world,' are gone.

"Whole books of the Old Testament are gone. Some of the richest portions of the books of the prophets are missing. From the New Testament they have omitted 4,000 verses. Other verses are cut in two, and a fragment left us, for which we are duly thankful. The great commission recorded in Matthew; the epistles of Titus, Jude, First and Second John, are entirely omitted, and but twenty-five verses of the second epistle of Timothy remain. The part of the third chapter of Romans which treats of human depravity, being 'of no practical value to the present age,' is omitted. Only one verse remains from the fourth chapter. The twenty-fourth chapter of Matthew and other passages upon which the premillenarians base their theory, are missing. All the passages which teach the atonement through the death of Christ are gone."

The campaigns of nearly three centuries against the Received Text did their work. The Greek New Testament of the Reformation was dethroned and with it the Versions translated from it, whether English, German, French, or of any other language. It had been predicted that if the Revised Version were not of sufficient merit to be authorized and so displace the King James, confusion and division would be multiplied by a crop of unauthorized and sectarian translations.[43] The Polychrome, the Shorter Bible, and a large output of heterogeneous Bibles verify the prediction. No competitor has yet appeared able to create a standard comparable to the text which has held sway for 1800 years in the original tongue, and for 300 years in its English translation, the King James.

---

[43] Dr. Schaff, In Bible Revision, p. 20.

CHAPTER VIII

How the Jesuits
Captured Oxford University

BEFORE the English people could go the way of the
Continent and be brought to question their great
English Bible, the course of their thinking must
be changed. Much had to be done to discredit, in their
eyes, the Reformation—its history, doctrines, and documents—which they looked upon as a great work of God.
This task was accomplished by those who, while working
under cover, passed as friends. In what numbers the
Jesuits were at hand to bring this about, the following
words, from one qualified to know, will reveal:

"Despite all the persecution they (the Jesuits) have
met with, they have not abandoned England, where there
are a greater number of Jesuits than in Italy; there are
Jesuits in all classes of society; in Parliament; among the
English clergy; among the Protestant laity, even in the
higher stations. I could not comprehend how a Jesuit
could be a Protestant priest, or how a Protestant priest
could be a Jesuit; but my Confessor silenced my scruples
by telling me, *omnia munda mundis,* and that St. Paul
became as a Jew that he might save the Jews; it was no
wonder, therefore, if a Jesuit should feign himself a Protestant, for the conversion of Protestants. But pay attention, I entreat you, to my discoveries concerning the
nature of the religious movement in England termed
Puseyism.

"The English clergy were formerly too much attached
to their Articles of Faith to be shaken from them. You
might have employed in vain all the machines set in motion by Bossuet and the Jansenists of France to reunite
them to the Romish Church; and so the Jesuits of England tried another plan. This was to demonstrate from
history and ecclesiastical antiquity the legitimacy of the

usages of the English Church, whence, through the exertions of *the Jesuits concealed among its clergy,* might arise a studious attention to Christian antiquity. This was designed to occupy the clergy in long, laborious, and abstruse investigation, and to alienate them from their Bibles." [1] (Italics mine)

So reported Dr. Desanctis, who for many years was a priest at Rome, Professor of Theology, Official Theological Censor of the Inquisition, and who later became a Protestant, as he told of his interview with the Secretary of the French Father Assistant of the Jesuit Order.

Why is it that in 1833, England believed that the Reformation was the work of God, but in 1883 it believed that the Reformation was a rebellion? In 1833, England believed that the Pope was Antichrist; in 1883, that the Pope was the successor of the apostles. And further, in 1833, any clergyman who would have used Mass, confession, holy water, etc., in the Church of England, would have been immediately dismissed, if he would not have undergone violent treatment at the hands of the people. In 1883, thousands of Masses, confessions, and other ritualistic practices of Romanism were carried on in services held in the Church of England. The historian Froude says:

"In my first term at the University (Oxford), the controversial fires were beginning to blaze. . . . I had learnt, like other Protestant children, that the Pope was Antichrist, and that Gregory VII had been a special revelation of that being. I was now taught that Gregory VII was a saint. I had been told to honor the Reformers. The Reformation became a great schism, Cranmer a traitor and Latimer a vulgar ranter. Milton was a name of horror." [2]

The beginning and center of this work was at Oxford University. The movement is known as the Oxford Movement. The movement also involved the revision of the Authorized Version. Kempson indicates the deep background and far-reaching effects of the movement in the following words:

---

[1] Desanctis, Popery and Jesuitism in Rome, pp. 128, 134, quoted in Walsh, Secret History of Oxford Movement, p. 33.
[2] J. A. Froude, Short Studies on Great Subjects, pp. 161, 167.

"Whoever, therefore, desires to get really to the bottom of what is commonly called the Catholic Revival in England is involved in a deep and far-reaching study of events: a study which includes not merely events of ecclesiastical history—some of which must be traced back to sources in the dawn of the Middle Ages or even in Apostolic times—but also the movements of secular politics." [3]

In order rightly to understand the immensity of what was done, the position at this time of the Church of England and of the University of Oxford must be understood. By the victory in 1588 of England over the Spanish Armada, England became the champion and defender of Protestantism. She became the impassable wall of defense which confined Catholicism to Europe, and by her possessions committed the continent of North America to a Protestant future. Whatever may be the defects in the doctrines and organization of the Church of England in the eyes of the large dissenting Protestant Churches, nevertheless, at the time when the Oxford Movement began, she was without question the strongest Protestant organization in the world. It was the Church of England, assisted by many Puritan divines, which gave us the Protestant Bible. The center of the Church of England was Oxford University. Mr. Palmer claims that half the rising clergymen of England were instructed in this seat of education. [4] This same writer speaks of Oxford as, "The great intellectual center of England, famed for its intellectual ascendency among all the churches of the world." [5] Catholics on the continent of Europe also recognized that Oxford was the heart of the Anglican Church. [6]

At the time the Oxford Movement began, a growing tide of Catholic reaction was running in Germany and France. Every turn of events in these two nations prof-

---

[3] F. C. Kempson, The Church in Modern England, p. 59.
[4] Wm. Palmer, Narrative of Events, p. 129.   [5] Idem. p. 7.
[6] Abbott, The Anglican Career of Cardinal Newman, Vol. II, pp. 282, 283.

ited for the Church of Rome. The strong influence in Germany of the Catholic writer, Möhler, and of Windhorst was carrying that erstwhile Protestant people toward the papal throne. The theories of Möhler on the Development of Doctrine became the basis on which the leaders of the movement toward Rome, in England, built.

At this same time in France, Lamennais, Lacordaire, and Montalembert were electrifying the youth of France with their brilliant and stirring leadership. The voice of Lacordaire was heard by enraptured audiences in the national Cathedral of Notre Dame. Montalembert, in his seat among the lawmakers of the French Legislature, was exercising an influence in favor of Catholic legislation. At the same time, Lamennais, with his pen, was idealizing the doctrines and plans of Rome, in the minds of fervent youth. The Jesuits had been restored in 1814. Was it possible that England could withstand this flood of Catholic advance which was devitalizing Protestantism on the Continent?

THE OXFORD MOVEMENT

All are agreed that the year 1833 marked the beginning of the Oxford Movement. The outstanding leader is generally recognized to have been J. H. Newman, who later went over to the Church of Rome, and who was the writer of the famous hymn, "Lead Kindly Light, Amid the Encircling Gloom."

Until the year 1833 there was no outward evidence other than that Newman belonged to the Evangelical party of the Church of England. We are told how he read those serious books which led him to make a profession of conversion and to look upon the Pope as Antichrist. He became a diligent student of the prophecies, and even participated, in some measure, in the current preaching and belief of the time in the soon return of Christ. From the moment, however, that he entered Oxford University, his earlier Evangelical beliefs passed under adverse influences. Hawkins, the Provost of Oriel

College, taught him that the Bible must be interpreted in the light of tradition. Whately led him to understand that the church, as an institution, was of God's appointment, independent of the State, and having rights which were the direct gift of heaven. Newman was led to investigate the creed of the Church of England, which was the Thirty-nine Articles. Of these Cadman says:

"They constituted an authoritative standard against the inroads of the Jesuit controversialists, and instilled those religious and political convictions which protected the integrity of the nation and of the Church against the intrigues of the Papacy."[7]

Shortly after Newman had taken his A. B. degree at Oxford, he was elected, in 1823, to a fellowship in Oriel College. This threw him into intimate touch with those eminent men of the day who were drinking in, and being molded by the intellectual influences coming from Germany.

As an illustration to show how agents from Germany and France were instrumental in changing thoughts and tastes of Oxford students, Mozley, the brother-in-law of Newman, tells us:

"In 1829 German agents, one of them with a special introduction to Robert Wilberforce, filled Oxford with very beautiful and interesting tinted lithographs of medieval paintings." And, "about the same time—that is, in 1829—there came an agent from Cologne with very large and beautiful reproductions of the original design for the cathedral, which it was proposed to set work on, with a faint hope of completing it before the end of the century. Froude gave thirty guineas for a set of drawings, went wild over them, and infected not a few of his friends with medieval architecture."[8]

The following year Newman became curate of a nearby church. It was while in the exercise of his duties there, he tells us, that he became convinced that the Evangeli-

---

[7] Cadman, Three Religious Leaders, p. 453.
[8] Mozley, Reminiscences, Vol. I, p. 32.

cal principles would not work. By far the greatest influence of the moment, however, in his life was the acquaintanceship which he formed in 1826 with Herrell Froude. Froude was the son of a High Churchman, "who loathed Protestantism, denounced the Evangelicals, and brought up his sons to do the same."[9] His attachment to Froude was so great that following the early death of this friend, he wrote endearing verses to his memory.

Another friendship formed in these Oxford days which equaled Froude's in its influence on Newman, was that of the gifted Keble, the author of the "Christian Year." In this book of beautiful poetry, according to Mr. Lock, will be found all the truths and tone, which came to the front in the movement.[10] Keble's parentage, like Froude's, was of the High Church party, strongly anti-Protestant, anti-Evangelical, which early turned the thoughts of Keble to those ideas and principles later to become outstanding features of the Oxford Movement. These three, Froude, Keble, and Newman, shared one another's isolation amid the dominant Protestantism of the hour, and encouraged one another in their longings for the sacraments and ritualism of the Papacy.

Newman, himself, early chose the celibate life, and no doubt Froude's passionate tendency toward Romanism answered in Newman's breast those social yearnings which men usually satisfy in married life. Thus, step by step, in a way most strange and mysterious, Newman, whom Cadman calls "the most brilliant and gifted son of the Church of England" was carried fast and early into that tide of Catholic enthusiasm which was running throughout the Continent.

Under these circumstances and in this frame of mind, he and Froude set out for a tour of the European countries in 1833, the principal point of their visit being the city of Rome. His mind had been prepared for sympa-

---

[9] Cadman, Three Religious Leaders, p. 459.
[10] Dr. Overton, The Anglican Revival, p. 24.

thetic participation in the scenes of Rome by the years
he previously had spent in reading the writings of the
Fathers. From them he had derived a philosophy which
would invest him with feelings of rapture as he viewed
the historical spots and ancient ruins of the Catholic
metropolis.

"Eventually," said Dr. Cadman, "the place of celestial
traditions subdued his questionings; the superstitions of
his youth that Rome was the 'Beast' which stamped its
image on mankind, the 'Great Harlot' who made drunk
the kings of the earth, were dispelled." [11]

Twice he and Froude sought an interview with Nicho-
las Wiseman, who later as Cardinal Wiseman, was to
exercise such a telling influence upon the revision of the
Bible, and the Romanizing of the English Church. We
are not informed of everything which passed between
them, but the question was submitted to the Papacy by
these two Oxford professors, to learn upon what terms
the Church of Rome would receive back into her bosom
the Church of England. The answer came straight, clear,
without any equivocation,—the Church of England must
accept the Council of Trent. The future now lay plain
before Newman. He left the city of Rome hastily, saying, "I have a work to do in England."

The man who was destined to bring forward successfully the greatest religio-political movement among the
children of men, since the Reformation, stood on the deck
of the vessel as it plowed its way through the Mediterranean waters toward the shores of England, and wrote
the hymn which more than any other thing in his life
has made him famous:

> "Lead, Kindly Light, amid the encircling gloom,
>   Lead thou me on!
> The night is dark and I am far from home;
>   Lead thou me on!

---

[11] Cadman, Three Religious Leaders, p. 496.

Keep thou my feet; I do not ask to see
      The distant scene;
One step's enough for me."

Or, as the scholarly secretary of the French Academy says:

"Newman landed in England, July 9, 1833. Some days afterwards what is called 'The Oxford Movement' began." [12]

TRACTARIANISM (1833-1841)

What the Movement meant the following will show:

"Romanism is known to have recently entered the Church of England in the disguise of Oxford Tractarianism; to have drawn off no inconsiderable number of her clergy and members; and to have gained a footing on British soil, from which the government and public opinion together are unable to eject her." [13]

Newman wrote in 1841 to a Roman Catholic, "Only through the English Church can you act upon the English nation. I wish, of course, our Church should be consolidated, with and through and in your communion, for its sake, and your sake, and for the sake of unity." [14] He and his associates believed that Protestantism was Antichrist. Faber, one of the associates of Newman in the Oxford Movement, himself a brilliant writer, said:

"Protestantism is perishing: what is good in it is by God's mercy being gathered into the garners of Rome. . . . My whole life, God willing, shall be one crusade against the detestable and diabolical heresy of Protestantism." [15]

Pusey, the well-known author of "Minor Prophets," and of "Daniel the Prophet," another member of the movement, and a fervent Romanizing apostle within the Protestant fold, said:

"I believe Antichrist will be infidel, and arise out of what calls itself Protestantism, and then Rome and England will be united in one to oppose it." [16]

[12] Thureau-Dangin, The English Catholic Revival, Vol. I, p. 57.
[13] *New Brunswick Review*, Aug. 1854.   [14] Newman, Apologia, p. 225.
[15] J. E. Bowden, Life of F. W. Faber (1869), p. 192.
[16] Walter Walsh, Secret History of the Oxford Movement, p. 292.

Of the movement, Pusey was the moral, as Keble was the poetic, and Newman the intellectual leader. Like the Methodist movement, it sprang from the University of Oxford, with this difference, that Wesleyanism strengthened the cause of Protestantism, while Tractarianism undermined it.

Newman ever gave the date of July 14, 1833, five days after he returned from Rome, as the beginning of the movement. From the very first, secrecy veiled a large measure of its activities. Its promoters at the beginning grouped themselves into a society called, "The Association of the Friends of the Church." All that went on under cover will never be known until the judgment day.

The immense transformation, which was wrought in the Church of England, enables us to single out certain prominent activities as its cause. The leaders banded themselves together with aggressive determination to attack weak points wherever they could make their presence felt, by precipitating crises in the control of the University, and by challenging fundamental relationships between church and state. Further, they grouped around them the students of the University and changed the course of Oxford thinking. They published a series of tracts which threw a flood of fermenting thought upon the English mentality. Amid all their varied and powerful engines of attack, possibly no one thing exercised a greater influence than the sermons Newman himself delivered weekly in the church of St. Mary's at Oxford.

By voice and pen, the teaching of Newman changed in the minds of many their attitude toward the Bible. Stanley shows us that the allegorizing of German theology, under whose influence Newman and the leaders of the movement were, was Origen's method of allegorizing.[17] Newman contended that God never intended the Bible to teach doctrines.[18] Much of the church history read, was on the Waldenses and how they had, through the

---

[17] Stanley, Church and State, pp. 135, 136.
[18] Tract 90, p. 11.

centuries from the days of the apostles, transmitted to us the true faith.[19] The Tractarians determined that the credit of handing down truth through the centuries, should be turned from the Waldenses to the Papacy.

Answering the general stir upon the question of Antichrist, Newman declared that the city of Rome must fall before Antichrist rises. That which saved Rome from falling, he averred, was the saving grace of the Catholic Church, the salt of the earth.[20]

Those who were promoting the movement seemed at times uncontrolled in their love for Romanism. Dr. Pusey, whose standing has given the name of "Puseyism" to this Tractarian Movement, scandalized some of the less ardent spirits by visiting the Catholic monasteries in Ireland to study monastic life, with a view to introducing it into England.[21] Whenever any of the Tractarians went abroad, they revelled in the scenes of Catholic ritualism as if they were starved. Dr. Faber, a talented and outstanding leader among them, gives a lengthy description of his experiences in Rome, in 1843. His visit to the church of St. John Lateran on Holy Thursday, he describes as follows:

"I got close to the altar, inside the Swiss Guards, and when Pope Gregory descended from his throne, and knelt at the foot of the altar, and we all knelt with him, it was a scene more touching than I had ever seen before. . . . That old man in white, prostrate before the uplifted Body of the Lord, and the dead, dead silence—Oh, what a sight it was! . . . On leaving St. John's by the great western door, the immense piazza was full of people; . . . and in spite of the noonday sun, I bared my head and knelt with the people, and received with joy the Holy Father's blessing, until he fell back on his throne and was borne away." [22]

Two of the Tracts especially created a public stir,— Tract 80 and Tract 90. Tract 80, written by Isaac Wil-

---

[19] Lathbury, Letters of Gladstone, Vol I, p. 7.   [20] Tract 83, pp. 30, 37.
[21] Walsh, Secret History, p. 282.   [22] Bowden, Life of Faber, p. 193.

liams on "Reserve in Communicating Knowledge," developed Newman's ideas of mental reservation, which he took from Clement of Alexandria. To Newman, the Fathers were everything; he studied them day and night; he translated them into English, lived with them, and in this Gnostic atmosphere of the early Christian centuries, he viewed all questions. Clement (about 200 A.D.), speaking of the rules which should guide the Christian, says, "He (the Christian) both thinks and speaks the truth; except when consideration is necessary, and then, as a physician for the good of his patient, he will be false, or utter a falsehood. . . . He gives himself up for the church." [23] On this point Mr. Ward, another prominent leader in the movement, is represented by his son as saying, "Make yourself clear that you are justified in deception and then *lie like a trooper.*" [24] Newman himself put this principle into practice, and was guilty of deception when he wrote against Popery, saying things as bitter against the Roman system as Protestants ever said, for the sole purpose of warding off suspicion that he was turning to Rome.

"If you ask me," he says, "how an individual could venture, not simply to hold, but to publish such views of a communion (i. e. the Church of Rome) so ancient, so wide-spreading, so fruitful in Saints, I answer that I said to myself, *'I am not speaking my own words,* I am but following almost a *consensus* of the divines of my own church.' . . . Yet I have reason to fear still, that such language is to be ascribed, in no small measure, to an impetuous temper, a hope of approving myself to persons I respect, and *a wish to repel the charge of Romanism.*"[25] (Italics mine).

Tract 80 created a widespread stir. The term "Jesuitical" might have been heard on the lips of Protestant England everywhere to express what they considered to be the source of such arguments.[26] But that stir was in-

---

23 Newman's Arians, p. 81.
24 Newman's Letters, Vol. II, p. 249, quoted in Walsh, Secret Hist., p. 16.
25 Newman, Apologia, p. 233.

significant compared with what was produced when New-man wrote Tract 90. In fact, if we were to single out any one outstanding event in the history of this Roman-izing Movement prior to the Revision of the Bible in 1870, we would point to Tract 90 as that event. The three great obstacles which stood in the way of Catholi-cism's crumpling up the mental defenses of English Prot-estantism, were: the King James Bible, the Prayer Book, and the Thirty-nine Articles. The Thirty-nine Articles stood for the Creed of the Church of England. These Articles were born in the days when English scholars were being burned at the stake for their adherence to Protestantism. They represented the questions which might be put to an adult before he received baptism or to a candidate for ministerial ordination. With Tract 90, Newman leveled his blow at the Thirty-nine Articles. With a surpassing skill which the Church of England never satisfactorily met, he, point by point, contended that Roman Catholicism could be taught in the Church of England under the Thirty-nine Articles.

The hostility aroused by the appearance of this Tract forced the Puseyites to a period of silence. The writing of tracts ceased. From 1841, the year in which Newman wrote Tract 90, until 1845, when he left the Church of England for Rome, his public activities were greatly les-sened. Newman was exultant. " 'No stopping of the tracts,' he said, 'can, humanly speaking, stop the spread of the opinions which they have inculcated.' Even Pusey, besides praising Newman's 'touching simplicity and humility,' writes hopefully on the general prospects:

" 'You will be glad to hear that the immediate excite-ment about Tract 90 seems subsiding, although I fear (in the minds of many) into a lasting impression of our Jesuitism.' " [27]

The effect, however, upon the world, through Oxford was tremendous. Newman, from the beginning, saw the

[26] Abbott, Anglican Career of Newman, Vol. I, p. 119.
[27] Abbott, Anglican Career of Newman, Vol. II, p. 261.

value of Oxford as a base. Some of his associates wanted to make London the center of the movement. Newman opposed the plan. He wished the tracts known as the Oxford Tracts.[28]

THE GORHAM CASE

Previous to this, Dr. Wiseman, who subsequently became Cardinal, had left Rome for England and had founded the *Dublin Review* in 1836, for the express purpose of influencing the Tractarians of Oxford and leading them on to Rome. [29] He said in his Essays:

"I have already alluded, in the preface of the first volume, as well as in the body of this, to the first circumstance which turned my attention to the wonderful movement then commenced in England—the visit which is recorded in Froude's 'Remains.' From that moment it took the uppermost place in my thoughts, and became the object of their intensest interest." [30]

Dr. Wiseman, when studying at Rome, had devoted himself to Oriental studies and investigations of the manuscripts. His books brought him into prominence, and in 1828, when he was only twenty-six years of age, he was elected Rector of the College in Rome for Catholic youth of the English language. His appearance in England in the midst of the violent excitement occasioned by Tract 90, is described thus by Palmer:

"Wiseman saw that there was an opening for the circulation of that false and plausible reasoning of Jesuitism in which he was an adept; skillful to put a plausible face upon the worst corruptions, and to instill doubt where there was no real doubt. He was instantly dispatched to England as Vicar Apostolic, to follow up the clue thus presented to him. He forthwith set on foot the *Dublin Review* as a means for reaching the class of minds at Oxford with which he had come in contact." [31]

---

[28] Dr. Overton, The Anglican Revival, p. 53.
[29] Thureau-Dangin, English Catholic Revival, Vol. I, p. 122.
[30] Wiseman's Essays, Vol. II, pp. VI, VII.
[31] Palmer, Narrative of Events, p. 73.

Dr. Wiseman found on his hands the task of welding together the Catholics of England, the Catholics of Ireland, so unlike them, influential Protestants of Catholic sympathies like Macaulay, Stanley, etc., as well as the Romanizing Movement in Oxford University. He was a textual critic of the first rank, and assisted by the information seemingly passed to him from Jesuits, he was able to furnish the facts well calculated to combat confidence in the Protestant Bible. Skillfully step by step, we are told, he led the Tractarian Movement toward Rome.

By this time, Stanley informs us, the Tractarians had become dominant at Oxford. Hort is thankful that the High Church movement is gaining ground in both Universities.—Oxford and Cambridge.[32] Stopping the Tracts seemed like a blow, but authorities recognize that it was a contribution to success. Oxford still retains her Romanizing tendencies, and many bishops of the Church of England have wholly surrendered to most of the Catholic positions which gained ground, and some of the bishops without leaving the Church of England, mentally have gone the whole way of Rome. Even the Privy Council, the highest court of appeal in the British Empire, did not pronounce upon a very important case in a way that would run directly counter to the Council of Trent.[33]

Public sentiment was again aroused to intensity in 1845 when Ward, an outstanding Tractarian, published his book which taught the most offensive Roman views,— Mariolatry, and mental reservation in subscribing to the Thirty-nine Articles. When Oxford degraded him from his university rights, he went over, in September, to the Church of Rome. It became very evident that Newman soon would follow. On the night of October 8, Father Dominic of the Italian Passionists, arrived at Newman's quarters in a downpouring rain. After being received, he was standing before the fire drying his wet garments. He turned around to see Newman prostrate at his feet,

[32] Life and Letters of Hort, Vol. I., p. 86.
[33] Stanley, Essays, p. 139.

begging his blessing, and asking him to hear his confession.[34] Thus the author of "Lead Kindly Light" passed over to Rome, and within one year, 150 clergymen and eminent laymen also had joined the Catholic Church.

It might be wondered why Newman went over to Rome, if by remaining at Oxford he would have more greatly advanced his Catholic project. There is, however, another phase to the situation.

Cardinal Wiseman found great difficulties in developing Roman Catholicism in England. He lacked leaders, so he urged Newman to take his stand publicly that the Oxonian might be made available for the training of clergymen.

After the passing from Oxford of Newman, the leadership of the Tractarians devolved upon Dr. Pusey. A change came over the movement. Oxford ceased to be its home and center. Nevertheless, Jesuitism had captured it long enough to change fundamentally the character of the Church of England. In its larger proportions, Tractarianism passed from the study to the street. The passion to introduce the Mass, the confession, the burning of candles, holy water, the blessing of oils, and all the other gorgeous accompaniments of Catholic ritualism went forward so strongly that the movement since 1845 is known rather under the name of Ritualism. It is now more an appeal to the eye, than, as it was formerly, an appeal to the ear.

In 1850, two events of outstanding importance occurred which hastened the change of English sentiment. The Bishop of Exeter, on the point of ordaining a clergyman by the name of Gorham, demanded that he subscribe to the doctrine of baptismal regeneration. He refused. The Bishop declined to admit him to the ministry. Mr. Gorham carried his case to the highest court in the Church of England, which decided against him. He then appealed to the Privy Council, which reversed the decision of the Ecclesiastical Court, and virtually decided that no

---

[34] Thureau-Dangin, Vol. I, p. 278.

man could be excluded from the Anglican ministry because he did not believe in baptismal regeneration. The effect on the country was tremendous. Even Gladstone, who had been drawn into the Oxford Movement, to whose thoughts and feelings it gave a new direction, wrote to his wife that it (the Gorham case) "may impose duties upon me which will separate forever between my path of life, public or private, and that of all political parties. The issue is one going to the very root of all teaching and all life in the Church of England." [35]

Gladstone felt that the bishops were to blame in not exercising a public influence strong enough to have secured a different decision. The bishops favored the Romanizing tendencies, but in order to make them prevalent, they were unwilling to pay the price, that is, to suffer a separation of church and state. There were still too many Protestant and non-religious influences to suffer the civil courts to be dictated to by the religious. The Privy Council would have been perfectly willing for the Church of England to have what it wished, even if it were Catholic ritualism, but was not willing to endorse such a change as long as the church received its salaries from the state. Stanley calls the Gorham decision the "Magna Charta" of the liberties of the English Church.

THE CATHOLIC AGGRESSION

While the mind of England was still being agitated by the Gorham case, it sustained another shock from an unsuspected quarter. In October, 1850, the Pope had advanced Dr. Wiseman to the princely position of Cardinal, at the same time creating him Archbishop of Westminster, and dividing England into twelve bishoprics. Cardinal Wiseman stood for hours in Rome receiving the congratulations of the ambassadors and representatives of other governments. After the round of ceremonies was over, he issued a letter to be published in the English newspapers announcing the establishment of a Catholic

---

[35] Lathbury, Letters of Gladstone, Vol. I, p. 83.

hierarchy in Great Britain. This is known as the famous letter of the Flaminian Gate. Not even Cardinal Wiseman was prepared to witness the explosion of wrath which shook the cities of England. Everywhere was heard the cry, "No Popery!" Press, Anglican clergymen, and leading statesmen raised indignant protest in terms of ever-increasing violence. Item by item the papal brief was analyzed by the press, each topic explained as a fresh insult to the English people. Some of the scenes in the different cities are described thus:

"The Church bells rang, the band played the 'Rose March,' and the procession, lighted by numerous torches, paraded the town. Placards were carried, inscribed, 'The brutal Haynau,' and 'Down with tyranny!' 'Down with Popery!' 'No Puseyites!' 'No Tractarians!' etc. There were several masked characters, and all made up such a sight as was never witnessed in this ancient borough before."

The scene in Salisbury is thus described:

"The effigies of his Holiness, the Pope, Cardinal Wiseman, and the twelve Bishops were completed. Friday evening, about five P. M., Castle Street was so densely crowded that no one could pass to the upper part of it. Shortly after, some hundreds of torches were lighted, which then exhibited a forest of heads. . . . The procession having paraded the city, the effigies were taken to the Green Croft, where, over a large number of fagots and barrels of tar, a huge platform was erected of timber; the effigies were placed thereon, and a volley of rockets sent up." [36]

In spite of public opposition, the object of the Catholic Church was gained. The creation of this hierarchy, with its titles and magnificent dwellings, pleased the aristocracy, and brought over to the Church of Rome, many of the wealthy and cultured, and of the nobility. Simple evangelical Christianity, as Jesus lived it, is not acceptable to the proud and worldly heart. The papal aggres-

---

[36] Ward, Life of Wiseman, Vol. I, pp. 551, 552.

sion of 1850 was another blow in favor of Rome. As Stanley says of it, "The general reaction of a large part of the religious sentiment of England and of Europe towards Rome was undoubted." [37]

THE CASE OF "ESSAYS AND REVIEWS"

Of the problems raised by the famous case, known as "Essays and Reviews," Westcott wrote:

"Of all cares, almost the greatest which I have had, has been 'Essays and Reviews,' and its opponents. The controversy is fairly turning me grey. I look on the assailants of the Essayists, from bishops downwards, as likely to do far more harm to the Church and the Truth than the Essayists." [38]

The period from 1850 to 1860 had seen a great forward movement among the Ritualists, and also considerable growth for the Catholics. In Cardinal Wiseman's address to the Congress of Malines in 1863, he reported that in 1830 the number of priests in England was 434; in 1863 they numbered 1242. The convents in 1830 amounted to only 16; in 1863 there were 162. [39] Parallel with this, the movement was going forward to introduce into England, German Biblical criticism. Something occurred in 1860 to test the inroads which had been made upon the English mind in its belief in the infallibility and inspiration of the Bible.

An enterprising publishing house put forth a volume containing seven essays and reviews written by prominent clergymen of the Church of England, some of whom were university professors. Dr. Hort was invited to be a contributor, but declined, fearing that the attempt was premature. These essays successively attacked such prominent Protestant doctrines as its position on the "inspiration of the Bible," "justification by faith," and "purgatory." A cry arose to demand the degradation of these writers from their positions as clergymen in the

[37] Stanley's Essays. p. 48.   [38] Life of Westcott, Vol. I, p. 215.
[39] Ward, Life of Wiseman, Vol. II, p. 459.

Church of England. A test case was carried before the highest court in the Church. The accused appealed from the judgment to a higher body. Although the indignation throughout the country was great, and a petition so voluminous as to be signed by eleven thousand clergymen was circulated, nevertheless the public mind was compelled to submit to this assault upon the beliefs held by Protestant England for three hundred years. One of these essays was written by Professor H. B. Wilson, who earlier had denounced Tract 90 for its views on the Thirty-nine Articles. Twenty years later, however, he argued in favor of the very views which he had denounced previously.

The case was carried still higher, to the secular court, the last court of appeal in the nation, the Privy Council. Here again the decision let the authors of these advanced views on higher criticism, go free. Such hostile attacks on inspiration were detaching the English mentality from its Protestant love of, and loyalty to, the Holy Scriptures. Now, campaigns favorable to the other side were needed to attach the English mind to the doctrines and practices of Rome. An event of this nature soon occurred.

NEWMAN'S MASTERPIECE

While Ritualism marched forward in the Church of England through the leadership of Dr. Pusey, Newman was aiding Cardinal Wiseman to increase the numbers and influence of Catholicism. For twenty years, apparently to the public, there had been little contact between him and his former associates. They retained for Newman, however, their old love and affection. In 1864 occurred an event which broke down this public distance between them and restored Newman to aristocratic favor. Charles Kingsley felt impelled to write upon the growing Catholic mentality throughout England, and lay the blame of it upon Newman. Newman took the pen; and master of the English language as he was, wrote the

"Apologia." An able controversialist, he handled Kingsley with a cruel invective that few can condone. With that subtlety of argument in which not many were his equal, he further advanced the cause of Catholic doctrine; while at the same time he placed himself so ably before the public as a martyr of honest convictions, that he threw open the door which admitted him, if it did not restore him, to a large place in public esteem. The publication of the "Apologia" added one more excitement to the many which, for a third of a century, had been stirring the Protestant mind of England.

Of the effect produced by this book in making acceptable the advance of Romanizing doctrines, Stanley says:

"The Hampdon controversy, the Gorham controversy, the 'Essays and Reviews' controversy, and the Colenso controversy—all have had their turn; but none excited such violent passions, and of none would the ultimate extinction have appeared so strange whilst the storm was raging, as the extinction of the controversy of Tract 90. . . . What has produced the calm? Many causes have contributed;—the recrudescence of the High Church party; the charm thrown over the history of that time by the 'Apologia.' " [40]

RITUALISM

By 1864, at the time of the "Apologia," the High Church party believed the divine authority of tradition, the inspiration of the Apocrypha, and escape from eternal punishment through purgatory. [41]

The decision of the Privy Council in 1864, in the case of "Essays and Reviews," legally declared to all intents and purposes that these views could be the doctrines of the Church of England. At the same time, the Protestant doctrine of Imputed Righteousness was condemned as it had been condemned by the Council of Trent. With public opinion placated by the "Apologia," with the voice of protest in the Church silenced by the judgment of the

---

[40] Stanley's Essays, pp. 238, 239.   [41] Idem, p. 111.

Privy Council, ritualism sprung forth with a suddenness that took the nation and church by surprise.

"At once in a hundred or more churches (so we are told) appeared colored vestments; candles lighted during the Communion in the morning, and during the Magnificat in the afternoon; a new liturgy interpolated into that established by law; prostrations, genuflections, elevations, never before seen; the transformation of the worship of the Church of England into a likeness of that of the Church of Rome, so exact as to deceive Roman Catholics themselves into the momentary belief that they were in their own places of worship." [42]

In other words, the Tractarianism of Oxford simply changed its character, and instead of being centered in the hands of notable scholars, it spread in the form of ritualism to the country parishes. As another author says:

"In fact, there appeared now a type of clergyman hitherto almost unknown in the Established Church—one who was less a man of the world, and less a scholar, but more clerical, more ascetic, more apostolic, one who came nearer to our ideal of a Catholic priest. Though seeming to contend about questions of candles and chasubles, they really began to revive in the Anglican Church the Sacramental life which had become almost extinct. In many ways they were truly the successors of the Tractarians, continuing and completing their work." [43]

Very early in the Tractarian Movement, the ritualistic activities connected with purgatory, pardons, images, relics, and prayers for the dead, had manifested themselves. But they were carried on secretly. Self-punishment by a scourge of five lashes having five knots on the lash was practiced by the most passionate Romanists; some had worn the haircloth girdle. [44] Sisterhoods, embracing girls who had vowed their life to the Church, as Catholic nuns do, were formed in the Church of England.

[42] Stanley's Essays, p. 253.
[43] Thureau-Dangin, The English Catholic Revival, Vol. II, pp. 587, 588.
[44] Walsh, Secret History, pp. 37, 40.

Throughout the years that ritualism had been advancing, different organizations were formed for attaining the different objectives sought by the Romanizers. The "Confraternity of the Blessed Sacrament" was formed for the purpose of influencing others to celebrate the Mass; the "Association for the Promotion of the Union of Christendom" was organized with the intent to bring all Christian churches under the leadership of the Pope; the "Order of Corporate Reunion" was an association created to bring about the joining of the Church of England with the Papacy; the "Society of the Sacred Cross" offered an organization into which clergymen of the Church of England might be enrolled, whose practices were the fervent performance of Catholic rituals; and the "English Church Union" was brought into existence to further the interests of Roman Catholicism in England.

The Movement has also affected other Protestant churches, and "there are many to-day who, though themselves rejecting Catholic belief, recognize that St. Paul's sacramental teaching is far more like that traditional among Catholics than like that of the 16th-century Reformers." [45]

Dr. Wylie indicates that these great changes were effected, not by a stirring message from God, but by indirection, little by little, as the Jesuits operate:

"Tract 90, where the doctrine of reserves is broached, bears strong marks of a Jesuit origin. Could we know all the secret instructions given to the leaders in the Puseyite movement,—the mental reservations prescribed to them,—we might well be astonished. 'Go gently,' we think we hear the great Roothan say to them. 'Remember the motto of our dear son, the *cidevant* Bishop of Autun, —"surtout, pas trop de zele," (above all, not too much zeal). Bring into view, little by little, the authority of the church. If you can succeed in rendering it equal to that of the Bible, you have done much. Change the table of the Lord into an altar; elevate that altar a few inches

---

[45] Biship Gore, A New Commentary, Part III, p. 420.

above the level of the floor; gradually turn around to it when you read the Liturgy; place lighted tapers upon it; teach the people the virtues of stained glass, and cause them to feel the majesty of Gothic basilisques. Introduce first the dogmas, beginning with that of baptismal regeneration; next the ceremonies and sacraments, as penance and the confessional; and, lastly, the images of the Virgin and the saints.' " "

It must not be supposed that this advance of ritualism went forward without opposition. There were riotous disturbances at Exeter and other places, chiefly directed against the use of the priestly robe in the pulpit, after a direction for its use had been given in a charge by the Bishop. The details of furniture and of Catholic garments worn by the priest, which had long since been discarded, and now were being used again by ritualistic priests, aroused great antagonism among the people. On one occasion in the church of St. Georges-in-the-East, the vast building was crowded with a furious congregation, trying to shout down the chanting of the liturgy. Policemen surrounded the clergy and choristers in their endeavor to carry on the ritualistic services. Anything in the recitation which appeared as a condemnation of idolatry was met with sounds of approval from the congregation. Congregations otherwise amiable, sociable, and friendly, were changed into bodies of wrath and resentment at Romanizing clergymen who persisted in services of ritualism repugnant to the worshipers.

A vast array of arguments, historical, legal, and ritualistic, were carried on between the clergy and their congregations. Who was to decide the question? This situation gave rise to a series of cases which were brought before the courts, both ecclesiastical and civil, amid tremendous excitement on the part of the people. Aided by the English Church Union, by eminent scholars of ritualistic sympathies, and by the strong Romanizing tendency among the bishops, the principal judgments

---

46 Dr. Wylie, The Papacy, pp. 527, 528.

went against the Protestants. Doctors Westcott and Hort, who come prominently before us later as leaders in connection with Bible revision, lent their influence on the side of the ritualists. "When consulted by a lady, as to the latitude admitted by the Church of England, which she thought tended towards Catholicism, Hort did not deny the divergencies, but thought they need not cause uneasiness." [47]

Dr. King, Bishop of Lincoln, whose influence multiplied converts to Catholicism, was cited by the Church Association (a society formed to support congregations imposed upon by the use of ritualism), before the Archbishop of Canterbury for his ritualistic enthusiasm. The Archbishop realized that if he decided in favor of the ritualists, and the case should be appealed, he risked the opposition of the Privy Council. He consulted with one of his most intimate friends, his former teacher, Bishop Westcott, and determined to take the risk. When, on November 21, 1890, before a numerous and excited throng, he left ritualism uncondemned and the door wide open for candles, absolution, eastward position, and other ritualistic activities, Protestants were greatly disturbed.

"They said that the Lincoln decision was the severest blow received by the Church of England since the Reformation." [48]

Or to sum the matter up in the words of another author:

"And so at present the ritualists have pretty nearly all the liberty of action they could desire." [49]

We are informed that so great was the increase of ritualism that it had spread from 2054 churches in 1844, to 5964 in 1896, and to 7044 in 1898. [50]

Relation of the Movement to Bible Revision

In the first place, had it not been for Jesuitism, Modernism might never have been a force in the Protestant

---

[47] Thureau-Dangin, The English Catholic Revival, Vol. II, p. 153.
[48] Idem, Vol. II, pp. 578, 579.
[49] McClintock and Strong, Encycl. Art. "Oxford Tracts."
[50] Thureau-Dangin, Vol. II, p. 583.

Church. As the historian Froude says: "But for the Oxford Movement, skepticism might have continued a harmless speculation of a few philosophers." [51]

The attitude of Roman Catholics to the King James Version has ever been one of bitter hostility. The Catholic Bishop of Erie, Pa., calls it that "vile" Protestant Version.[52] This attitude is further evinced through the feelings expressed by two eminent characters connected with the Oxford Movement; one who critically described the Authorized Version before revision was accomplished; the other, after revision was well under way. Dr. Faber, the brilliant associate of Newman, and a passionate Romanizer, called the King James Version, "that stronghold of heresy in England;" and when revision began to appear as almost certain, Cardinal Wiseman expressed himself in these words:

"When we consider the scorn cast by the Reformers upon the Vulgate, and their recurrence, in consequence, to the Greek, as the only accurate standard, we cannot but rejoice at the silent triumph which truth has at length gained over clamorous error. For, in fact, the principal writers who have avenged the Vulgate, and obtained for it its critical preëminence are Protestants." [53]

The famous Tract 90 did not leave this question untouched. Though Cardinal Newman argued strongly for the orthodox Catholic position, that tradition is of equal, if not of superior authority to the Bible, nevertheless, he put a divine stamp on the Vulgate and a human stamp upon the Authorized Version. These are his words:

"A further question may be asked, concerning our Received Version of the Scriptures, whether it is in any sense imposed on us as a true comment on the original text; as the Vulgate is upon the Roman Catholics. It would appear not. It was made and authorized by royal commands, which cannot be supposed to have any claim upon our interior consent." [54]

---

[51] Froude, Short Studies, p. 164.
[52] Bishop Tobias Mullen, (Erie, Pa.) The Canon of the Old Testament, p. 335.
[53] Wiseman, Essays, Vol. I, p. 104.   [54] Newman, Tract 90.

Furthermore, in the *Dublin Review* (June 1883), Newman says that the Authorized Version "is notoriously unfair where doctrinal questions are at stake," and speaks of its *"dishonest renderings."* This shows the Catholic attitude of mind toward the King James Version.

Cardinal Newman was invited to sit with the English New Testament Revision Committee. He refused. Nevertheless, with his reputation for Biblical knowledge, with the profound admiration Dr. Hort never failed to express for him, and with his Napoleonic leadership in breaking down Protestantism, the fact that he was invited is indicative of the influence which the Oxford Movement had on Revision.

How anxious Roman Catholicism was to do something to break the spell which the King James Version held over English speaking people, and through them over the world, was revealed in what happened as soon as Cardinal Newman had quit the Church of England for the Church of Rome. At that time he had been invited to Rome—which invitation he accepted—to imbibe the atmosphere of his new affiliations and relate himself to the Papacy in ways which might be deemed best for future service. How he was requested at that time to revise the King James, may be seen in a letter written from Rome to Wiseman by Newman, January 17, 1847. He says:

"The Superior of the Franciscans, Father Benigno, in the Trastevere, wishes us out of his own head to engage in an English Authorized Translation of the Bible. He is a learned man, and on the Congregation of the Index. What he wished was, that we would take the Protestant translation, correct it by the Vulgate . . . and get it sanctioned here. This might be our first work if your Lordship approved of it. If we undertook it, I should try to get a number of persons at work (not merely our own party). First, it should be overseen and corrected by ourselves, then it should go to a few select revisers, e. g., Dr. Tait of Ushaw, Dr. Whitty of St. Edmunds," (a Jesuit).[55]

---

[55] Ward, Life of Wiseman, Vol. I, p. 454.

It is a remarkable fact that Newman, now a Catholic, once a Protestant, is seeking for a revision of the King James Bible, for England, that will conform to the Vulgate, and is suggesting a well-defined plan to Cardinal Wiseman who rejoices that Protestant revisers are vindicating the Vulgate, as previously noted.

We have already spoken of the influence of the movement on certain Revisers, when we brought forward Doctors Hort and Westcott, as in sympathy with, and assisting the movement of ritualism.   One need only to scan the list of the men who sat on the English New Testament Revision Committee, review certain acts in their history and read their writings, to know all too well that the majority were actually of the Oxford Movement, (Tractarians and Ritualists), or in sympathy with the same.   Dr. Thirlwall, who has been pointed out as the leader in introducing German textual criticism into England, and who has been described by two authors as a man of princely intellect, came out strongly in defense of the Tractarians when they were assailed.[66]

When Newman and Froude, in 1833, were in Rome and had presented their inquiry to the Papacy to learn upon what terms the Church of England would be received back into the Roman fold, they had the direct answer,— only by accepting the Council of Trent.   Previously, we have shown that the first four resolutions passed by that Council, settled, first, that no one should say it is wicked to put tradition on a level with Scripture; second, that the Apocryphal books were equal to the Canonical; third, that there were no errors in the Vulgate; and finally, that the right of interpretation of Holy Writ belonged to the clergy.   Newman left Rome saying, "I have a work to do for England."   He could not bring the Church of England to accept the Council of Trent without establishing those books of the Catholic Bible which are rejected by Protestants and without securing endorsement for those Catholic readings of the accepted

[66] Cadman, Three Religious Leaders, p. 424.

books which had been rejected by the Reformers. Revision became the inevitable outcome of the Oxford Movement.

That this was so understood by the participants in Tractarianism, I will now quote from Mozley, the brother-in-law of Cardinal Newman:

"The Oxford Movement, unforeseen by the chief movers, and to some extent in spite of them, has produced a generation of ecclesiologists, ritualists, and religious poets. Whatever may be said of its priestcraft, it has filled the land with churchcrafts of all kinds. Has it not had some share in the restoration of Biblical criticism and in the revision of the Authorized Version?" [57]

It ought to be further noticed that Dr. Pusey, who succeeded to the leadership of the Oxford Movement upon the defection of Newman to Rome, he who pushed forward ritualism, established nunneries and monasteries, and was passionate in Romanizing, was also invited to sit on the English New Testament Revision Committee. The fact that he refused, does not in any way lessen the mental attitude of sympathy with Tractarianism which possessed the dominant majority of that committee. And we are told that so strong were the efforts on the Revision Committee to revise different passages of the New Testament in favor of Rome, that on one occasion the Dean of Rochester remarked that it was time they raised a cry of "No Popery." [58]

The Oxford Movement had created great discontent with existing theology and had emphasized the apparent contradictions and inconsistencies of the Bible. At the same time textual criticism had cast discredit upon the Received Text and the King James Version translated from it. There had been enough agitation to arouse an expectancy that some kind of revision would be attempted. But even then, revision of such a revolutionary na-

---

[57] Mozley, Vol. II, p. 42.
[58] Hemphill, A History of the Revised Version, p. 55.

ture, as happened, could never have been brought about, unless men who long had policies of a nature little suspected, were at hand to do the deed. These men were Westcott and Hort. Let us now throw some sidelights upon their surprising beliefs and purposes.

CHAPTER IX

Westcott and Hort

I T IS interesting at this juncture to take a glance at Doctors Westcott and Hort, the dominating mentalities of the scheme of Revision, principally in that period of their lives before they sat on the Revision Committee. They were working together twenty years before Revision began, and swept the Revision Committee along with them after work commenced. Mainly from their own letters, partly from the comments of their respective sons, who collected and published their lives and letters, we shall here state the principles which affected their deeper lives.

THEIR HIGHER CRITICISM

WESTCOTT writes to his fiancée, Advent Sunday, 1847:

"All stigmatize him (Dr. Hampden) as a 'heretic'. . . . If he be condemned, what will become of me! . . . The battle of the Inspiration of Scripture has yet to be fought, and how earnestly I could pray that I might aid the truth in that." [1]

WESTCOTT'S son comments, 1903:

"My father . . . believed that the charges of being 'unsafe' and of 'Germanizing' brought against him were unjust." [2]

HORT writes to Rev. Rowland Williams, October 21, 1858:

"Further I agree with them (authors of "Essays and Reviews") in condemning many leading specific doctrines of the popular theology. . . . Evangelicals seem to me perverted rather than untrue. There are, I fear, still more serious differences between us on the subject

---

[1] Life of Westcott, by his son, Vol. I, pp. 94, 95.
[2] Idem, Vol. I, p 218.

of authority, and especially the authority of the Bible."[3]

HORT writes to Rev. John Ellerton, April 3, 1860:

"But the book which has most engaged me is Darwin. Whatever may be thought of it, it is a book that one is proud to be contemporary with. . . . My feeling is strong that the theory is unanswerable. If so, it opens up a new period."[4]

THEIR MARIOLATRY

WESTCOTT writes from France to his fiancée, 1847:

"After leaving the monastery, we shaped our course to a little oratory which we discovered on the summit of a neighboring hill. . . . Fortunately we found the door open. It is very small, with one kneeling-place; and behind a screen was a 'Pieta' the size of life (i. e. a Virgin and dead Christ). . . . Had I been alone I could have knelt there for hours."[5]

WESTCOTT writes to Archbishop Benson, November 17, 1865:

"I wish I could see to what forgotten truth Mariolatry bears witness."[6]

HORT writes to Westcott:

"I am very far from pretending to understand completely the oft-renewed vitality of Mariolatry."[7]

HORT writes to Westcott, October 17, 1865:

"I have been persuaded for many years that Mary-worship and 'Jesus'-worship have very much in common in their causes and their results."[8]

HORT writes to Westcott:

"But this last error can hardly be expelled till Protestants unlearn the crazy horror of the idea of priesthood."[9]

HORT writes to Dr. Lightfoot, October 26, 1867:
"But you know I am a staunch sacerdotalist."[10]

[3] Life of Hort, by his son, Vol. I, p. 400. [4] Idem, Vol. I, p. 416.
[5] Life of Westcott, Vol. I, p. 81. [6] Idem, Vol. I, p. 251.
[7] Life of Hort, Vol. II, p. 49. [8] Idem, Vol. II, p. 50.
[9] Idem, Vol. II, p. 51. [10] Idem, Vol. II, p. 86.

DR. HORT FALLS UNDER THE INFLUENCE OF MAURICE, COLERIDGE, WINER, AND COMTE

HORT writes to Dr. Harold Brown, (Bishop of Eli), November 8, 1871:

"Moreover, Mr. Maurice has been a dear friend of mine for twenty-three years, and I have been deeply influenced by his books." [11] Frederick Maurice, the son of a Unitarian minister, and brilliant student of Oxford and Cambridge Universities, became a clergyman in the Church of England. He had a commanding influence upon the leaders of his day, especially upon Dr. Hort. Maurice was dismissed from his position as principal of King's College, London, on charges of heresy.

HORT'S son says of his father:

"In undergraduate days, if not before, he came under the spell of Coleridge." [12]

HORT writes to Rev. John Ellerton, October 21, 1851:

"You cannot imagine his (Carlyle's) bitter hatred of Coleridge, to whom he (truly enough) ascribes the existence of 'Puseyism.' " [13]

HORT writes to W. F. Moulton, July 17, 1870:

"It has long been on my mind to write and thank you for a copy of your *Winer* which reached me, I am shocked to find, four months ago. . . . We shall all, I doubt not, learn much by discussion in the New Testament Company." [14]

WESTCOTT says in the preface to a volume of Westminster Sermons:

"Those who are familiar with recent theories of social morality will recognize how much I owe to two writers who are not often joined together in an acknowledgment of deep gratitude—Comte and Maurice." [15]

THEIR SPIRITUALISM

WESTCOTT'S son writes:

"The 'Ghostlie Guild,' which numbers amongst its

---

[11] Idem, Vol. II, p. 155.   [12] Idem, Vol. I, p. 42.
[13] Idem, Vol. I, p. 205.   [14] Life of Hort, Vol. II, pp. 134, 135.
[15] Life of Westcott, Vol. II, p. 11.

members A. Barry, E. W. Benson, H. Bradshaw, the Hon. A. Gordon, F. J. A. Hort, H. Luard, and C. B. Scott, was established for the investigation of all supernatural appearances and effects. Westcott took a leading part in their proceedings, and their inquiry circular was originally drawn up by him." [16]

WESTCOTT'S son writes, speaking of his father:

"The Communion of Saints, seems peculiarly associated with Peterborough. . . . He had an extraordinary power of realizing this communion. It was his delight to be alone at night in the great Cathedral, for there he could meditate and pray in full sympathy with all that was good and great in the past. I have been with him there on a moonlight evening, when the vast building was haunted with strange lights and shades, and the ticking of the great clock sounded like some giant's footsteps in the deep silence. Then he had always abundant company. Once a daughter, in later years, met him returning from one of his customary meditations in the solitary darkness of the chapel at Auckland Castle, and she said to him, 'I expect you do not feel alone?' 'Oh no,' he said, 'it is full.' " [17]

HORT writes to Rev. John Ellerton, December 29, 1851:

"Westcott, Gorham, C. B. Scott, Benson, Bradshaw, Luard, etc., and I have started a society for the investigation of ghosts and all supernatural appearances and effects, being all disposed to believe that such things really exist, and ought to be discriminated from hoaxes and mere subjective disillusions." [18]

THEIR ANTI-PROTESTANTISM

WESTCOTT wrote to the Archbishop of Canterbury:

"It does not seem to me that the Vaudois claim an ecclesiastical recognition. The position of the small Protestant bodies on the Continent, is, no doubt, one of great difficulty. But our church can, I think, only deal with churches growing to fuller life." [19]

HORT writes to Westcott, September 23, 1864:

---

[16] Idem, Vol. I, p. 117.
[18] Life of Hort, Vol. I, p. 211.
[17] Idem, Vol. I, p. 312.
[19] Life of Westcott, Vol. II, p. 53.

"I believe Coleridge was quite right in saying that Christianity without a substantial church is vanity and disillusion; and I remember shocking you and Lightfoot not so long ago by expressing a belief that 'Protestantism' is only parenthetical and temporary." [20]

"Perfect Catholicity has been nowhere since the Reformation." [21]

THEIR ANTI-ANGLICANISM

WESTCOTT writes to his fiancée, January 6, 1848:

"You can scarcely tell how I felt when I found we had to sign some declaration before the degree (A.B.). I feared it might be of an assent to the Thirty-nine Articles, and that I dare not give now." [22]

WESTCOTT'S son writes:

"In 1881 he was appointed by Mr. Gladstone a member of the Ecclesiastical Courts Commission. . . . It did valuable service to the Church of England in that it asserted its continuity, and 'went behind the Reformation.' In speaking of Archbishop Benson's work on this Commission, my father says: 'It was my happiness to sit by Benson's side, and to watch as he did with unflagging interest the gradual determination of the relations in which a national church must stand to the nation. . . . The ruling ideas of the Lincoln Judgment were really defined by these inquiries.' " [23]

It will be remembered that Archbishop Benson's ruling in this judgment constituted the greatest victory for ritualism, and the most serious defeat for Protestantism. In fact it discouraged the Protestants.

WESTCOTT:

"Nothing remains but to assert our complete independence of Convocation. . . . If the (Revision) Company accept the dictation of Convocation, my work must end." [24] These words he wrote to Dr. Hort when Southern Convocation practically asked them to dismiss the Unitarian scholar from the New Testament Revision Committee.

---

[20] Life of Hort, Vol. II, p. 30.
[22] Life of Westcott, Vol. I, p. 99.
[24] Life of Westcott, Vol. I, p. 394.
[21] Idem, Vol. II, p. 32.
[23] Idem, Vol. I, pp. 315, 316.

HORT writes to Westcott, September 23, 1864:

"Within that world Anglicanism, though by no means without a sound standing, seems a poor and maimed thing beside great Rome." [25]

THEIR ANTI-METHODISM

HORT writes to his father, December 14, 1846:

"In fact his (Dr. Mill's) whole course lay in misrepresentation, confounding Evangelicalism with Methodism, which last is worse than popery, as being more insidious." [26]

THEIR ANTI-AMERICANISM

HORT writes to Rev. John Ellerton, September 25, 1862:

"It cannot be wrong to desire and pray from the bottom of one's heart that the American Union may be shivered to pieces." [27]

"Lincoln is, I think, almost free from the nearly universal dishonesty of American politicians (his letter to Greely I know nothing about). I cannot see that he has shown any special virtues or statesmanlike capacities." [28]

THEIR ANTI-BIBLE DOCTRINES

WESTCOTT writes to Mr. Wickenden, October 26, 1861:

"I was much occupied with anxious thoughts about the possible duty of offering myself for the Hulsean Professorship at Cambridge. I had little wish, and no hope, for success, but I was inclined to protest against the imputations of heresy and the like which have been made against me." [29]

HORT writes to Mr. A. Macmillan:

"About Darwin, I have been reading and thinking a good deal, and am getting to see my way comparatively clearly, and to be also more desirous to say something." [30]

HORT writes to Westcott:

"You seem to me to make (Greek) philosophy worthless for those who have received the Christian revelation.

[25] Life of Hort, Vol. II, p. 30.   [26] Idem, Vol. I, p. 49.
[27] Idem, Vol. I, p. 459.   [28] Idem, Vol. I, p. 458.
[29] Life of Westcott, Vol. I, p. 222.   [30] Life of Hort, Vol. I, p. 424.

To me, though in a hazy way, it seems full of precious truth of which I find nothing, and should be very much astonished and perplexed to find anything, in revelation." [31]

THEIR TENDENCY TO EVOLUTION

WESTCOTT writes to the Archbishop of Canterbury on O. T. Criticism, March 4, 1890:

"No one now, I suppose, holds that the first three chapters of Genesis, for example, give a literal history —I could never understand how any one reading them with open eyes could think they did." [32]

HORT writes to Mr. John Ellerton:

"I am inclined to think that no such state as 'Eden' (I mean the popular notion) ever existed, and that Adam's fall in no degree differed from the fall of each of his descendants, as Coleridge justly argues." [33]

THEIR TRACTARIANISM

WESTCOTT writes to his fiancée:

"To-day I have again taken up Tracts for the Times and Dr. Newman. Don't tell me that he will do me harm. At least to-day he will, has, done me good, and had you been here I should have asked you to read his solemn words to me. My purchase has already amply repaid me. I think I shall choose a volume for one of my Christmas companions." [34]

WESTCOTT writes to Hort, September 22, 1864:

"My summer was not as fruitful as I had wished; or rather, it was not fruitful in the way I had wished. Dr. Newman's 'Apologia' cut across it, and opened thoughts which I thought had been sealed forever. These haunted me like spectres and left little rest." [35]

HORT writes to Rev. John Ellerton, February 25, 1869:

"It is hard to resist a vague feeling that Westcott's going to Peterborough will be the beginning of a great movement in the church, less conspicuous, but not less powerful, than that which proceeded from Newman." [36]

[31] Idem, Vol. I, p. 449.
[33] Life of Hort, Vol. I, p. 78.
[35] Idem, Vol. I, p. 285.
[32] Life of Westcott, Vol. II, p. 69.
[34] Life of Westcott, Vol. I, p. 223.
[36] Life of Hort, Vol. II, p. 108.

HORT writes to his wife, July 25, 1864:

"How inexpressibly green and ignorant (Blank) must be, to be discovering Newman's greatness and goodness now for the first time." [37]

The above quotation shows Hort's contempt for anyone who is slow in discovering Newman's greatness and goodness.

THEIR RITUALISM

We have already noticed Westcott's associated work with Archbishop Benson in protecting ritualism and giving the most striking blow which discouraged Protestantism.

HORT writes to Mr. John Ellerton, July 6, 1848:

"The pure Romish view seems to me nearer, and more likely to lead to, the truth than the Evangelical. . . . We should bear in mind that that hard and unspiritual medieval crust which enveloped the doctrine of the sacraments in stormy times, though in a measure it may have made it unprofitable to many men at that time, yet in God's providence preserved it inviolate and unscattered for future generations. . . . We dare not forsake the sacraments or God will forsake us." [38]

THEIR PAPAL ATONEMENT DOCTRINE

WESTCOTT writes to his wife, Good Friday, 1865:

"This morning I went to hear the Hulsean Lecturer. He preached on the Atonement. . . . All he said was very good, but then he did not enter into the great difficulties of the notion of sacrifice and vicarious punishment. To me it is always most satisfactory to regard the Christian as in Christ—absolutely one with him, and then he does what Christ has done: Christ's actions become his, and Christ's life and death in some sense his life and death." [39]

Westcott believed that the death of Christ was of His human nature, not of His Divine nature, otherwise man could not do what Christ did in death. Dr. Hort agrees in the following letter to Westcott. Both rejected the

---

[37] Idem, Vol. II, p. 18.   [38] Idem, Vol. I, p. 76.
[39] Life of Westcott, Vol. I, p. 231.

atonement of the substitution of Christ for the sinner, or vicarious atonement; both denied that the death of Christ counted for anything as an atoning factor. They emphasized atonement through the Incarnation. This is the Catholic doctrine. It helps defend the Mass.

HORT writes to Westcott, October 15, 1860:

"To-day's post brought also your letter. . . . I entirely agree—correcting one word—with what you there say on the Atonement, having for many years believed that 'the absolute union of the Christian (or rather, of man) with Christ Himself' is the spiritual truth of which the popular doctrine of substitution is an immoral and material counterfeit. . . . Certainly nothing could be more unscriptural than the modern limiting of Christ's bearing our sins and sufferings to his death; but indeed that is only one aspect of an almost universal heresy." [40]

THEIR COLLUSION PREVIOUS TO REVISION

WESTCOTT writes to Hort, May 28, 1870:

"Your note came with one from Ellicott this morning. . . . Though I think that Convocation is not competent to initiate such a measure, yet I feel that as 'we three' are together it would be wrong not to 'make the best of it' as Lightfoot says. . . . There is some hope that alternative readings might find a place in the margin." [41]

WESTCOTT writes to Lightfoot, June 4, 1870:

"Ought we not to have a conference before the first meeting for Revision? There are many points on which it is important that we should be agreed." [42]

WESTCOTT writes to Hort, July 1, 1870:

"The Revision on the whole surprised me by prospects of hope. I suggested to Ellicott a plan of tabulating and circulating emendations before our meeting which may in the end prove valuable." [43]

HORT writes to Lightfoot:

"It is, I think, difficult to measure the weight of acceptance won beforehand for the Revision by the single fact of our welcoming an Unitarian." [44]

---

[40] Life of Hort, Vol. I, p. 430.
[42] Idem, Vol. I, p. 391.
[44] Life of Hort, Vol. II, p. 140.
[41] Life of Westcott, Vol. I, p. 390.
[43] Idem, Vol. I, pp. 392, 393.

HORT writes to Williams:

"The errors and prejudices, which we agree in wishing to remove, can surely be more wholesomely and also more effectually reached by individual efforts of an indirect kind than by combined open assault. At present very many orthodox but rational men are being unawares acted on by influences which will assuredly bear good fruit in due time, if the process is allowed to go on quietly; and I cannot help fearing that a premature crisis would frighten back many into the merest traditionalism." [45]

Although these last words of Dr. Hort were written in 1858, nevertheless they reveal the method carried out by Westcott and himself as he said later, "I am rather in favor of indirect dealing." We have now before us the sentiments and purposes of the two men who entered the English New Testament Revision Committee and dominated it during the ten years of its strange work. We will now be obliged to take up the work of that Committee, to behold its battles and its methods, as well as to learn the crisis that was precipitated in the bosom of Protestantism.

---

[45] Life of Hort, Vol. I, p. 400.

CHAPTER X

Revision at Last!

B Y the year 1870, so powerful had become the influence of the Oxford Movement, that a theological bias in favor of Rome was affecting men in high authority. Many of the most sacred institutions of Protestant England had been assailed and some of them had been completely changed. The attack on the Thirty-nine Articles by Tract 90, and the subversion of fundamental Protestant doctrines within the Church of England had been so bold and thorough, that an attempt to substitute a version which would theologically and legally discredit our common Protestant Version would not be a surprise.

The first demands for revision were made with moderation of language. "Nor can it be too distinctly or too emphatically affirmed that the reluctance of the public could never have been overcome but for the studious moderation and apparently rigid conservatism which the advocates of revision were careful to adopt." [1] Of course, the Tractarians were conscious of the strong hostility to their ritualism and said little in public about revision in order not to multiply the strength of their enemies. The friends and devotees of the King James Bible, naturally wished that certain retouches might be given the book which would replace words counted obsolete, bring about conformity to more modern rules of spelling and grammar, and correct what they considered a few plain and clear blemishes in the Received Text, so that its bitter opponents, who made use of these minor disadvantages to discredit the whole, might be answered. Nevertheless, universal fear and distrust of revision pervaded the public mind, who recognized in it, as Archbishop Trench

---

[1] Hemphill, History of the R. V., p. 25.

said, "A question affecting . . . profoundly the whole moral and spiritual life of the English people," and the "vast and solemn issues depending on it." [2]   Moreover, the composition of the Authorized Version was recognized by scholars as the miracle of English prose, unsurpassed in clearness, precision, and vigor. The English of the King James Bible was the most perfect, if not the only, example of a lost art. It may be said truthfully that literary men as well as theologians frowned on the revision enterprise. [3]

For years there had been a determined and aggressive campaign to take extensive liberties with the Received Text; and the Romanizing Movement in the Universities of Oxford and Cambridge, both ritualistic and critical, had made it easy for hostile investigators to speak out with impunity. Lachmann had led the way by ignoring the great mass of manuscripts which favored the printed text and built his Greek New Testament, as Salmon says, of scanty material. [4]   Tregelles, though English, "was an isolated worker, and failed to gain any large number of adherents." [5]   Tischendorf, who had brought to light many new manuscripts and had done considerable collating, secured more authority as an editor than he deserved, and in spite of his vacillations in successive editions, became notorious in removing from the Sacred Text several passages hallowed by the veneration of centuries. [6]

The public would not have accepted the extreme, or, as some called it, "progressive" conclusions of these three. The names of Westcott and Hort were not prominently familiar at this time although they were Cambridge professors. Nevertheless, what was known of them, was not such as to arouse distrust and apprehension. It was not until the work of revision was all over, that the world awoke to realize that Westcott and Hort had outdistanced Lachmann, Tischendorf, and Tregelles. As Salmon says, "Westcott and Hort's Greek Testament has

---

[2] Hemphill, History of the R. V., p. 24.   [3] Idem, p. 26.
[4] Salmon, p. 7.   [5] Idem, p. 8.   [6] Idem, p. 8,

been described as an epoch-making book; and quite as correctly as the same phrase has been applied to the work done by Darwin." [7]

The first efforts to secure revision were cautiously made in 1857 by five clergymen (three of whom, Ellicott, Moberly, and Humphrey, later were members of the New Testament Revision Committee), who put out a "Revised Version of John's Gospel." Bishop Ellicott, who in the future, was to be chairman of the New Testament Revision Committee, believed that there were clear tokens of corruptions in the Authorized Version.[8] Nevertheless, Ellicott's utterances, previous to Revision, revealed how utterly unprepared was the scholarship of the day to undertake it. Bishop Coxe, Episcopal, of Western New York, quotes Ellicott as saying about this time:

"Even critical editors of the stamp of Tischendorf have apparently not acquired even a rudimentary knowledge of several of the leading versions which they conspicuously quote. Nay, more, in many instances they have positively misrepresented the very readings which they have followed, and have allowed themselves to be misled by Latin translations which, as my notes will testify, are often sadly, and even perversely, incorrect." [9]

The triumvirate which constantly worked to bring things to a head, and who later sat on the Revision Committee, were Ellicott, Lightfoot, and Moulton. They found it difficult to get the project on foot. Twice they had appealed to the Government in hopes that, as in the case of the King James in 1611, the King would appoint a royal commission. They were refused.[10]

There was sufficient aggression in the Southern Convocation, which represented the Southern half of the Church of England, to vote Revision. But they lacked a leader. There was no outstanding name which would suffice in the public eye as a guarantee against the dangers possible. This difficulty, however, was at last over-

[7] Salmon, p. 5. [8] Dr. Ellicott, Addresses, p. 70.
[9] Dr. Bissell, Origin of Bible, p. 357.
[10] Historical Account of the Work of the American Committee of Revision, pp. 3, 5.

come when Bishop Ellicott won over "that most versatile and picturesque personality in the English Church, Samuel Wilberforce, the silver-tongued Bishop of Oxford." [11]   He was the remaining son of the great Emancipator who was still with the Church of England; the two other sons, Henry and Robert, influenced by the Oxford Movement, had gone over to the Church of Rome. Dr. Wilberforce had rendered great service to the English Church in securing the resurrection of the Southern Convocation, which for a hunderd years had not been permitted to act.   "When Ellicott captured the persuasive Wilberforce, he captured Convocation, and revision suddenly came within the sphere of practical politics." [12]

First came the resolution, February 10, 1870, which expressed the desirability of revision of the Authorized Version of the New Testament:

"Whether by marginal notes or otherwise, in all those passages where plain and clear errors, whether in the Hebrew or Greek text originally adopted by the translators, or in translation made from the same, shall, on due investigation, be found to exist." [13]

An amendment was passed to include the Old Testament.   Then a committee of sixteen—eight from the Upper House, and eight from the Lower House—was appointed.   This committee solicited the participation of the Northern Convocation, but they declined to cooperate, saying that "the time was not favorable for Revision, and that the risk was greater than the probable gain." [14]

Later the Southern Convocation adopted the rules which ordered that Revision should touch the Greek text only where found necessary; should alter the language only where, in the judgment of most competent scholars, such change was necessary; and in such necessary changes, the style of the King James should be followed; and also, that Convocation should nominate a commit-

---

[11] Hemphill, p. 28.   [12] Hemphill, p. 28.
[13] W. F. Moulton, The English Bible, p. 215.   [14] Idem, p. 216.

tee of its own members who would be at liberty to invite
the coöperation of other scholars in the work of Revision. This committee when elected consisted of eighteen
members. It divided into two bodies, one to represent
the Old Testament, and the other to represent the New.
As the majority of the most vital questions which con-
cern us involve New Testament Revision, we will follow
the fortunes of that body in the main.

The seven members of this English New Testament
Revision Committee sent out invitations which were accepted by eighteen others, bringing the full membership
of the English New Testament Committee to the number of twenty-five. As we have seen before, Dr. Newman, who later became a cardinal, declined, as also did
the leader of the Ritualistic Movement, Dr. Pusey. It
should be mentioned here also that Canon Cook, editor
of the "Speakers Commentary," declined. W. F. Moulton, who had spent some years in translating, from the
German into English, Winer's Greek Grammar, and himself a member of the Committee, exercised a large influence in the selection of members. Dr. Moulton favored
those modern rules appearing in Winer's work which, if
followed in translating the Greek, would produce results
different from that of the King James. How much Dr.
Moulton was a devotee of the Vulgate may be seen in the
following words from him:

"The Latin translation, being derived from manuscripts more ancient than any we now possess, is frequently a witness of the highest value in regard to the
Greek text which was current in the earliest times, and
. . . its testimony is in many cases confirmed by Greek
manuscripts which have been discovered or examined
since the 16th century." [15]

From this it is evident that Dr. Moulton looked upon
the Vulgate as a witness superior to the King James,
and upon the Greek manuscripts which formed the base
of the Vulgate as superior to the Greek manuscripts

---

[15] Moulton, The English Bible, p. 184.

which formed the base of the King James. Furthermore, he said, speaking of the Jesuit New Testament of 1582, "The Rhemish Testament agrees with the best critical editions of the present day." [16]   Dr. Moulton, therefore, not only believed the manuscripts which were recently discovered to be similar to the Greek manuscripts from which the Vulgate was translated, but he also looked upon the Greek New Testaments of Lachmann, Tischendorf, and Tregelles, built largely upon the same few manuscripts, as "the best critical editions." Since he exercised so large an influence in selecting the other members of the Committee, we can divine at the outset, the attitude of mind which would likely prevail in the Revision Committee.

The Old Testament Committee also elected into its body other members which made the number in that company twenty-seven. Steps were now taken to secure coöperation from scholars in America. The whole matter was practically put in the hands of Dr. Philip Schaff of the Union Theological Seminary in New York City. Of Dr. Schaff's revolutionary influence on American theology through his bold Romanizing policy; of his trial for heresy; of his leadership in the American "Oxford Movement," we will speak later. An appeal was made to the American Episcopal Church to take part in the Revision, but that body declined.[17] Through the activities of Dr. Schaff, two American Committees were formed, the Old Testament Company having fourteen members, and the New Testament, thirteen. These worked under the disadvantage of being chosen upon the basis that they should live near New York City in order that meetings of the committee might be convenient. The American Committee had no deciding vote on points of revision. As soon as portions of the Holy Book were revised by the English committees, they were sent to the American committees for confirmation or amendment. If the suggestions returned by the American committees

---

[16] Idem, p. 185.   [17] Ellicott, Addresses, p. 39.

were acceptable to their English coworkers, they were adopted; otherwise they had no independent claim for insertion. In other words, the American committees were simply reviewing bodies.[18] In the long run, their differences were not many. They say:

"The work then went on continuously in both countries, the English Companies revising, and the American Committees reviewing what was revised, and returning their suggestions. . . . When this list is fully considered, the general reader will, we think, be surprised to find that the differences are really of such little moment, and in very many cases will probably wonder that the American divines thought it worth while thus to formally record their dissent." [19]

Dr. Schaff, who was to America what Newman was to England, was president of both American committees.[20]

The story of the English New Testament Revision Committee is a stormy one, because it was the battle ground of the whole problem. That Committee finished its work three years before the Old Testament Company, and this latter body had three years to profit by the staggering onslaught which assailed the product of the New Testament Committee. Moreover the American Revised Bible did not appear until twenty years after the work of the English New Testament Committee, so that the American Revisers had twenty years to understand the fate which would await their volume.

When the English New Testament Committee met, it was immediately apparent what was going to happen. Though for ten long years the iron rule of silence kept the public ignorant of what was going on behind closed doors, the story is now known. The first meeting of the Committee found itself a divided body, the majority being determined to incorporate into the proposed revision the latest and most extreme higher criticism. This majority was dominated and carried along by a triumvirate

[18] Hemphill, History of the R. V., p. 41.
[19] Historical Account of the Work of the American Committee of Revision, pp. 10, 11.
[20] *New Brunswick (N. J.) Review*, August, 1854, pp. 322, 282, 283.

consisting of Hort, Westcott, and Lightfoot. The dominating mentality of this triumvirate was Dr. Hort. Before the Committee met, Westcott had written to Hort, "The rules though liberal are vague, and the interpretation of them will depend upon decided action at first." [21] They were determined at the outset to be greater than the rules, and to manipulate them.

The new members who had been elected into the body, and who had taken no part in drawing up the rules, threw these rules completely aside by interpreting them with the widest latitude. Moreover, Westcott and Hort, who had worked together before this for twenty years, in bringing out a Greek New Testament constructed on principles which deviated the farthest ever yet known from the Received Text,[22] came prepared to effect a systematic change in the Protestant Bible. On this point Westcott wrote to Hort concerning Dr. Ellicott, the chairman:

"The Bishop of Gloucester seems to me to be quite capable of accepting heartily and adopting personally a thorough scheme." [23]

And as we have previously seen, as early as 1851, before Westcott and Hort began their twenty years labor on their Greek text, Hort wrote, "Think of that vile Textus Receptus." [24]   In 1851, when he knew little of the Greek New Testament, or of texts, he was dominated with the idea that the Received Text was "vile" and "villainous." The Received Text suffered fatal treatment at the hands of this master in debate.

We have spoken of Bishop Ellicott as the chairman. The first chairman was Bishop Wilberforce. One meeting, however, was sufficient for him. He wrote to an intimate friend, "What can be done in this most miserable business?" [25]   Unable to bear the situation, he absented himself and never took part in the proceedings.

----

[21] Hemphill, History of the R. V., p. 44.
[22] Salmon, Some Criticism, pp. 10, 11.   [23] Life of Westcott, Vol. I, p. 393.
[24] Life of Hort, Vol. I, p. 211.   [25] Hemphill, History, p. 36.

His tragic death occurred three years later. One factor had disturbed him considerably,—the presence of Dr. G. Vance Smith, the Unitarian scholar. In this, however, he shared the feelings of the people of England, who were scandalized at the sight of a Unitarian, who denied the divinity of Christ, participating in a communion service held at the suggestion of Bishop Westcott in Westminster Abbey, immediately preceding their first meeting.

The minority in the Committee was represented principally by Dr. Scrivener, probably the foremost scholar of the day in the manuscripts of the Greek New Testament and the history of the Text. If we may believe the words of Chairman Ellicott, the countless divisions in the Committee over the Greek Text, "was often a kind of critical duel between Dr. Hort and Dr. Scrivener." [26] Dr. Scrivener was continuously and systematically outvoted.

"Nor is it difficult to understand," says Dr. Hemphill, "that many of their less resolute and decided colleagues must often have been completely carried off their feet by the persuasiveness, and resourcefulness, and zeal of Hort, backed by the great prestige of Lightfoot, the popular Canon of St. Paul's, and the quiet determination of Westcott, who set his face as a flint. In fact, it can hardly be doubted that Hort's was the strongest will of the whole Company, and his adroitness in debate was only equaled by his pertinacity." [27]

The conflict was intense and ofttimes the result seemed dubious. Scrivener and his little band did their best to save the day. He might have resigned; but like Bishop Wilberforce, he neither wished to wreck the product of revision by a crushing public blow, nor did he wish to let it run wild by absenting himself. Dr. Hort wrote his wife as follows:

"July 25, 1871. We have had some stiff battles to-day in Revision, though without any ill feeling, and usually

---

[26] Ellicott, Addresses, p. 61.
[27] Hemphill, History of the R. V., pp. 49, 50.

with good success. But I, more than ever, felt how impossible it would be for me to absent myself." [28]

On the other hand, Westcott wrote:

"March 22, 1886. I should be the last to rate highly textual criticism; but it is a little gift which from school days seemed to be committed to me." [29]

Concerning the battles within the Committee, Dr. Westcott writes:

"May 24, 1871. We have had hard fighting during these last two days, and a battle-royal is announced for tomorrow." [30]

"January 27, 1875. Our work yesterday was positively distressing. . . . However, I shall try to keep heart to-day, and if we fail again I think that I shall fly, utterly despairing of the work." [30]

Same date. "To-day our work has been a little better —only a little, but just enough to be endurable." [30]

The "ill-conceived and mismanaged" attempts of the Revision Committee of the Southern Convocation to bring in the radical changes contemplated [31] violated the rules that had been laid down for its control. Citations from ten out of the sixteen members of the Committee, (sixteen was the average number in attendance), show that eleven members were fully determined to act upon the principle of exact and literal translation, which would permit them to travel far beyond the instructions they had received. [32]

The Committee being assembled, the passage for consideration was read. Dr. Scrivener offered the evidence favoring the Received Text, while Dr. Hort took the other side. Then a vote was taken. [33] Settling the Greek Text occupied the largest portion of time both in England and in America. [34] The new Greek Testament upon which Westcott and Hort had been working for twenty years was, portion by portion, secretly committed into the hands of the Revision Committee. [35] Their Greek

---

[28] Life of Hort, Vol. II, p. 146.   [29] Life of Westcott, Vol. II, p. 84.
[30] Idem, Vol. I, pp. 396, 397.   [31] Bissell, Origin of Bible, p. 356.
[32] Hemphill, History of the R. V., pp. 67-70.   [33] Newth, Revision, p. 120.
[34] Ellicott, Addresses, p. 118.   [35] Idem, p. 56.

Text was strongly radical and revolutionary.[36] The Revisers followed the guidance of the two Cambridge editors, Westcott and Hort, who were constantly at their elbow, and whose radical Greek New Testament, deviating the farthest possible from the Received Text, is to all intents and purposes the Greek New Testament followed by the Revision Committee.[37] And this Greek text, in the main, follows the Vatican and Sinaiticus manuscripts.[38] It is true that three other unicals, the Codices Beza, Ephraemi and Alexandrinus were occasionally used, but their testimony was of the same value as the other two.

Hort's partiality for the Vatican Manuscript was practically absolute.[39] We can almost hear him say, The Vaticanus have I loved, but the Textus Receptus have I hated. As the Sinaiticus was the brother of the Vaticanus, wherever pages in the latter were missing, Hort used the former. He and Westcott considered that when the consensus of opinion of these two manuscripts favored a reading, that reading should be accepted as apostolic.[40] This attitude of mind involved thousands of changes in our time-honored Greek New Testament because a Greek text formed upon the united opinion of Codex B and Codex (א) would be different in thousands of places from the Received Text. So the Revisers "went on changing until they had altered the Greek Text in 5337 places." [41] Dr. Scrivener, in the Committee sessions, constantly issued his warning of what would be the outcome if Hort's imaginary theories were accepted. In fact, nine-tenths of the countless divisions and textual struggles around that table in the Jerusalem Chamber arose over Hort's determination to base the Greek New Testament of the Revision on the Vatican Manuscript.[42] Nevertheless, the Received Text, by his own admission,

---

[36] Dr. Salmon, Some Criticism, pp. 11, 12.
[37] Hemphill, History of the R. V., pp. 54, 55.
[38] Gore, New Commentary, Part III, p. 721.
[39] Hort's Introduction, p. 238.
[40] Idem, pp. 225, 251.
[41] Dr. Everts, The Westcott and Hort Text Under Fire, Bibliotheca Sacra, Jan., 1921.
[42] Hemphill, History of the R. V., pp. 55, 56.

had for 1400 years been the dominant Greek New Testament.[43]

It was of necessity that Westcott and Hort should take this position. Their own Greek New Testament upon which they had been working for twenty years was founded on Codex B and Codex (ℵ), as the following quotations show:

"If Westcott and Hort have failed, it is by an overestimate of the Vatican Codex, to which (like Lachmann and Tregelles) they assign the supremacy, while Tischendorf may have given too much weight to the Sinaitic Codex."[44]

Dr. Cook, an authority in this field, also says:

"I will ask the reader to compare these statements with the views set forth, authoritatively and repeatedly, by Dr. Hort in his 'Introduction,' especially in reference to the supreme excellence and unrivalled authority of the text of B—with which, indeed, the Greek text of Westcott and Hort is, with some unimportant exceptions, substantially identical, coinciding in more than ninetenths of the passages which, as materially affecting the character of the synoptic Gospels, I have to discuss."[45]

Another quotation from Dr. Hoskier, an authority who worked in this field many years after the appearance of the Revised Version:

"We always come back to B, as Westcott and Hort's text is practically B."[46]

Of course the minority members of the Revision Committee, and especially the world in general, did not know the twenty years' effort of these two Cambridge professors to base their own Greek New Testament upon these two manuscripts. Hort's "excursion into cloudland," as one authority describes his fourth century revisions, was apparent to Dr. Scrivener, who uttered his protest. Here is his description of Hort's theory as Scrivener later published it:

---

[43] Hort's Introduction, p. 92.
[44] Schaff, Companion to the Greek Test, p. 277.
[45] Cook, Revised Version, p. 6.
[46] Hoskier, Genesis of the Versions, p. 416.

"There is little hope for the stability of their imposing structure, if its foundations have been laid on the sandy ground of ingenious conjecture: and since barely the smallest vestige of historical evidence has ever been alleged in support of the views of these accomplished editors, their teaching must either be received as intuitively true, or dismissed from our consideration as precarious, and even visionary." [47]

As Westcott and Hort outnumbered Scrivener two to one, so their followers outnumbered the other side two to one, and Scrivener was systematically outvoted. As Professor Sandy writes:

"They were thus able to make their views heard in the council chamber, and to support them with all the weight of their personal authority, while as yet the outer public had but partial access to them." [48]

As a consequence, the Greek New Testament upon which the Revised Version is based, is practically the Greek New Testament of Westcott and Hort. Dr. Schaff says:

"The result is that in typographical accuracy the Greek Testament of Westcott and Hort is probably unsurpassed, and that it harmonizes essentially with the text adopted by the Revisers." [49]

THE REVISERS PROFESSEDLY LIBERAL, ACTUALLY NARROW

We meet the paradox in the Revisers, as they sit assembled at their task, of men possessing high reputation for liberalism of thought, yet acting for a decade with extreme narrowness. Stanley, Thirlwall, Vaughan, Hort, Westcott, Moberly—men of leading intellect—would naturally be expected to be so broad as to give most sacred documents fair consideration. Dean Stanley had glorified the Church of England because within her ranks both ritualists and higher critics could officiate as well as the regular churchmen. When Bishop Colenso, of Natal, was on trial, amid great excitement throughout all Eng-

---

[47] Scrivener's Introduction, Vol. II, p. 285.
[48] Professor Sandy, quoted in Hemphill, p. 59.
[49] Schaff, Companion, p. 279.

land, for his destructive criticism of the first five books of Moses, Dean Stanley stood up among his religious peers and placed himself alongside of Colenso. He said:

"I might mention one who . . . has ventured to say that the Pentateuch is not the work of Moses; . . . who has ventured to say that the narratives of those historical incidents are colored not unfrequently by the necessary infirmities which belong to the human instruments by which they were conveyed,—and that individual is the one who now addresses you. If you pronounce against the Bishop of Natal on grounds such as these, you must remember that there is one close at hand whom . . . you will be obliged to condemn." [50]

Bishop Thirlwall, of "princely intellect," had a well-known reputation for liberalism in theology. He introduced both the new theology of Schleiermacher and higher criticism into England. In fact, when Convocation yielded to public indignation so far as essentially to ask Dr. Smith, the Unitarian scholar, to resign, Bishop Thirlwall retired from the committee and refused to be placated until it was settled that Dr. Smith should remain. Evidence might be given to show liberalism in other members. These men were honorably bound to do justice to thousands of manuscripts if they assumed to reconstruct a Greek Text. We are informed by Dr. Scrivener that there are 2,864 cursive and uncial manuscripts of the New Testament in whole or in part. Price says there are 112 uncials and 3,500 cursives. These represent many different countries and different periods of time. Yet astonishing to relate, the majority of the Revisers ignored these and pinned their admiration and confidence practically to two,—the Vaticanus and Sinaiticus.

Doctor Moberly, Bishop of Salisbury, Bishop Westcott, and Dr. G. Vance Smith, came to the Committee with past relationships that seriously compromised them. Bishop Moberly "belonged to the Oxford Movement, and, it is stated in Dean Church's 'Life and Letters' that he

---

[50] Stanley, Essays, pp. 329, 330.

wrote a most kind letter of approval to Mr. Newman as
to the famous Tract 90." [51] During the years when he was
a schoolmaster, the small attendance at times under his
instruction was credited to the fact that he was looked
upon as a Puseyite. [52] While with regard to Dr. Westcott,
his share in making the Ritualistic Movement a success
has been recognized. [53] Dr. Vaughan, another member
of the Revision Committee was a close friend of Westcott. [54] The extreme liberalism of Dr. G. Vance Smith,
the Unitarian member of the Committee, is well known
through his book on the "Bible and Theology." This
amounted practically to Christianized infidelity. Nevertheless, the worshipful attitude of these men, as well as
that of Lightfoot, Kennedy, and Humphrey toward Codex
B, was unparalleled in Biblical history. The year 1870
was marked by the Papal declaration of infallibility. It
has been well said that the blind adherence of the Revisionists to the Vatican manuscript proclaimed "the
second infallible voice from the Vatican."

THE RUTHLESS CHANGES WHICH RESULTED

Even the jots and tittles of the Bible are important.
God has pronounced terrible woes upon the man who
adds to or takes away from the volume of Inspiration.
The Revisers apparently felt no constraint on this point,
for they made 36,000 changes in the English of the King
James Version, and very nearly 6,000 in the Greek Text.
Dr. Ellicott, in submitting the Revised Version to the
Southern Convocation in 1881, declared that they had
made between eight and nine changes in every five verses,
and in about every ten verses three of these were made
for critical purposes. [55] And for the most of these changes
the Vatican and Sinaitic Manuscripts are responsible.
As Canon Cook says:

"By far the greatest number of innovations, including
those which give the severest shocks to our minds, are

[51] F. D. How. Six Great Schoolmasters, p. 69. [52] Idem, p. 82.
[53] Kempson, Church in Modern England, p. 100.
[54] How, Six Great Schoolmasters, pp. 179, 180.
[55] Ellicott, Submission of Revised Version to Convocation, p. 27.

adopted on the authority of two manuscripts, or even of one manuscript, against the distinct testimony of all other manuscripts, uncial and cursive. . . . The Vatican Codex, . . . sometimes alone, generally in accord with the Sinaitic, is responsible for nine-tenths of the most striking innovations in the Revised Version." [56]

WRECKERS, NOT BUILDERS

A force of builders do not approach their task with swords, spears, bombs, cannons, and other instruments of destruction. If the Greek New Testament of Westcott and Hort marks a new era, as we are repeatedly informed, then it was intended that the Revised Version would mark a new era. The appointees to the task of Revision evidently approached their work with the intention of tearing down the framework of the teachings which sprang from the Received Text and of the institutions erected for the spread of such teachings. The translators of 1611 organized themselves into six different companies. Each company allotted to each of its members a series of independent portions of the Bible to translate, so that all would act as checks and counterchecks on one another, in order that the truth might be transmitted. Above all, their inter-relations were so preserved that the world would receive the gift of a masterpiece. Their units were organizations of construction. The units of the 1881 Revision did not make for protection and independence, but rather for the suppression of individuality and freedom, and for tryannical domination.

The instruments of warfare which they brought to their task were new and untried rules for the discrimination of manuscripts; for attacking the verb; for attacking the article; for attacking the preposition, the pronoun, the intensive, Hebraisms, and parallelisms. The following quotations show that literal and critically exact quotations frequently fail to render properly the original meaning:

[56] Cook, Revised Version, pp. 227, 231.

"The self-imposed rule of the Revisers," says the *Forum*, "required them invariably to translate the aoristic forms by their closest English equivalents; but the vast number of cases in which they have forsaken their own rule shows that it could not be followed without in effect changing the meaning of the original; and we may add that to whatever extent that rule has been slavishly followed, to that extent the broad sense of the original has been marred." [57]

One of the Revisers wrote, after the work was finished:

"With reference to the rendering of the article, similar remarks may be made. As a rule, it is too often expressed. This sometimes injures the idiom of the English, and in truth impairs or misrepresents the force of the original." [58]

The obsession of the Revisionists for rendering literally Hebraisms and parallelisms have often left us with a doctrine seriously, if not fatally, weakened by their theory. "The printing in parallelisms spoils the uniformity of the page too much and was not worth adopting, unless the parallelism was a good one." [59]

Probably no one act of Germany during the war brought down upon her more ill feeling than the bombing of Rheims Cathedral. We felt sad to see the building splintered and marred. It was the work of centuries. The Revisionists approached the beautiful cathedral of the King James Version and tunneled underneath in order that they might destroy the Received Text as its foundation, and slip into its place another composed of the Vatican and Sinaitic Manuscripts. In thousands of places the grandeur of the sacred building was chipped and splintered by the substitution of various readings. In the form of the Revised Version we no longer recognize the strong foundation and glorious features of the old edifice.

This is a case where a little means much. "If one wonders whether it is worth while," says Dr. Robertson,

---

[57] *Forum*, June, 1887, p. 357.
[58] Dr. G. Vance Smith, *Nineteenth Century*, June, 1881.   [59] Idem.

speaking of the Revision, "he must bear in mind that some of the passages in dispute are of great importance." The Bible should more probably be compared to a living organism. Touch a part and you spoil it all. To cut a vital artery in a man might be touching a very small point, but death would come as truly as if he were blown to pieces. Something more than a crushing mass of accumulated material is needed to produce a meritorious revision of God's Holy Book.

THE REVISERS' GREATEST CRIME

Ever since the Revised Version was printed, it has met with strong opposition. Its devotees reply that the King James met opposition when it was first published. There is a vast difference, however. Only one name of prominence can be cited as an opponent of the King James Version at its birth. The King, all the church of England, in fact, all the Protestant world was for it. On the other hand, royal authority twice refused to associate itself with the project of revision, as also did the northern half of the Church of England, the Episcopal Church of North America, besides a host of students and scholars of authority.

When God has taught us that "all Scripture is given by Inspiration" of the Holy Spirit and that "men spake as they were moved by the Holy Ghost," the Holy Spirit must be credited with ability to transmit and preserve inviolate the Sacred Deposit. We cannot admit for a moment that the Received Text which, by the admission of its enemies themselves, has led the true people of God for centuries, can be whipped into fragments and set aside for a manuscript found in an out-of-the-way monastery, and for another of the same family, which has lain, for man knows not how long, upon a shelf in the library of the Pope's palace. Both these documents are of uncertain ancestry, of questionable history, and of suspicious character. The Received Text was put for centuries in its position of leadership by divine Providence, just as truly as the star of Bethlehem was set in the heavens to guide the wise men. Neither was it the product of certain technical rules of textual criticism which some men have chosen the last few decades to exalt as divine principles.

The change of one word in the Constitution of the United States, at least the transposition of two, could vitally affect thousands of people, millions of dollars, and many millions of acres of land. It took centuries of training to place within that document a combination of words which cannot be tampered with, without catastrophic results. It represents the mentality of a great people, and to change it would bring chaos into their well-ordered life. Not of one nation only, but of all great nations, both ancient and modern, is the Bible the basis of the Constitution. It foretold the fall of Babylon; and when that empire had disappeared, it survived. It announced beforehand the creation of the empires of Greece and Rome, and lived to tell their faults and why they failed. It warned succeeding kingdoms. All ages and continents have their life inwrought into the fabric of this Book. It is the handiwork of God through the centuries. Only those whose records are lifted high above suspicion, can be accepted as qualified to touch it. Certainly no living being or any number of them ever had authority to make such astounding changes, as were made by those men who were directly or indirectly influenced by the Oxford Movement.

The history of the Protestant world is inseparable from the Received Text. A single nation could break loose and plunge into anarchy and license. The Received Text shone high in the heavens to stabilize surrounding peoples. Even many nations at one time might fall under the shadow of some great revolutionary wave. But there stood the Received Text to fill their inner self with its moral majesty and call them back to law and order.

On what meat had this great critic, Dr. Hort, fed, when, even by his own confession, at the time he had read little of the Greek New Testament, and knew nothing of texts and certainly nothing of Hebrew, he dared, when only twenty-three years old, to call the Received Text "villainous" and "vile"? What can be the most charitable estimate we can put upon that company of men who submitted to his lead, and would assure us in gentle words that they had done nothing, that there was really no great difference between the King James Bible and the Revised, while in another breath, they reject as "villainous" and "vile" the Greek New Testament upon which the King James Bible is built? Did they belong to a superior race of beings, which entitled them to cast aside, as a thing of naught, the work of centuries? They gave us a Version which speaks with faltering tones, whose music is discordant. The Received Text is harmonious. It agrees with itself, it is self-proving, and it creeps into the affections of the heart.

But, they say, there are errors in the Received Text. Yes, "plain and clear errors," as their instructions informed the Revisers. It is to the glory of the Textus Receptus that its errors are "plain and clear." When God showed us these errors were "plain and clear," we recognized them as errors of the copyists and therefore, like printer's errors, they can be promptly and certainly corrected. They are not errors of the Author. Man made them and man can correct them. Neither are they "errors" which man made and only God can correct. They do not enter into the core of any question. They are not, like the errors of the Vaticanus and Sinaiticus, the product of Systematic Depravation. They are the scars which witness to the terrible struggles endured by the Holy Word throughout the centuries.

The glorified body of Christ will always have five scars where the nails pierced His hands and feet, and where the sword entered His side. A captious critic might cry out that the eternal form of Christ is not perfect; it has five scars. But another of deeper insight would point out that by those scars we know that Christ does not

bear an untried form. Those reminiscences of His humiliation testify to His struggle and His triumph.
Christ's perfection would not have been complete without those scars. Without them, He would not have been
our Saviour. The errors of the Received Text, are the
scars which tell of its struggles throughout the centuries
to bring us light, life, and immortality. The Living
Word and the Written Word correspond.

How vastly different are the errors of the Revised!
They are the product of a well-laid, designing scheme to
incorporate in the text the theology of the Revisers.
Westcott, writing to Hort before the committee was under way, rejoiced that the future chairman, Dr. Ellicott,
was "quite capable of accepting heartily and adopting
personally a *thorough* scheme." And when the new book
was published, Bishop Westcott recommended it to the
Bible student, because the profound effect on doctrine
was produced by changing "here a little, there a little."
He clearly convicted the Revised Version of being the
product of a designing scheme with an ulterior purpose.
He said:

"But the value of the Revision is most clearly seen
when the student considers together a considerable group
of passages, which bear upon some article of the Faith.
The accumulation of small details then produces its full
effect. Points on which it might have seemed pedantic
to insist in a single passage become impressive by repetition. . . . The close rendering of the original Greek in
the Revised Version appears to suggest ideas of creation
and life and providence, of the course and end of finite
being and of the Person of the Lord, who is the source of
all truth and hope, which are of deepest interest at the
present time." [60]

All must see that it was a *"thorough scheme."* The
dominant minds on the Revision Committee approached
their task, committed beforehand to this *"thorough
scheme."* The errors therefore of the Revised Version
are not incidental and accidental, as those of the Re-

---

[60] Westcott, Some Lessons, pp. 184, 185.

ceived Text, but are so systematically interlinked that they constitute with cumulative effect vital changes in doctrine. The Revised Version bears the stamp of intentional Systematic Depravation.

When we consider the men who dominated the Committee and consequently determined the content of the Revised work, and when we consider their critical bias, their sympathy with the germinal ideas of modern religious liberalism, their advocacy of Ritualism, and their fondness for Rome, simple intelligence compels us to wonder if the "scheme" does not embrace a subservience to these predilections.

When a company of men set out faithfully to translate genuine manuscripts in order to convey what God said, it is one thing. When a committee sets itself to revise or translate with ideas and a "scheme," it is another thing. But it may be objected that the translators of the King James were biased by their pro-Protestant views. The reader must judge whose bias he will accept, that of the influence of the Protestant Reformation, as heading up in the Authorized Version, or that of the influence of Darwinism, higher criticism, incipient modern religious liberalism, and a reversion back to Rome, as heading up in the Revised Version. If we select the latter bias, we must remember that both higher criticism and Romanism reject the authority of the Bible as supreme.

The predominant ideas of the respective times of their births influenced and determined the essential characteristics of the Authorized and Revised Versions. The following chapters will establish the truthfulness of the position just stated.

CHAPTER XI

Blow After Blow Against the Truth
(*Revised Texts and Margins*)

THERE are many who claim that the changes in the Revised Version did not affect any doctrine. Bishop Westcott reveals the contrary. His utterances prove that the Revisers worked systematically during the ten years of their task to make alterations that by a repetition of details they might alter articles of faith. This we have shown in the previous chapter.[1]

They did not use the margin to indicate changes in the Greek text as directed by Convocation; on the contrary they choked the margin with preposterous readings designed to carry out "the scheme" of Westcott, Hort, and Lightfoot. "There is some hope," wrote Westcott to Hort, before revision began, when prospects of a complete textual revision seemed small, "that alternative readings might find a place in the margin."[2] And they did, only to sow, broadcast, doubts about the sacred utterances.

A further word from Bishop Westcott to show how systematically the Revisers worked in making changes:

"For while some of the variations which we have noticed are in themselves trivial, some are evidently important; but they all represent the action of the same law; they all hang together; they are samples of the general character of the Revision. And, even if we estimate differently the value of the particular differences which they express, we can certainly see that they do express differences; and they are sufficient, I cannot doubt, to encourage the student to consider in any case of change which comes before him, whether there may

---

[1] Westcott, Some Lessons, p. 184.
[2] Westcott, Life and Letters, Vol. I, p. 390.

not have been reasons for making it which are not at once clear." [3]

To show that it was the settled purpose as well as the definite expectation on the part of the leaders in the movement for revision, that doctrine should be changed, I will now quote from the outstanding agitator for revision, who was also chairman of the English New Testament Revision Committee, Bishop Ellicott:

"Passages involving doctrinal error. Here our duty is obvious. Faithfulness, and loyalty to God's truth, require that the correction should be made unhesitatingly. This class of cases, will, however, embrace many different instances; some of real and primary importance, some in which the sense will be but little affected, when the error, grammatically great as it really may be, is removed, and the true rendering substituted. For instance, we shall have, in the class we are now considering, passages in which the error is one of a doctrinal nature, or, to use the most guarded language, involves some degree of liability to doctrinal misconception." [4]

I. *Tradition Equals Scripture According to the Revised*

1. 2 Tim. 3:16

KING JAMES: "All Scripture is given by inspiration of God."
REVISED: "Every Scripture inspired of God is also profitable."

In this, the Revised follows the thought of the Douay. This change in the Revised indicates that parts of the Scriptures may not have been inspired. Therefore, as we are not able to judge what is, and what is not inspired, the Catholics say that tradition tests the inspiration and gives us the correct meaning. The tradition of the Catholic Church corresponds to the higher criticism of the so-called Protestants, only with this difference, that the Catholics claim their higher criticism to be infallible. On this point we will quote the note in the Douay on this very passage, *2 Tim. 3:16,*—

"Every part of divine Scripture is certainly *profitable* for all these ends. But, if we would have the *whole*

---

[3] Westcott, *Some Lessons*, p. 158.   [4] Ellicott, *Considerations*, p. 88.

rule of Christian faith and practice, we must not be content with those Scriptures, which Timothy *knew from his infancy*. That is, with the Old Testament alone; nor yet with the New Testament, without taking along with it the traditions of the apostles, and the interpretation of the Church, to which the apostles delivered both the book, and the true meaning of it."

The *Dublin Review* (Catholic), July, 1881, speaking of the changes in the Revised Version, shows clearly that Catholics see how the Revised reading robs Protestantism of its stronghold, the Bible. It says:

"It (Protestantism) has also been robbed of its only proof of Bible inspiration by the correct rendering of 2 Tim. 3:16."

Also the *Interior* says on this change,—

"It is not very probable that Paul would utter an inconsequential truism of that kind. No one need be told that a Scripture inspired of God would be profitable—that would be taken for granted; but what has needed to be known was just the truth that Paul wrote, that 'all Scripture is given by inspiration of God.' " [5]

Knowing the views held by the Revisers, such a change as this could be expected. Many controlling members of the English New Testament Revision Committee believed that "there may be parts of the canonical books not written under the inspiration of the Holy Spirit." [6]

2.   John 5:39

KING JAMES: "Search the Scriptures; for in them ye think ye have eternal life."

REVISED: "Ye search the Scriptures, because ye think that in them," etc.

The command of the Saviour to search the Scriptures, as given in the King James, establishes them as the source of life eternal and the authority of true doctrine. The Revisers destroyed this command. Is not this changing a fundamental doctrine?

---

[5] Dr. Warfield's Collection of Opinions and Reviews, Vol. II, p. 77.
[6] Stanley, Church and State, p. 123.
  Also, Hort's Life and Letters, Vol. I, p. 424.

On this point the *Dublin Review* (Catholic), July, 1881, says:

"But perhaps the most surprising change of all is John 5:39. It is no longer 'Search the Scriptures,' but 'Ye search;' and thus Protestantism has lost the very cause of its being."

Other changes of passages, which we investigate following this, affect the great doctrines of truth; the change now under consideration affects the very citadel of truth itself. The Church of England Convocation, which called the Revision Committee into existence, authorized that Committee to correct only "plain and clear errors" in the Received Text. Neither Convocation, nor Protestant England expected it to be changed in thousands of places.

When the Revised Version declares that parts of the Bible may not have been inspired of God, (as in 2 Tim. 3:16), the defendant is forced to bear witness against itself. So far as the Revised Version is concerned, the change destroys the infallibility of that glorious citadel of revelation which for centuries had been the standard of truth.

II.　*A Deadly Blow Against Miracles*
I.　John 2:11

KING JAMES: "This beginning of miracles did Jesus in Cana of Galilee."

REVISED: "This beginning of signs did Jesus in Cana of Galilee."

The word "miracle" is found, singular and plural, thirty-two times in the Authorized Version of the New Testament. Alas! What desolation has been wrought by the Revised! In twenty-three of these instances, the word "miracle" has entirely disappeared. In the case of the other nine, although the term is used in the text, its force is robbed by a weakening substitute in the margin. While in the Old Testament, it has disappeared from the Revised in the five instances where it occurs in the Authorized. Modern religious liberalism finds consolation here. So the Revisers have exposed believers in the Bible to the ridicule of unbelievers because they describe the supernatural events of the New Testament by belittling words. To describe the supernatural in terms of the natural, indicates doubt in the supernatural. If we persist in calling a mountain a molehill, it is evident that we do not believe it is a mountain. The Revisers, in persistently describing supernatural events by ordinary terms, have changed doctrines respecting miracles. And if they made such fundamental changes in these thirty-two New Testament texts,—all there was on the subject,—what is this, but systematic depravation of doctrine?

III.   Doctrine of Conversion Undermined
1.   Matt. 18:2,3

KING JAMES: "And Jesus . . . said, . . . Except ye be converted, and become as little children."

REVISED: "And He . . . said, . . . Except ye turn, and become as little children."

FERRAR FENTON: "Then Jesus . . . said: I tell you indeed, that if you do not turn back."

Not only in this text but in all the rest (seven texts altogether), "be converted" has been changed to "turn." On this point we will use the following quotation which speaks for itself:

"The Rev. Homersham Cox writes to the *Church Times* in favor of the New Revision because (as he says) it alters 'be converted' into 'turn,' the former implying that the sinner *is* converted by another, that is, the Holy Spirit, and the latter that he turns or converts himself. He says:

" 'I have here given every passage without exception in which the word 'converted' in the passive voice occurs in the older translation. In every one of these instances the passive form is avoided in the new translation. The change seems to be one of incalculable importance. The former version teaches men that they are converted by a power external to themselves; the later version teaches them to turn themselves. In other words, the doctrine of superhuman conversion disappears from the New Testament, and thus the main foundation of modern Evangelicalism is destroyed. Only a few Sundays ago it was my misfortune to have to listen to a long "Evangelical" sermon, the whole burden of which was that men could not convert themselves. This pernicious tenet is preached every year in myriads of sermons, books, and tracts. I rejoice that it is now shown to be unscriptural.' " [7]

Also Dr. Milligan, commenting on this change in Matt. 18:3 and in Acts 3:19, says that "the opening verb, though passive in form, is properly rendered actively, and the popular error of men being mere passive instruments in the hands of God thereby exploded." [8]

The dangerous doctrine of salvation by our own effort is exalted; and the miracle-saving power of God in conversion, so far as these texts are concerned, is thrust out of the New Testament. The Revised changes the doctrine of conversion, and that change is a complete reversal of the doctrine.

IV. No Creation: Evolution Instead

We shall present a series of Scripture texts to exhibit how the Revisers made the Bible teach the origin of the material universe by evolution instead of by creation.

S. Parkes Cadman explains clearly how the German brain, working in theology and higher criticism, manifested itself in science and history, thus influencing Sir Charles Lyell to produce his "Principles of Geology," which heralded the advent of Evolution and contravened the cosmogonies of Genesis. Lyell altered the whole tone of Darwin's thinking, and Darwin's inquiries were vindicated in a revolution foreshadowed by Newman's "Essay on the Development of Christian Doctrine." [9] In this, Newman followed Möhler of Germany, and started the great ritualistic movement in the Church of England, which blossomed out into Revision. Both Westcott and Hort leaned heavily toward Ritualism and Evolution. Bishop Westcott says:

"Again 'world' answers to a plural or singular, 'the

---

[7] Dr. Warfield's Collection of Opinions and Reviews, Vol. II, pp. 28, 29.
[8] Milligan, Expository Value, p. 180.
[9] Cadman, Three Religious Leaders, pp. 409, 410.

ages,' or 'the age,' (Greek οἱ αἰῶνες, ὁ αἰών), in which creation is regarded as a vast system unfolded from æon to æon, as an immeasurable and orderly development of being under the condition of time, of which each 'age,' or 'this age,' and 'the age to come,' has its distinguishing characteristics, and so far is 'the world.' " [10]

This truth, he says, is "consistently preserved" in the margin.[11] That is, the unfolding of the "vast system" from "age to age" (evolution), is consistently preserved in the margin. In other words, the Revisers consistently, consciously, and intentionally, by their own confession, maintained the basal theory of evolution in the margin. On the importance of "age" and "ages" in the margin, I quote from Dr. Samuel Cox, editor of the *Expositor*:

"And here I may remark, in passing, that in such marginal readings as 'this age' and 'the coming age' which abound in our New Version, there lie the germs, latent for the present, of far larger doctrinal changes than either of those which I am now suggesting." [12]

1.   Hebrews 11:3

KING JAMES: "Through faith we understand that the worlds were framed by the word of God."

REVISED: By faith we understand that the ages have been framed by the word of God." (Margin.)

On this Westcott says:

"In this connection we see the full meaning of the words used of creation in Hebrews 11:3: *By faith we understand that the worlds* (*the ages,* i. e. the universe under the aspect of time) *have been formed by the Word of God.* . . . The whole sequence of life in time, which we call 'the world' has been 'fitted together' by God. His one creative word included the harmonious unfolding on one plan of the last issues of all that was made. That which is in relation to Him 'one act at once' is in relation to us an EVOLUTION apprehended in orderly succession." [13] (Caps. Mine).

Bishop Westcott's interpretation of God's work in creation is evolution, making room for the long geological

---

[10] Westcott, Some Lessons, p. 127.   [11] Idem, p. 186.
[12] Expositor, Vol. III, 2nd Series, p. 451, note.
[13] Westcott, Some Lessons, p. 187.

ages. Hort considered Darwin's theory of evolution unanswerable.[14] Westcott and Hort, whose Greek New Testament was the basis of the Revised, injected evolution into the Revised Version.

2. Col. 1:15,16

KING JAMES: "Who is the image of the invisible God, the first-born of every creature: For by Him were all things created."
REVISED: "Who is the image of the invisible God, the firstborn of all creation; for in Him were all things created."

Dr. G. Vance Smith, a member of the English New Testament Revision Committee, commenting on Colossians 1:15,16 says:

"Is it not therefore probable that, in the very different phraseology of Colossians, he is speaking of the promulgation of Christianity and its effects under the figure of a spiritual creation? . . . Is it possible to think that this language can refer to the material creation?"[15]

The new language of the Revised in the judgment of this Reviser, hinders the application of these texts to a material creation, as in the King James, and limits them as a spiritual application to Christianity.

3. Hebrews 1:2 (last part)

KING JAMES: "By whom also He made the worlds."
REVISED: "Through whom also He made the ages." (Margin.)

By this change the door is opened to spiritualizing away creation.

V. *The Person of Christ*

The "Person of Christ" is the evangelical phraseology used to express a doctrine which is taught in a way that tends to Rome. Some make it the central principle of all doctrines, and especially of ritualistic practices. This is shown by the following words from a ritualistic clergyman:

"Let every one who hears you speak, or sees you worship, feel quite sure that the object of your devotion is

---

[14] Hort's Life and Letters, Vol. I, pp. 414, 416.
[15] G. Vance Smith, The Bible and Its Theology, pp. 196, 197.

not an idea or a sentiment, or a theory, . . . but a real personal King and Master and Lord: present at all times everywhere in the omnipresence of His *Divine* nature, present by His own promise, and His own supernatural power in His *Human* Nature too upon His Altar-Throne, there to be worshiped in the Blessed Sacrament as really, and literally, and actually, as you will necessarily worship Him when you see Him in His beauty in Heaven." [16]

This ritualistic clergyman believed that preachers (or priests) have power to change the wafer into the actual body of Christ.

1. 1 Tim. 3:16

KING JAMES: "And without controversy great is the mystery of godliness: God was manifest in the flesh," etc.

AMERICAN REVISED: "And without controversy great is the mystery of godliness; He who was manifest in the flesh," etc.

On the change of "He who" for "God," Bishop Westcott says:

"The reader may easily miss the real character of this deeply instructive change. The passage now becomes a description of the essential character of the gospel, and not simply a series of historical statements. The gospel is personal. The gospel—'the revelation of godliness'— is, in a word, Christ Himself, and not any propositions about Christ." [17]

The Revisers made this change which confounds Christ with the movement He instituted, the gospel, and leads our minds away from Christ, the person on His heavenly throne, to Christ, the bread of the Lord's supper, (Mass), on the ritualistic altar-throne. What is this, if not a change of doctrine? Bishop Westcott was conscious of the change the Revisers were making in this reading. On this the *Princeton Review* says:

"Making Christianity a life—the divine-human life of Christ—has far-reaching consequences. It confounds and contradicts the Scriptural and church doctrine as to the Person of Christ." [18]

---

[16] Quoted in Walsh, Secret History, p. 385.
[17] Westcott, Some Lessons, p. 198.   [18] *Princeton Review*, Jan. 1854.

2. Acts 16:7

KING JAMES: "But the Spirit suffered them not."
AMERICAN REVISED: "And the Spirit of Jesus suffered them not."

The Douay is like the Revised. On this change Dr. George Milligan says:

"Acts 16:7, . . . the striking reading, 'the Spirit of Jesus' (not simply as in the Authorized Version 'the Spirit') implies that the Holy Spirit had so taken possession of the Person of the Exalted Jesus that He could be spoken of as 'the Spirit of Jesus.' " [19]

By this change they identified Jesus, the second Person of the Trinity, with the Holy Spirit, the third Person. The evident purpose of this change is to open the way to teach ideas of the Person of Jesus different from the generally accepted Protestant view. As the *Princeton Review* says concerning the doctrine of the Person of Christ as held by Dr. Philip Schaff, President of both American Committees of Revision, and by his former associate, Dr. Nevin:

"It is impossible to understand the writings of Drs. Nevin and Schaff on this whole subject without a knowledge of the pantheistic philosophy. . . . It led men to look on the church as the development of Christ, very much as that philosophy regards the universe as the development of God." [20].

VI. *The Virgin Birth*
1. Isaiah 7:14

KING JAMES: "Behold a virgin shall conceive, and bear a son."
REVISED: "Behold the maiden (margin) shall conceive and bear a son."

This change gives room to doubt the virgin birth of Christ. Dr. G. Vance Smith says:

"The meaning of the words of Isaiah may, therefore, be presented thus: 'Behold the young wife is with child.' " [21]

---

[19] Milligan, Expository Value, p. 99.
[20] *Princeton Review*, Jan., 1854.
[21] Smith, Bible and Theology, p. 26.

VII. *Change in the Doctrine of Atonement*
1. 1 Cor. 5:7

KING JAMES: "For even Christ our passover is sacrificed for us."
REVISED: "For our Passover also hath been sacrificed, even
Christ."

One writer thus registers his indignation upon the
change made in this passage:

"Mad? Yes; and haven't I reason to be mad when I
find that grand old passage, 'For even Christ our passover is sacrificed for us'—a passage which sounds the
keynote of the whole doctrine of redemption—unneces-
sarily changed into, 'For our Passover also hath been
sacrificed, even Christ'? And we have such changes
everywhere. They are, I believe, called improvements
in style by their authors—and certainly by no one else." [22]

That Christ our Passover was sacrificed is an historical fact; that He was sacrificed "for us" is a doctrine and
the very basis on which the gospel rests. Take away the
fact that He died "for us," as the Revisers did in this
text, and there is no gospel left.

The leading Revisers, in particular, Westcott and Hort,
rejected the idea that Christ was our substitute and sacrifice.[23] Of course, Dr. G. Vance Smith, the Unitarian
member of the Revision Committee, did the same. The
widespread refusal to-day by Christian ministers of
many churches to admit we owe this debt to our Lord
Jesus Christ, who in His divine Person died in our place,
is largely due to those influences which gave us the Revised Version. Changes which on first reading seem
slight, when examined and read in the light of the intentional change, are seen to be fatal.

VIII. *A Blow Against the Resurrection of the Body*
1. Job 19:25,26

KING JAMES: "I know that my Redeemer liveth, and that He shall
stand at the latter day upon the earth: and though after my
skin worms destroy this body, yet in my flesh shall I see God."

---

[22] Rev. E. B. Birks in Dr. Warfield's Collection of Opinions, Vol. 2, p. 80.
[23] Hort's Life and Letters, Vol. I, p. 430; Vol. II, pp. 50, 213.

AMERICAN REVISED: "But as for me, I know that my Redeemer
     liveth, and at last He will stand up upon the earth: and after
     my skin, even this body, is destroyed, then without my flesh
     shall I see God."

What need is there of a resurrection of the body, if,
without our flesh, we can see God? The tendency to
make the resurrection from the tomb only a spiritual
event is as great to-day as in the first Christian centuries.

2.   Acts 24:15

KING JAMES: "That there shall be a resurrection of the dead both
     of the just and unjust."
REVISED: "That there shall be a resurrection both of the just and
     unjust."

The omission of the phrase "of the dead" makes it
easier to spiritualize away the resurrection.

IX.   Doctrine of the Second Coming of Christ Radically Changed

1.   Matt. 24:3

KING JAMES: "What shall be the sign of Thy coming, and of the
     end of the world?"
REVISED: "What shall be the sign of Thy presence (margin) and
     of the consummation of the age." (Margin.)

"The consummation of the age" in no sense means the
same thing as "the end of the world." "The end of the
world" is the appointed time for human history, under
the reign of sin, to close. The earth must be purified by
fire before being again inhabited by man. "The consummation of the age" might mean only some change from
one epoch to another,—national, scientific, educational,
or dispensational. How systematically this substitution
is thrust forward in the margin by the Revisers is shown
by its recurrence in the other passages in which the
phrase "end of the world" occurs, namely,—Matt. 13:39,
40,49; 24:3; 28:20. A similar substitution is found in
Heb. 13:21.

Another depravation in the doctrine of the Second
Coming of Christ is the substitution of "presence" for
"coming" in the margin of the text under consideration.

"Presence" does not mean return; it rather signifies continuous nearness. But "coming" refers to Christ's Second Advent in glory, at the end of the world, to raise the righteous dead and confer immortality on all righteous living or resurrected. How systematically the Revisers have gone about this, displacing the true idea of the Advent, may be seen in the twenty other verses where "coming" as it refers to Christ's Second Advent is changed into "presence," namely,—Matt. 24:27,37,39; 1 Cor. 15:23; 2 Cor. 7:7; Phil. 1:26; 2:12; 1 Thess. 2:19; 3:13; 4:15; 5:23; 2 Thess. 2:1,8,9; Jas. 5:7,8; 2 Peter 1:16; 3:4,12; 1 Jno. 2:28. These marginal changes give notice that the ordinary orthodox interpretation of these verses is not a sure one. Westcott, one of the Revisers, says:

"His advent, if it is in one sense future, is in another sense continuous." [24]

According to Westcott, Christ came at the time of Genesis, first chapter, at the fall of Jerusalem, and many times in the past: in fact, is "coming" to us now.[25]

2. Phil. 3:20,21

KING JAMES: "Who shall change our vile body that it may be fashioned like unto His glorious body."

REVISED: "Who shall fashion anew the body of our humiliation that it may be conformed to the body of His glory."

The change in us indicated by the King James according to this and other Scriptures, is a change that occurs only at the Second Coming of Christ; it is a physical change of tangible reality. But the change called for by the Revised may occur at any time before His Coming, or be continuous; it may be a change from abstract vices to abstract virtues.

3. 2 Thess. 2:2

KING JAMES: "That you be not soon shaken in mind . . . as that the day of Christ is at hand."

REVISED: "That ye be not quickly shaken from your mind . . . as that the day of the Lord is now present."

---

[24] Westcott. Some Lessons, p. 44.
[25] Life of Westcott, Vol. II, pp. 307, 308.

When an event is "at hand" it has not yet come; but when it is "now present" it is here. Without offering an opinion which is the correct rendering, there is certainly here a change of doctrine. If the day of the Lord "is now present," it is in no sense, "at hand."

4.   Titus 2:13

KING JAMES: "Looking for that blessed hope and the glorious appearing of the great God and our Saviour, Jesus Christ."

REVISED: "Looking for the blessed hope and appearing of the glory of the great God and our Saviour Jesus Christ."

By changing the adjective "glorious" to the noun "glory," the Revisers have removed the Second Coming of Christ from this text. In the King James Version the object of our hope is the appearing of Christ, which is a personal and a future and an epochal event. In the Revised Version, the object of our hope is changed to be the appearing of the glory of Christ, which may be the manifestation among men, or in us, of abstract virtues, which may appear at any time and repeatedly in this present life.

5.   Rev. 1:7

KING JAMES: "He cometh with clouds . . . and all kindreds of the earth shall wail because of Him."

REVISED: "He cometh with the clouds . . . and all the tribes of the earth shall mourn over Him."

How great is the change intended here, let the Reviser, Bishop Westcott himself, state:

"All the tribes of the earth shall mourn over Him in penitential sorrow, and not, as the Authorized Version, shall wail because of Him, in the present expectation of terrible vengeance." [26]

It is well known that many of the Revisers believed in what they called, The Larger Hope, or Universal Salvation, which the translators of the King James did not believe. Westcott admits the Revisers made the change, in order to make the change of doctrine.

---

[26] Westcott, Some Lessons, p. 196.

6. Acts 3:19

Here again the Revisers plead guilty to changing doctrine. That the reading of Acts 3:19,20 was changed because the Revisers held different views on the Second Coming of Christ from the men of 1611, a member of the English New Testament Committee, Dr. Alexander Roberts, testifies:

"Acts 3:19,20. An impossible translation here occurs in the Authorized Version, in which we read: 'Repent ye therefore, and be converted, that your sins may be blotted out, when the times of refreshing shall come from the presence of the Lord; and He shall send Jesus Christ, which before was preached unto you.' *For eschatological reasons*, it is most important that the true rendering of this passage should be presented. It is thus given in the Revised Version: 'Repent ye, therefore, and turn again, that your sins may be blotted out, that so seasons of refreshing may come from the presence of the Lord; and that He may send the Christ who hath been appointed for you, (even) Jesus.' " [27] (Italics mine.)

"For eschatological reasons" he says, that is, for reasons springing from their view on last things, not for textual reasons, it was "most important" to change the rendering. Most of the Revisers did not believe there would be a personal return of Jesus before the restitution of all things, which the Authorized rendering of this passage teaches.

Hort, another Reviser, says: "There is a present unveiling of Him simply as He is, without reference to any special action of His, such as came to St. Paul on his conversion. There are apparently successive unveilings of Him, successive Days of the Lord. There is clearly indicated, a supreme unveiling, in which glory and judgment are combined." [28]

G. Vance Smith, another Reviser, says: "This idea of the Second Coming ought now to be passed by as a merely temporary incident of early Christian belief. Like many another error, it has answered its transitory purpose in

---

[27] Roberts, Companion, pp. 80, 81.
[28] Hort, The Apocalypse of St. John, p. 4.

the providential plan, and may well, at length, be left to rest in peace." [29]

Thus this Reviser dismisses the Second Coming of Christ as a temporary, erroneous idea among the early Christians.

X. Blows Against the Law of God—The Ten Commandments

1. Rev. 22:14

KING JAMES: "Blessed are they that do His commandments, that they may have right to the tree of life."

REVISED: "Blessed are they that wash their robes, that they may have the right to the tree of life."

Man keeping the commandments of God, and man washing his robes in the blood of Christ, are two different doctrines,—the latter applies to forgiveness for past sins, the former applies to so abiding in Christ as to avoid sinning, or breaking the commandments. No man washes his robes by keeping the commandments; that would be salvation by works. Shall we be sinning and repenting (that is, washing our robes) as we enter through the gates into the eternal city? Evidently not, since three verses previous, verses 11 to 13, present the eternally redeemed as settled in a holy and righteous condition obedient to His commandments and ready to enter through the gates into the city. The Revisers have dislocated this verse from its place in the scheme of the last chapter of the Bible. If, instead of being holy and righteous still,—that is, keeping God's commandments,— the redeemed are sinning and repenting still, or "washing their robes," they are not ready to say, "Even so, Lord Jesus, come quickly." The entire book of Revelation is in agreement with the King James translation of this verse, since commandment keeping is an outstanding characteristic of those who wait for the return of their Lord. (See Rev. 12:17; 14:12.) Revelation 22:14 gives final emphasis to this characteristic. The Authorized

---

[29] Smith, Bible and Theology, p. 281.

rendering is clear and definite, but the Revised is obscure and misleading.

2. Acts 13:42

KING JAMES: "And when the Jews were gone out of the synagogue, the Gentiles besought that these words might be preached to them the next sabbath."

REVISED: "And as they went out, they besought that these words might be spoken to them the next sabbath."

The Authorized Version pictures to us the congregation, composed of Jews and Gentiles. By this distinction it reveals that a number of the Gentiles were present and desired all their Gentile friends to hear the same message the next Sabbath. Since the Sabbath came in for special mention (see verse 27), and since the Gentiles requested a special meeting on the following Sabbath, and waited for it, we see that the great truth announced by Christ, that "the Sabbath was made for man" (Mark 2:28), was brought home to the Gentiles. All this is lost in the Revised Version by failing to mention the Jews and the Gentiles. Thus the Authorized Version is consistent with itself throughout, a divine harmony. Here the Revised strikes an absolute discord. Does not this affect fundamental doctrine?

XI. Affecting Scientific Teaching of the Bible
1. Mark 7:19

KING JAMES: "Because it entereth not into his heart, but into the belly, and goeth out into the draught, purging all meats?"

REVISED: "Because it goeth not into his heart, but into his belly, and goeth out into the draught? This he said, making all meats clean."

In the Old Testament system of sacrifices, God never accepted the offering of an unclean beast. Moreover, He forbade the use of unclean meats as food. In translating the above Scripture, there is nothing in the King James which breaks down this distinction. Who said that the Revisers had the right to alter what God anciently ordained?

"But by the change of a single letter in the Greek," says Milligan on this passage, "a new reading is gained, and the verse now concludes—'*This He said,* making all meats clean,' being the Evangelist's comment upon what he has just recorded, a comment that gains still further in significance when we remember that St. Mark's Gospel was in all probability largely dependent upon the recollections of the apostle Peter, who was taught in so striking a manner that in God's sight nothing is common or unclean. Acts 10:9-16." [30]

Peter said that by the vision of Acts 10, "God hath shewed me that I should not call any man common or unclean." *Acts 10:28.* And later he said that "God made choice amongst us, that the Gentiles by my mouth should hear the word of the gospel." *Acts 15:7.* Who gave the Revisers the right to say that the vision sent by God to Peter to break down the differences between Jew and Gentile was sent to abolish the age-long distinction between clean and unclean meats, and which exists in the very nature of the unclean animals as contrasted with the clean?

2.   Luke 23:44,45

KING JAMES: "And there was a darkness over the whole earth until the ninth hour. And the sun was darkened."

REVISED: "A darkness came over the whole land until the ninth hour, the sun's light failing."

MOFFATT: "And darkness covered the whole land till three o'clock, owing to an eclipse of the sun."

The Greek text of the Revisers on this passage and the Greek text of Moffatt is the same; the Greek text of the King James is different. The Greek text of the Revisers says there was an eclipse of the sun, ($\tau o \hat{v}$ $\dot{\eta} \lambda \acute{\iota} o v$ $\dot{\epsilon} \kappa \lambda \epsilon \grave{\iota}$ $\pi o v \tau o \varsigma$). Moffatt honestly translated his mutilated Greek thus, "owing to an eclipse of the sun." The Revisers failed to do it. Since an eclipse of the sun is physically impossible at the time of a full moon which was shining the night of Christ's burial, this shows that the Greek text of the Revisers, heralded among us with high praises, was scientifically incorrect and impossible. Moffatt was true to his Greek, even if he had adopted the

---

[30] Milligan, Expository Value, p. 62.

same Greek MS. as the Revisers.   The Revisers were not.

XII.   The Ascension
1.   Mark 16:9-20

These verses which contain a record of the ascension
are acknowledged as authority by the King James, but
separated by the Revised from the rest of the chapter to
indicate their doubtful value.   This is not surprising.
Dr. Hort, the evil genius of the Revision Committee,
cannot say anything too derogatory of these twelve
verses.[31]   In this he is consistent; for he believes the
story of the ascension was not entitled to any place in
any Gospel:

"The violence of Burgon's attack on the rejectors of
the conclusion of St. Mark's Gospel seems somewhat to
have disturbed Hort's calmness of judgment, and to have
made him keen-sighted to watch and close every possible
door against the admission of the disputed verses.   In
this case he takes occasion to profess his belief not only
that the story of the Ascension was no part of St. Mark's
Gospel, but that it ought not to find a place in any Gospel." [32]

The rejection of the last twelve verses of Mark's Gospel, or rather setting them off to one side as suspicious,
either indicts the church of past ages as a poor keeper
and teacher of Holy Writ, or indicts the Revisers as
exercising an extreme and unwarrantable license.

WHOLE SECTIONS OF THE BIBLE AFFECTED BY THE REVISED VERSION

The Revised Version mutilates the main account of
the Lord's prayer in the Gospel of Matthew, by leaving
out the words, "For thine is the kingdom, and the power
and the glory forever, Amen." *Matt. 6:13.*

It mutilates the subsidiary account of the Lord's
prayer in Luke 11:2-4, so that this last prayer could be
prayed to any man-made god.   It omits "which art in
heaven," from "Our Father, which art in heaven;" leaves

---

[31] Hort's Introduction, Select Notes, pp. 30-51.
[32] Salmon, Some Criticism of the Text, pp. 95, 96.

out the words, "thy will be done, as in heaven so in earth," etc. It is worthy to remark here that this mutilation of the Lord's prayer in both these places was the subject of fierce controversy between the Reformers and the Jesuits from 1534-1611, the Reformers claiming Jerome's Vulgate and the Jesuit Bible in English translated from the Vulgate were corrupt. The Revisers joined the Jesuits in this contention, against the Reformers. Dr. Fulke, Protestant, said in 1583:

"What your vulgar Latin translation hath left out in the latter end of the Lord's prayer in St. Matthew, and in the beginning and midst of St. Luke, whereby that heavenly prayer is made imperfect, not comprehending all things that a Christian man ought to pray for, besides many other like omissions, whether of purpose, or of negligence, and injury of time, yet still by you defended, I spare to speak of in this place." [33]

Matthew 17:21 is entirely omitted. Compare also Mark 9:29 and 1 Cor. 7:5. On this the *Dublin Review* says: "In many places in the Gospels there is mention of 'prayer and fasting.' Here textual critics suspect that 'an ascetic bias,' has added the fasting; so they expunge it, and leave in prayer only. If an 'ascetic bias' brought fasting in, it is clear that a bias, the reverse of ascetic, leaves it out." [34]

It sets off to one side and brands with suspicion, the account of the woman taken in adultery. *Jno. 8:1-11.*

See how Luke 9:55,56 is shortened:

KING JAMES: "But He turned, and rebuked them and said, Ye know not what manner of spirit ye are of. For the Son of man is not come to destroy men's lives, but to save them. And they went to another village."

AMERICAN REVISED: "But He turned, and rebuked them. And they went to another village."

Acts 8:37. This text is omitted in the English and American Revised.

Notice Eph. 5:30:

---

[33] Fulke, Defense of Translations of the Bible, (1583), pp. 57, 58.
[34] *Dublin Review* (Catholic), July, 1881.

KING JAMES: "For we are members of His body, of His flesh, and of His bones."

AMERICAN REVISED: "Because we are members of His body."

Behold how greatly this verse is cut down in the Revised!

See how, in 2 Timothy 4:1, the time of the judgment is obliterated, and Christ's Second Coming is obscured:

KING JAMES: "I charge thee therefore before God, and the Lord Jesus Christ, who shall judge the quick and the dead at His appearing and His kingdom."

AMERICAN REVISED: "I charge thee in the sight of God, and of Christ Jesus, who shall judge the living and the dead, and by His appearing and His kingdom."

It changes Revelation 13:10 from a prophecy to a general axiomatic statement, and, in the margin, places a black mark against the passage:

KING JAMES: "He that leadeth into captivity, shall go into captivity."

AMERICAN REVISED: "If any man is for captivity, into captivity he goeth."

Without presenting any more examples,—and the changes are many,—we will offer the words of another which will sum up in a brief and interesting way, the subject under consideration:

"By the sole authority of textual criticism these men have dared to vote away some forty verses of the inspired Word. The Eunuch's Baptismal Profession of Faith is gone; and the Angel of the Pool of Bethesda has vanished; but the Angel of the Agony remains—till the next Revision. The Heavenly Witnesses have departed, and no marginal note mourns their loss. The last twelve verses of St. Mark are detached from the rest of the Gospel, as if ready for removal as soon as Dean Burgon dies. The account of the woman taken in adultery is placed in brackets, awaiting excision. Many other passages have a mark set against them in the margin to show that, like forest trees, they are shortly destined for the critic's axe. Who can tell when the destruction will cease?" [35]

---

[35] *Dublin Review*, July, 1881.

CHAPTER XII

Blow After Blow in Favor of Rome

(*Revised Texts and Margins*)

IT is now necessary to present the Revised Version in a new phase. To do this, we will offer some passages of Scripture the Revisers have changed to those Catholic readings which favor the doctrines of Rome. On this Dr. Edgar says:

"It is certainly a remarkable circumstance that so many of the Catholic readings in the New Testament, which in Reformation and early post-Reformation times were denounced by Protestants as corruptions of the pure text of God's Word, should now, in the last quarter of the nineteenth century, be adopted by the Revisers of our time-honored English Bibles." [1]

Tobias Mullen, Catholic Bishop of Erie, Pa., calls attention to a number of passages, whose readings in the Catholic and in the Revised Version are identical in thought. He comments on one of these as follows:

"It will be perceived here, that the variation between the Catholic Version and the Revision is immaterial, indeed no more than what might be found between any two versions of different but substantially identical copies of the same document." [2]

I. *Human Knowledge Exalted Above the Divine Word by the Revision*
1. John 1:3,4

KING JAMES: "Without Him was not anything made that was made. In Him was life."

REVISED: "Without Him was not anything made. That which hath been made was life in Him." (Margin.)

Let it be remembered that the marginal readings were considered of great importance by the Revisers. Many

---

[1] Edgar, Bibles of England, pp. 347, 348. [2] Mullen, Canon, p. 333.

of them would be in the body of the text but for lack of a two-thirds majority vote.

The principal defect of Romanism was the assumption of wisdom communicated to it apart from, and superior to the written Word. This is essentially the Gnostic theory, that false knowledge which was spoken of by the apostle Paul in I Tim. 6:20. To this Gnostic theory, must be laid the blame for the great apostasy in the early Christian Church. This same Gnostic theory which Newman had, according to S. Parkes Cadman, led him into the arms of Rome. To show that the offensive marginal reading of the Revised on John 1:3 is the product of Gnosticism, I will quote from Dean Burgon:

"In the third verse of the first chapter of St. John's Gospel, we are left to take our choice between,—'without Him was not anything made that hath been made. In Him was life; and the life,' etc.,—and the following absurd alternative,—'without Him was not anything made. That which hath been made was life in Him; and the life,' etc. But we are not informed that this latter monstrous figment is known to have been the importation of the Gnostic heretics in the second century, and to be as destitute of authority as it is of sense. *Why is prominence given only to the lie?*" [3]

It is the Catholic doctrine that the lay members of the church are devoid of a certain capacity for understanding divine things, which capacity is bestowed upon their cardinals, bishops, and priesthood,—transmitted to them by the laying on of hands. They claim the people cannot secure this knowledge by direct personal contact with the Bible. This theory of a knowledge hidden from the many and open only to the few is that ancient Gnosticism which developed into the Catholic Church. It separated official Catholicism from the great body of members, and this is the reason for the power of the priests over the people. In other words, as in the case of Cardinal Newman, they substituted superstition for faith; be-

---

[3] Burgon, Revision Revised, p. 132.

cause faith does not come by ordinances of men, but by hearing the Word of God. (Rom. 10:17.)   True Protestantism has faith in the Bible as supreme.

II.   *Protestantism Condemned by the Change Affecting the Sacraments*

1.   I Cor. 11:29

KING JAMES: "For he that eateth and drinketh unworthily, eateth and drinketh damnation to himself, not discerning the Lord's body."

REVISED: "For he that eateth and drinketh, eateth and drinketh judgment unto himself, if he discern not the body."

Why were the two expressions "unworthily" and "Lord's" left out?   By the presence of the word "unworthily" the one partaking of the bread would be guilty of condemnation upon some other count than not discerning the body.   And if the word "Lord's" remained, Protestants could still claim that they discerned their absent Lord in a spiritual sense.   The omission of "unworthily" and "Lord's" therefore condemns Protestants who do not believe that the bread has been turned into the body of Christ.

III.   *The Change Restoring the Confessional*

1.   James 5:16

KING JAMES: "Confess your faults one to another."

REVISED: "Confess therefore your sins one to another."

In order to make the change from "faults" to "sins" the Greek was changed.   The Greek word meaning "faults" was rejected and replaced by the Greek word meaning "sins."   If man is commanded by Scripture to confess his "sins" to man, what objection is there to the auricular confession of the priests?   On this revised reading the *Dublin Review* (Catholic), July, 1881, says:

"The Apostles have now power to 'forgive' sins, and not simply to 'remit' them.   'Confess therefore your sins' is the new reading of James 5:16."

IV. *The Exaltation of the Priesthood Made Easy*
1. Hebrews 10:21

KING JAMES: "And having an high Priest over the house of God."
REVISED: "And having a great priest over the house of God."

This change may seem unimportant; nevertheless the wording carries with it, its effect. To single out Jesus as our "high Priest" in heaven, as the King James Version does, makes Him so outstanding, that we instinctively regard Him, since His ascension, as our only Priest, so far outdistancing other persons as to rate them unnecessary. The expression "great priest" exalts the order of the priesthood among whom Jesus happens to be the greatest one. The word "great" is a comparative word and implies a degree of the same order; the expression "high priest" signifies an office. There can be many great priests, but only one high priest. The reading of the King James puts Christ in a class by Himself. Just what singular position would that of Christ be as a "great priest" if He were not the high Priest? Moreover Christ is distinctly designated ten times in this same epistle as the high Priest. The change in the Revised leaves the conclusion possible that this change provided a priest for the Confessional, which, in turn, was restored by the change in James 5:16.

We know of one dominating Reviser—Dr. Hort—who exalted the necessity of an earthly priesthood and who bitterly assailed Protestantism for not having it.[4]

Since the Greek word "mega" was translated "high," in John 19:31, by the Revisers, why did they not so translate it here?

V. *Church Government—Separating the Priesthood from the Laity*
1. Acts 15:23

KING JAMES: "And wrote letters by them after this manner, The apostles and elders and brethren, send greeting unto the brethren."

---

[4] See Chapter IX.

AMERICAN REVISED: "And they wrote thus by them, The apostles and the elders, brethren, unto the brethren who are of the Gentiles."

In the King James, the word "brethren" is a noun making the lay people a third class separate from the apostles and elders. In the Revised it is a noun in apposition applying alike to apostles and elders,—two classes only.

This passage is used as a foundation on which to base an argument for a clergy separated by God in their function from the lay brethren. It makes a vast difference, in sending out this authoritative letter, from the first council of the Christian Church, whether it issued from the apostles and elders only, or issued from the apostles, elders, *and the brethren.* Here again to effect this change the Revisers omitted two Greek words.

The Jesuitical translators of 1582 strongly denounced Puritans for failing, in their translation, to make the distinction between the priesthood and the laity. As we read:

"This name then of 'priest' and 'priesthood' properly so called, as St. Augustine saith, which is an order distinct from the laity and vulgar people, ordained to offer Christ in an unbloody manner in sacrifice to His heavenly Father for us, to preach and minister the sacraments, and to be the pastors of the people, they wholly suppress in their translations." [5]

VI. *Changes to Support the Teaching of the Intermediate State*
1. Hebrews 9:27

KING JAMES: "And as it is appointed unto men once to die, but after this the judgment."

REVISED: "And inasmuch as it is appointed unto men once to die, and after this cometh judgment."

Canon Farrar claims that this change was deliberately made to emphasize the doctrine of the intermediate state of men after death, before being summoned to their final

---

[5] Fulke's Defense, p. 242.

reward or punishment. Canon Farrar ought to know, because he was a member of that brilliant organization, the "Apostles Club," dominant in its influence at Cambridge University, where Hort, Westcott, and other Revisers discussed questions of doctrine and church reform. Farrar said on this change:

"There is positive certainty that it does not mean '*the* judgment' in the sense in which that word is popularly understood. By abandoning the article which King James translators here incorrectly inserted, the Revisers help, as they have done in so many other places, silently to remove deep-seated errors. At the death of each of us there follows 'a judgment,' as the sacred writer says: *the* judgment, the final judgment, may not be for centuries to come. In the omission of that unauthorized little article from the Authorized Version by the Revisers, lies no less a doctrine than that of the existence of an Intermediate State." *

In the above quotation, note the use of the word "silently."

VII. The Larger Hope—Another Chance After Death
1. John 14:2

KING JAMES: "In my Father's house are many mansions."
REVISED: "In my Father's house are many abiding places." (Margin.)

In the following quotation from the *Expositor*, the writer points out that, by the marginal reading of the Revised, Dr. Westcott and the Committee referred, not to a final future state, but to intermediate stations in the future before the final one.

"Dr. Westcott in his Commentary on St. John's Gospel gives the following explanation of the words, '*In my Father's house are many mansions.*' 'The rendering comes from the Vulgate *mansiones*, which were "resting places," and especially the "stations" on a great road, where travelers found refreshment. This appears to be the true meaning of the Greek word here; so that the

---

* Canon F. W. Farrar, Contemporary Review, Mar. 1882.

contrasted notions of repose and progress are combined in this vision of the future.' " [7]

"For thirty years now," said Dr. Samuel Cox, in 1886, "I have been preaching what is called 'the larger hope,' through good and ill report." [8]

The "larger hope" meant a probation after this life, such a time of purifying, by fire or otherwise, after death as would insure another opportunity of salvation to all men. Dr. Cox, like others, rejoices that the changes in the Revised Version sustain this doctrine. "Had the new Version then been in our hands, I should not have felt any special gravity in the assertion," he said. [8] Doctors Westcott and Hort, both Revisers, believed this "larger hope." [9]

We have seen how Dr. G. Vance Smith, another Reviser, proved that the change of "hell fire" in the Authorized to "the hell of fire" in the Revised opened the way to introduce several hells. With this, Catholic theology agrees, as it teaches four different places of punishment after death, either intermediate places for purification, or the final place. Dr. Samuel Cox rejoices that the changes in the Revised Version make it possible to find these different stations. He says:

"The states of being, shadowed forth by the words, Gehenna, Paradise, Hades cannot, therefore, be final or everlasting; they are only intermediate conditions, states of discipline in which the souls of men await, and may be prepared for, their final award." [10]

2. Luke 1:72

KING JAMES: "To perform the mercy promised to our fathers."
REVISED: "To show mercy to our fathers."

To perform the mercy promised to our fathers long ago, Christ came, is the meaning of the King James. The Revised means that Christ came to shew to our dead fathers the mercy they need now. As Bishop Mullen says:

---

[7] T. Sterling Berry, Expositor, Vol. III, 2nd series, p. 397.
[8] Dr. Samuel Cox, Idem, p. 446.   [9] Hort's Life and Letters, Vol. I, p. 275.
[10] Dr. Samuel Cox, Expositor, Second Series, Vol. III, p. 447.

"For the text was one which, if rendered literally, no one could read without being convinced, or at least suspecting, that the 'fathers' already dead needed 'mercy'; and that 'the Lord God of Israel' was prepared 'to perform' it to them. But where were those fathers? Not in heaven, where mercy is swallowed up in joy. And assuredly not in the hell of the damned, where mercy could not reach them. They must therefore have been in a place between both, or neither the one nor the other. What? In Limbo or Purgatory? Why, certainly. In one or the other." [11]

The bishop further claims that the Revisers, in making this change, vindicated the Jesuit New Testament of 1582, and convicted the King James of a perversion.[12] Dr. Westcott also finds the "larger hope" in the change made in Luke 1:72 by the revision.[13] We will now quote from a well-known church historian who briefly describes the different intermediate states according to papal doctrine:

"This power of the Church through the Pope extends —'indirectly,' says Aquinas—to Purgatory. This was one of the five abodes in the invisible world. These are: 1. Hell, a place of eternal suffering, the abode of those who die in mortal sin, without absolution. The Schoolmen unite in affirming torment by eternal fire. 2. The *limbus* of infants dying unbaptized—*limbus* signifying literally a border, as, for instance, the bank of a river. In this abode the inmates are cut off from the vision of God, but, it was generally held, are not subject to positive inflictions of pain. 3. The *limbus patrum*—the abode of the Old Testament Saints, now, since the advent of Christ, turned into a place of rest. 4. Purgatory, for souls not under condemnation for mortal sin, yet doomed to temporal, terminable punishments. These served the double purpose of an atonement and of a means of purification. 5. Heaven, the abode of the souls which at death need no purification and of souls cleansed in the fires of Purgatory." [14]

---

[11] Mullen, Canon, p. 332.   [12] Idem, p. 331.
[13] Westcott, Some Lessons, p. 195.
[14] Fisher, History of Christian Doctrine, p. 259.

3.   I Peter 4:6

KING JAMES: "For, for this cause was the gospel preached also to them that are dead."

REVISED: "For unto this end was the gospel preached even to the dead."

The King James Version presents the truth of this passage to be that the gospel was preached (past tense) to them that are dead now (present tense); multitudes now dead had the gospel preached to them while they were living.   There is no hint that there is any preaching going on now to them that are now dead. The reverse is the teaching of the passage as changed by the Revised Version.   This is another contribution by the new Version, which, with other passages of the same import, reveals a systematic presentation of the doctrine of Purgatory.

Still another passage, this time from the Old Testament, reveals the tendency which the Revisers had in this direction.

4.   Job 26:5

KING JAMES: "Dead things are formed from under the waters, and the inhabitants thereof."

REVISED: "They ("the shades" margin) that are deceased tremble beneath the waters and the inhabitants thereof."

It is very evident here that the Revisers did not have a Protestant mentality.   On this passage we will quote from a member of the Old Testament Revision Committee (American):

"In Chapter 26 the senseless rendering of verse 5, 'Dead things are formed from under the waters,' etc., is replaced by a vivid reference to God's control over departed spirits." [15]

5.   II Peter 2:9

KING JAMES: "The Lord knoweth how to deliver the godly out of temptations, and to reserve the unjust unto the day of judgment to be punished."

REVISED: "The Lord knoweth how to deliver the godly out of temptation, and to keep the unrighteous under punishment unto the day of judgment."

---

[15] Chambers, Companion, p. 116.

By the change of this passage, the Revisers have gone beyond even the Douay Version, which agrees here with the King James. This change puts the wicked at once, after death, under continuing punishment, even before they have had a fair trial at the judgment seat. Speaking of I Peter 4:6, a reviewer of an article (1882) by Professor Evans, of Lane Seminary, says:

"In the department of eschatology, the work of the revision has been severely criticized. Its terms of gehenna, paradise, and hades, it is claimed, are not sharply defined and lead to confusion; . . . and probation after death to be favored by its rendering of I Peter 4:6, and from a passage in the book of the Revelation." [16]

VIII. The Different Regions of the Conscious Dead, as Roman Catholics Teach, Supported by the Revised

1. Rev. 13:8

KING JAMES: "And all that dwell upon the earth shall worship him, whose names are not written in the book of life of the Lamb slain from the foundation of the world."

AMERICAN REVISED: "And all that dwell on the earth shall worship him, every one whose name hath not been written from the foundation of the world in the book of life of the Lamb that hath been slain."

Even in 1583, thirty years before the King James Version was published, this text with all its possibilities was the subject of heavy controversy between the Jesuits and the Puritans. The Protestants, even then, rejected the way it is now written in the American Revised Version." [17]

IX. A Substitute Number for the Beast: "616" or "666"

1. Rev. 13:18

KING JAMES: "And his number is six hundred threescore and six."

REVISED: "And his number is six hundred and sixteen" (margin).

Throughout the ages, the certainty of this number, "666," and the certainty of applying it to the Papacy, has been a source of strength and comfort to Protestant

---

[16] Dr. Warfield's Collection of Opinions and Reviews, Vol. I, p. 62.
[17] Fulke's Defense, pp. 278, 329, 330.

martyrs.   Behold the uncertainty and confusion brought into the interpretation of this prophecy by offering in the margin the substitute number "616."   Did not the Revisers by this change strike a blow in favor of Rome?

"But why is not the *whole* truth told? viz., why are we not informed that *only one* corrupt uncial (C) :—*only one* cursive copy(11) :—*only one* Father (Tichonius) : and *not one* ancient Version—advocates this reading?— which, on the contrary, Irenaeus (A.D. 170) knew, but rejected; remarking that 666, which is 'found in all the best and oldest copies and is attested by men who saw John face to face,' is unquestionably the true reading. Why is not the ordinary reader further informed that the same number (666) is expressly vouched for by Origen,—by Hippolytus,—by Eusebius:—as well as by Victorinus—and Primasius,—not to mention Andreas and Arethas?   To come to the moderns, as a matter of fact the established reading is accepted by Lachmann, Tischendorf, Tregelles,—even by Westcott and Hort.   *Why* therefore—for what possible reason—at the end of 1700 years and upwards, is this which is so clearly nothing else but an ancient slip of the pen, to be forced upon the attention of 90 millions of English speaking people?

"Will Bishop Ellicott and his friends venture to tell us that it has been done because 'it would not be safe to accept' 666, 'to the absolute exclusion of' 616? . . . 'We have given *alternative readings* in the margin,' (say they,) 'wherever they seem to be of sufficient importance or interest to deserve notice.' Will they venture to claim either 'interest' or 'importance' for *this*? or pretend that it is an 'alternative reading' *at all*? Has it been rescued from oblivion and paraded before universal Christendom in order to perplex, mystify, and discourage 'those that have understanding,' and would fain 'count the number of the Beast,' if they were able?   Or was the intention only to insinuate one more wretched doubt—one more miserable suspicion—into minds which have been taught (*and rightly*) to place absolute reliance in the textual accuracy of all the gravest utterances of the SPIRIT: minds which are utterly incapable of dealing with the subtleties of Textual Criticism; and, from a one-sided statement like the present, will carry away none but entirely mistaken inferences, and the most unreasonable distrust? . . . Or, lastly, was it only because, in their opinion, the margin of every Englishman's N. T. is the fittest place for reviving the memory of obsolete blunders, and ventilating forgotten perversions of the Truth? . . . We really pause for an answer." [18]

X. The Entire Meaning Touching Old Testament Prophecies Changed
1. Matt. 2:15

KING JAMES: "Out of Egypt have I called my son."
REVISED: "Out of Egypt did I call my son."

The comment of Dean Farrar on this change proves how systematically the Old Testament prophecies were robbed of their typical meaning by the "modern rules" used to translate that Greek tense known as the aorist. He says:

" 'Out of Egypt did I call my son.' What could the Revisers do but alter the incorrect rendering of the Authorized Version? The Authorized Version confuses the entire meaning of the passage, and hides the invariable method of St. Matthew in his references to Old Testament prophecies. Hosea's reference, Hosea 11:1, is to the calling forth of the Israelites from Egypt. . . . It is by a restoration of the tenses actually used that we may expect, in this and HUNDREDS OF OTHER TEXTS, to rekindle a light of understanding which has long faded away." [19]   (Capital letters mine.)

When Hosea, who prophesied 700 years after Moses, said, "Out of Egypt have I called my son," was he talking history or prophecy? Did he refer back to the Israelites leaving Egypt, or forward to the flight of the infant Jesus into and out of Egypt? The King James translators considered it a prophecy and wrote "have called;" the Revisers wrote "did call" to express history. The King James translated it by the perfect, "have called," which shows the action to have effects still continuing. The Revisers said that this was wrong, claiming that

[18] Burgon, Revision Revised, pp. 135-137.
[19] *Contemporary Review*, March 1882.

the aorist should always be translated by the past tense and not by the perfect. This new rule, Farrar claims, changed hundreds of texts affecting both Old Testament prophecies and "the great crises of Christian life."

As to the unfairness of this rule, we could quote from many witnesses. We will let only one testify. Sir Edmund Beckett, LL.D., says:

"No one rule of that kind has produced so many alterations in the Revised Version as that an aorist always means an action past and gone, while a perfect tense implies action continuing up to the present time. . . . But if we find that forcing the English translation to conform to those rules produces confusion, or such English as no master of it writes, and no common person uses; that it is neither colloquial or solemn, nor impressive, nor more perspicuous than the old phrases, and often less so: such facts will override all general rules in the minds of men of common sense, not bewildered by too much learning or the pedantry of displaying it." [20]

How serious have been the effects upon doctrine by this "self-imposed rule," as the *Forum* says, in the Revised Version, we will now proceed to show.

XI.   *Entire Meaning of Great Crises in Christian Life Changed*

1.   I Cor. 15:3,4

KING JAMES: "For I delivered unto you first of all that which I also received, how that Christ died for our sins according to the Scriptures; and that He was buried, and that He rose again the third day."

REVISED: " . . . that He was buried; and that He hath been raised on the third day."

In this text, "He rose," has been changed to, "He hath been raised," for a definite purpose. We lay a charge against the triumvirate who swept the Revision Committee along with them, of deliberately making changes in order to introduce a new set of doctrines which would be neither Presbyterianism (Protestantism) or Episcopalianism, but which would favor Romanism. Before

---

[20] Beckett, Revised N. T., p. 15.

the proof is given that this text, I Cor. 15:3,4, is one of them, a letter of Bishop Westcott to Dr. Hort will reveal the full scheme. Thus he writes concerning "we three":

"Just now I think we might find many ready to welcome the true mean between the inexorable logic of the Westminster and the skeptical dogmatism of orthodoxy. At any rate, I am sure that there is a true mean, and that no one has asserted its claims on the allegiance of faithful men. Now, I think that Lightfoot, you, and I are in the main agreed, and I further think that with our convictions, we are at such a time bound to express them. The subjects which had occurred to me are—1. The development of the doctrine of Messiah, including the discussion of the selection of one people out of many. 2. Miracles and history. 3. The development of Christian doctrine out of the apostolic teaching. In other words, I should like to have the Incarnation as a center, and on either side the preparation for it, and the apprehension of it in history." [21]

The term "Westminster" referred to the Westminster Confession, the Presbyterian articles of faith, while by the term "orthodoxy" Bishop Westcott could refer only to his own faith, Episcopalianism. What third set of doctrines different from these two, did they have in mind, in using the word "mean"? When the Oxford Movement, with its revolutionary results, was the background to this situation, when the admiration of this triumvirate for Newman is considered, as well as the expressed convictions of Westcott and Hort for sacramental salvation and Mariolatry, it can be seen that the new set of doctrines they planned to advocate could be nothing else than Ritualism and Romanism. Evidently, the Revisers incorporated their theology into the Scriptures. This is not the function of revisers or translators.

Many Protestants are not aware of the serious difference between the papal doctrine of Atonement and theirs; nor of the true meaning of the Mass. Catholics teach that only the humanity of Christ died on the cross, not

---

[21] Life and Letters of Westcott, Vol. I, p. 214.

His divine nature. Therefore, in their eyes, His death was not, in a primary sense, a vicarious atonement to satisfy the wrath of God against sin and pay the claims of a broken law.[22] Because of this, His death is to them only a momentary event; while His coming in the flesh, or the doctrine of the Incarnation, is supreme. Its effects are continual and daily, a source of saving grace, as they believe. The turning of the bread into the body of Christ, by the priest in the ceremony of the Mass, represents His birth in the flesh, or the Incarnation, repeated in every Mass.

So fundamental to all their beliefs is this different view of the Atonement and of the Mass, as held by Roman Catholics, that it profoundly affects all other doctrines and changes the foundation of the Christian system. When the triumvirate approached their task of revision, with their scheme to advocate their new system of doctrines, Dean Farrar says that "hundreds of texts" were so changed that the Revisers restored conceptions "profound and remarkable" in the "verbs expressive of the great crises of Christian life."[23]

The great crises of Christian life are set forth by Protestants in words and practices different from Catholics. In the great crisis, when the Protestant is under conviction of sin, he reveals it by deep sorrow and contrition; the Catholic by going to Mass. In the crisis of that moment when the soul is moved by repentance, the Protestant speaks forth his heart to God, alone or in the assembly of fellow-believers; the Catholic goes to confess to a priest and so exalts the confessional to the doctrine of the Sacrament of Confession. In that crisis, when forgiveness of sins is experienced, the Protestant is conscious of God's pardon by faith in His Word; the Catholic hears the priest say, "I absolve thee," which indicates the power of the supernatural priesthood. In those deep wrestlings of the spirit, the crises which come

---

[22] Catholic Encyclopedia, Vol. II, p. 58.
[23] *Contemporary Review*, March 1882.

from the demands of Christian obedience, the Protestant leans on the infallibility of the Bible to tell him what he should, or should not, do; the Catholic, through the priest, gets his light from the infallibility of the Pope, the crown of the supernatural priesthood.

The Revisers may not have had, in detail, these phases in their minds as we have enumerated them. But they had, in purpose, the principle which would lead to them. Westcott said, in the quotation above, when planning for a new set of doctrines on which the triumvirate was agreed, "I should like to have the Incarnation as a center." And on the text under consideration—I Cor. 15:3,4—Dean Farrar, interpreting it in the new meaning the Revisers intended it to have, said:

"When St. Paul says that 'Christ was buried and hath been raised,' he emphasizes, by a touch, that the death and burial of Christ were, so to speak, but for a moment, while His Resurrection means nothing less than infinite, permanent, and continuous life." [24]

It is apparent by this translation they mean to minimize the death of Christ and to magnify His resurrection, which to them is substantially a repeated Incarnation. This tends to the Roman idea of Transubstantiation in the Mass. They belittle the death of Christ when they rule out the death of His divine nature. That leads to the conclusion that there was no divine law to be satisfied. Dr. Farrar ought to know what was intended, for he was one of the coterie in which Westcott and Hort moved.

This translation is purely arbitrary. Why did they not say, "hath been dead," and "hath been buried," as well as "hath been raised"? "The aorist, the aorist," we are told. Previously, we have sufficiently answered this unwarranted plea.

Take another text upon which Bishop Westcott has spoken expressly to inform us what is the superior reading of the Revised:

---

[24] *Contemporary Review*, March 1882.

2.   Matt. 27:46

KING JAMES: "My God, my God, why hast thou forsaken me."
REVISED: "My God, my God, why didst thou forsake me." (Margin.)

According to their self-imposed rules, the Revisers considered that the meaning of this text, in the Authorized, was that the effects of Christ's death were supreme and were continuous.   This thought they believed of Christ's resurrection which opened the way for repeated Incarnations, as previously shown.   Therefore, in the Revised (margin), they changed the tense to the past in order to make the death of Christ a temporary event, as of a moment.   Bishop Westcott, on this text, shows in the following words that he believed Christ's passion was the death of a human, not of a divine being:

"If, then, we may represent suffering as the necessary consequence of sin, so that the sinner is in bondage, given over to the Prince of Evil, till his debt is paid, may we not represent to ourselves our Lord as taking humanity upon Him, and as man paying this debt—not as the debt of the individual, but as the debt of the nature which He assumed?   The words in St. Matthew 27:46 seem to indicate some such view." [25]

He wrote to Benson, "In a few minutes I go with Lightfoot to Westminster (Revision Committee Session). More will come of these meetings, I think, than simply a revised version." [26]

As to the "more" which might come of these revision meetings, two incidents of Westcott's life within the five years previous to revision are significant,—his visit to the Shrine of the Virgin Mary at LaSalette, France, (1865), and his suspicious Tract of 1867.

LaSalette was one of the more famous shrines of France where the Catholics claim that the spirit of the Virgin Mary wrought miracles.   Westcott reports that, while there, a miracle of healing took place.   "The eager energy of the father," he writes, "the modest thankful-

---

ness of the daughter, the quick glances of the spectators from one to the other, the calm satisfaction of the priest, the comments of look and nod, combined to form a scene which appeared hardly to belong to the nineteenth century. An age of faith was restored before our sight in its ancient guise. . . . In this lay the real significance and power of the place." [27]

So thorough was the impression of a "restored age of faith," made by this Catholic shrine miracle, on him, that he wrote a paper and sent it in for publication. Dr. Lightfoot besought him to withdraw it. He feared, "that the publication of the paper might expose the author to a charge of Mariolatry and even prejudice his chance of election to a Divinity Professorship at Cambridge." [28]

Again, in 1867, Westcott wrote a tract entitled, "The Resurrection as a Fact and a Revelation." It was already in type, his son tells us, when he was obliged to withdraw it because of the charge against it of heresy. [29]

Thus the Revisers revealed how they were influenced by exhibitions of what they considered the channel of divine power,—shrines and sacraments. This came from their incorrect view of the Atonement. For if Christ paid not the debt for our sins by the death of His divine being on Calvary, then, from their viewpoint, satisfaction for our sins must logically be made to God by some other means. Catholics find it in the sacrifice of the Mass and also by their own works of penance, while the Ritualists and leading Revisers look to the sacraments, which is in reality the same thing. This leads to the power of the priest and the practices of Ritualism. These views of doctrines so different from those held by Protestants in 1611, would fundamentally affect, not only the foundation truth of the Atonement, that Christ's death paid the debt for our sins, but all other doctrines, and pave the way for a different mentality, a different gospel, wherever the ascendancy of the King James Bible was broken

---

[27] Life and Letters of Westcott. Vol. I, p. 254.
[28] Idem, p. 255.   [29] Idem, p. 256.

down. The evidences produced in connection with the American Revisers will show this more fully.

XII. *The Jesuitical Doctrines of the Sacraments Favored by the Revised*

1. I Cor. 11:24

KING JAMES: "And when He had given thanks, He brake it, and said, Take, eat: this is my body, which is broken for you."

REVISED: "And when He had given thanks, He brake it, and said, This is my body, which is for you: This do in remembrance of me."

Why were the two expressions, "take, eat" and "broken" omitted from the Revised? Before answering this question, let us consider further some fundamental viewpoints of the Revisers.

The word "sacrament" is not found in the Bible. The Lord's Supper and Baptism are never called "sacraments." The observance of these memorials of Christ's death, burial and resurrection indicate the Christian's faith, but the Scriptures nowhere teach that they bring salvation or the forgiveness of sin. The mystic power of the priest by means of the so-called "sacraments" is a human invention. Therefore, sacramental salvation is no salvation. We do not wish to offend, or wound, but to us it looks like an empty delusion.

It is a most significant fact that of the system of doctrines with which the Cambridge trio of Revisers—Westcott, Hort and Lightfoot—set out to permeate Christendom, the central one was what they call the "Person of Christ." This doctrine teaches, first, that the only true way to do God's will is by "good works," in dependence upon "the Person of Christ;" second, it involves a clearer grasp of the fact that as the "God Incarnate," Christ is thus "mighty to save;" third, that the believer's incorporation into Christ is by means of the Sacraments; fourth, that the principal Sacraments are three in number,—Baptism, the Lord's Supper (the Mass), and the Confessional. Rev. Kempson, a Church of England clergyman, while admitting that others look upon the

Movement of the Jesuits as counter to the Reformation, himself, holds a different view. He says:

"I say the Reformation, because I can see no sound reason for calling the events of that period which occurred within the Roman Communion a 'Counter-Reformation.' It was a movement which involved a great revival of personal piety and devotion to God and desire to do His will, and an equally clear realization of the fact that that desire could only be realized in good works in dependence on the *Person of Christ*. Thus far we have a remarkable parallel to our own Evangelical Revival. But in this case there was a clearer grasp of the fact that it is as the God Incarnate of the Creed that Christ is mighty to save, and that He communicates Himself to those who desire to live through Him *by means of the Sacraments*. That is, that the individual is grafted into Christ in the New Birth of Baptism, that he feeds on Christ, 'Who is verily and indeed taken and received by the faithful in the Lord's Supper,' and that His healing grace is applied to the sinner and the results of sin by the receiving of the 'Benefit of Absolution.' " [30] (Italics mine.)

In Catholic theology, "Absolution" means the forgiveness which follows confession to a priest. Another quotation by the same author, presents the strong part Westcott had in this work: "Maurice and Kingsley, and Bishop Westcott, in his insistence on the social significance of the Incarnation, have done their work." [31]

The significant remarks above, that "Christ is mighty to save," only "as the God incarnate of the creed,"—which is made available to us in the Lord's Supper or in the Mass, the reincarnation,—and that "He communicates Himself to those who desire to live through Him by means of the Sacraments," were the central doctrines of the Counter-Reformation, or the world-wide movement of the Jesuits. The Revisers changed the words of the King James Version to embody the very same sentiments. On this, Milligan, in his book on the Revised Version, says:

---

[30] Kempson, Church in Modern England, pp. 88, 89.   [31] Idem, p. 100.

"The doctrine of the Sacraments may next engage our attention, and here again the variations in the renderings of familiar texts, though they may not appear at first of great importance, involve far-reaching truths. . . . The Bread—that is, the Body of Christ—recalls more particularly His Incarnation, apart from His sufferings." [32]

Now we see why the word "broken" was left out of the Revised text under consideration, as it is also in the Douay. A footnote of Milligan, in connection with the above quotation, emphasizes the disappearance of "broken." [33]

How we are supposed to come in touch with the "Person of Christ," and receive His power and blessing, is shown by the following quotation from a ritualistic clergyman:

"Now there are, of course, many Catholic practices that necessarily result from a belief in the Real Presence of our dear Lord upon the Altar. . . . Bowing and genuflecting. Bowing to the Altar at all times . . . because the Altar is the throne of God Incarnate, where *daily* now, thank God, in many a Church in the land He deigns to rest. . . . And genuflecting, not to the Altar, but to the *Gift that is upon it*; to the God-man, Christ Jesus, when He is there." [34]

This is the doctrine of the "Person of Christ," as taught by the Ritualists and Revisers. The priest in every Mass creates from bread the very body, the "Person of Christ," and then worships, and causes others to worship, the work of his own hands. We would not wish to offend or speak unfeelingly when we express our opinion that this is as truly idolatry as was ancient paganism, or as is the heathenism of to-day. This localizing of the literal body and "Person of Christ," by making Him present in every particle of the bread and wine of the Lord's Supper, or the Mass, is exactly the opposite, and contrary to the statement of the Saviour when about to bid fare-

---

[32] Milligan, Expository Value, pp. 120, 122.
[33] Idem, p. 122 (note).
[34] Six Plain Sermons, by Richard Wilkins, quoted in the Secret Hist. of the Oxford Movement, p. 410.

well to His disciples,—"It is expedient for you that I go away: for if I go not away, the Comforter will not come unto you; but if I depart, I will send him unto you." *John 16:7.*

When Christ ascended, He withdrew His personal presence from the disciples, and the era of the ministration of the Holy Spirit began. His words indicate that it was necessary for His person to go away, that His Spirit might come to His disciples. He who, like doubting Thomas, depends only on the local, personal, literal, presence of Christ, walks by sight and not by faith and deprives himself of the ministry of the Holy Spirit. "God is a Spirit: they that worship Him must worship Him in spirit and in truth." *John 4:24.* No Scripture commands us to worship in the Lord's supper the "Person of Christ." The Romanists, the Ritualists, and the Revisers invented this unspiritual dogma. Christ is with us always, not in "person," but by His Spirit. We receive Him by receiving His Word, for "they are Spirit, and they are life." *John 6:63.*

Nineteen hundred years ago, Christ journeyed on this earth from Bethlehem to Calvary in "person." When He departed from this world and ascended up on high, He left the glorious promise that He would come the "second time" in "person." His Second Coming is yet future. But if He comes personally in every Mass, or the Lord's Supper, He has already come not only the "second" time but the millionth time. The Revisers' doctrine of the Incarnation (the Mass), therefore, makes unnecessary and destroys the truth that He shall come "the second time without sin unto salvation." *Hebrews 9:28.* How feeble is the coming of the "Person of Christ" in the Mass, or Lord's Supper, compared with His Second Coming in His own glory and the glory of His Father with all the holy angels! The fact that He came once in person and that His "second" personal coming is still future, proves untrue, the doctrine of the "Person of Christ" in the Mass.

This doctrine is a weak substitute for, and counterfeit of, the glorious Second Coming of Christ.

Here a little, and there a little, the Westcott-Hort generalship moved forward, changing the divine Word to bear the impress of their doctrines, until they had changed the Greek in 5,337 places, and the English of the King James in 36,000 places. These 5,337 mutilations of the Greek and 36,000 metamorphoses of the English, in working out their scheme, stamp many of the readings of the Revised Version with the marks of Systematic Depravation.

CHAPTER XIII

Catholics Rejoice That the Revised Version Vindicates Their Bible

PREVIOUSLY we have shown how Catholics were elated over the readings in the Revised Version that undermined Protestantism, and criticized the Revisers for wanton omissions.[1] We shall now show how they rejoiced that Catholic readings rejected by the Reformers have been restored by the Revisers, and their Catholic Bible vindicated.

A Catholic bishop says that the Revisers were not as Protestant as the translators of 1611:

"It must be admitted that either the Revisers wished to withdraw several important passages of the Holy Scripture from Protestants, or that the latter, in their simplicity, have all along been imposed upon by King James' translators, who, either through ignorance or malice, have inserted in the Authorized Version a number of paragraphs which were never written by an apostle or other inspired author." [2]

Cardinal Wiseman exults that the Revision Movement vindicates the Catholic Bible:

"When we consider the scorn cast by the Reformers upon the Vulgate, and their recurrence, in consequence, to the Greek, as the only accurate standard, we cannot but rejoice at the silent triumph which truth has at length gained over clamorous error. For, in fact, the principal writers who have avenged the Vulgate, and obtained for it its critical preëminence, are Protestants." [3]

A Catholic Magazine claims Revision for Higher Criticism and Catholicism:

"How bitter to them must be the sight of their Anglican bishops sitting with Methodists, Baptists, and Uni-

[1] Chapter XI.
[2] Bishop Tobias Mullen, Erie, Pa., The Canon of the Old Test., p. 366.
[3] Wiseman, Essays, Vol. I, p. 104.

tarians to improve the English Bible according to modern ideas of progressive Biblical Criticism! Who gave these men authority over the written Word of God? It was not Parliament or Privy Council, but the Church of England acting through Convocation. To whom do they look for the necessary sanction and approval of their work, but to public opinion? One thing at least is certain, the Catholic Church will gain by the new Revision both directly and indirectly." [4]

A Catholic priest indicates that the changes agree with the Latin Vulgate:

"It is very pleasant to read the commendation given by the learned reviewer, the Very Rev. James A. Corcoran, D.D., in the American Catholic *Quarterly Review,* of the new Revision. He devotes a considerable space to proving that the earlier English translations corrupted the text, for the purpose of attacking the Roman Catholic faith, and that even King James' Version retained many of these odious mistranslations. Of the Revision he says: 'One of the greatest benefits conferred by the Revision on the English Protestant world, though very few or none seem to realize it, is that all the wicked translations, whether by falsification of meaning, or by interpolation, or by foisting of glosses into the text, have been ruthlessly swept away by the besom of the Revisers. And why? Solely on the ground that they were corruptions. They do not explicitly say that they were sectarian corruptions, nor need we insist on their saying it; but they recognized them as such, and every honest man, every friend of religious truth must be thankful that they have with unsparing hand driven these unholy abominations out of the book of God's revelation. This proves that their honesty was wholesome, not partial or interested.' " [5] The above quotation shows the hostile attitude of Romanists to the King James Version, and their endorsement of the Revision.

A Catholic Bishop says that Protestants have prayed the Lord's prayer wrong for 300 years:

---

[4] *Dublin Review* (Catholic), July 1881.
[5] Dr. Warfield's Collection of Opinons and Reviews, Vol. II, p. 82.

"This writer (Dr. Alexander Roberts) notifies his readers in one place, that, because the Revisers made use of an amended Greek text, 'a vast multitude of changes will be found in the Revised English Version' of the New Testament. Next he reminds them of 'the entire omission of the doxology of the Lord's prayer of Matt. 6:13,' so that all English speaking Protestants have been all along adding to that prayer words which the Lord never dictated. Indeed, they are likely to continue the practice, as the Revision of the Authorized Version will probably never be generally adopted by them." [6]

A Catholic priest says that the Revised Version confirms readings of the Catholic Version:

"From the Very Rev. Thomas S. Preston, of St. Ann's (R. C.) Church of New York,—'The brief examination which I have been able to make of the Revised Version of the New Testament has convinced me that the Committee have labored with great sincerity and diligence, and that they have produced a translation much more correct than that generally received among Protestants.

" 'It is to us a gratification to find that in very many instances they have adopted the reading of the Catholic Version, and have thus by their scholarship confirmed the correctness of our Bible.' " [7]

A Catholic Magazine says that the Revised readings do justice to Catholics:

"We have next to examine the new Version in detail to see how it will affect Catholic truth. In the first place, there are several important corrections and improved renderings. The Revisers have done an act of justice to Catholics by restoring the true reading of 1 Cor. 11:27." [8]

A Catholic Bishop considers that the Revised Version is like the Douay Bible:

"And there is no reason to doubt that, had King James' translators generally followed the Douay Version, the convocation of Canterbury would have been saved the

[6] Mullen, Canon of the O. T., pp. 365, 366.
[7] Dr. Warfield's Collection of Opinions, Vol. II, p. 21.
[8] *Dublin Review* (Catholic), July 1881.

trouble of inaugurating a movement for the purpose of expurgating the English Protestant Bible of the errors and corruptions by which its pages are defiled." [9]

French and German Catholic authorities approve the critical features of the Greek text which underlies the Revised Version:

"In the *Bulletin Critique* of Paris for Jan. 15, 1881, the learned Louis Duchesne opens the review of Westcott and Hort with these words: 'Voici un livre destine a faire epoque dans la critique du Nouveau-Testament.' (Here is a book destined to create a new epoch in New Testament criticism.) To this Catholic testimony from France may be added German Catholic approval, since Dr. Hundhausen, of Mainz, in the 'Literarischer Handweiser,' 1882, No. 19, col. 590, declares: 'Unter allen bisher auf dem Gebiete der neu-testamentlichen Textkritik erschienenen Werken gebuhrt dem Westcott-Hortschen unstreitig die Palme.' " (Among all printed works which have appeared in the field of New Testament textual criticism, the palm belongs unquestionably to the Westcott-Hort Text.) [10]

A Catholic magazine claims that the Revised Version is the death knell of Protestantism:

"On the 17th of May the English speaking world awoke to find that its Revised Bible had banished the Heavenly Witnesses and put the devil in the Lord's Prayer. Protests loud and deep went forth against the insertion; against the omission none. It is well, then, that the Heavenly Witnesses should depart whence their testimony is no longer received. The Jews have a legend that shortly before the destruction of their Temple, the Shechinah departed from the Holy of Holies, and the Sacred Voices were heard saying, 'Let us go hence.' So perhaps it is to be with the English Bible, the Temple of Protestantism. The going forth of the Heavenly Witnesses is the sign of the beginning of the end. Lord Panmure's prediction may yet prove true—the New Version will be the death knell of Protestantism." [12]

[9] Mullen. Canon of the O. T., pp. 369, 370.
[10] Dr. Warfield's Collection of Opinions, Vol. I, p. 48.
[12] *Dublin Review* (Catholic), July 1881.

CHAPTER XIV

The American Revision Committee and Its Influence Upon the Future of America

A S THE influence of the Oxford Movement crossed the ocean and began to spread in the United States, Dr. Hort could not refrain from writing to Westcott:

"A most singular movement is taking place among the German 'Reformation' settled in America, the center of the Movement being Mercersburg. The leading man is Dr. Nevin. . . . I can compare him to no one but Newman, and higher praise it would be difficult to give. I fear he is fast drifting Romewards." Easter Eve, 1854.[1]

So wrote from England one who knew. The "Mercersburg Movement," or the "Mercersburg Theology," made a revolutionary and permanent change in American Theological colleges and American theology. Dr. Nevin, however, was not the American Newman. He was only the forerunner. The outstanding leader, his associate, was Dr. Philip Schaff, President of both American Committees of Revision, Old and New Testament.

The following quotation will show, in an introductory way, how the Mercersburg Movement stood related to American churches, to the Oxford Movement, and to Dr. Schaff:

"The works of the Mercersburg professors are fraught with dangerous tendencies. The Reformed Dutch Church has, by a public and solemn act, withdrawn from ecclesiastical relations with the German Reformed Church, her ancient ally, on account of her countenance of those works and of their authors. The General Assembly of the Presbyterian Church (O.S.) has suspended her

---

[1] Life and Letters of Dr. Hort, Vol. I, p. 277.

relations with that denomination for the present year, and awaits further developments. This painful step has, in both cases, been taken after much deliberation, and with the calmness and dignity which befit a Christian Church. . . .

"Romanism is known to have recently entered the Church of England in the disguise of Oxford Tractarianism, to have drawn off no inconsiderable number of her clergy and members, and to have gained a footing on British soil, from which the government and public opinion together are unable to eject her. The Mercersburg writers began with decided commendation of the system which is called Puseyism. Their own course has thus far strongly resembled that which has marked its history. Step by step they have advanced, till Romanism stands forth almost unveiled in the 'Apostles' Creed,' 'Early Christianity,' and 'Cyprian,' of Dr. Nevin in the *Mercersburg Review*. . . . Yet *Dr. Nevin and these very works are commended and endorsed by Dr. Schaff in this 'History of the Apostolic Church,' and that without caution or reserve.*" [2]

Before the part played by Dr. Schaff in contaminating American theology is presented, the fundamental doctrines which formed the issues of the Mercersburg Movement, as well as the background of its birth, must be considered. While on a visit to Germany in 1854, Dr. Schaff lectured before several organizations, on Dr. Nevin and the Mercersburg Movement. From a report of his remarks we quote the following:

"The 'Mystical Presence' published in 1846, was his (Dr. Nevin's) first dogmatic-polemic work, a Vindication of the Mystical Presence of Christ in the Lord's Supper, and of the actual participation of believers in the power of His divine-human life, in opposition to the prevalent symbolical view in America, which sees in this sacrament only a commemoration of the death of Christ now absent in heaven. . . .

"But the Movement did not here stop. Already in the Mystical Presence, the idea of the Incarnation of Christ

---

[2] *New Brunswick Review*, Aug. 1854, pp. 282, 283.

came to the front very clearly, as the central truth of Christianity. . . .

"In the same track with the more recent German theology, he (Dr. Nevin) studied with the deepest interest the entire Puseyite controversy, foremost the writings of Dr. John H. Newman, with whom he had many points of resemblance, and read the works of the most important Roman Catholic apologists and polemics, such as Bellarmine, Bossuet, Möhler, Wiseman, and Balmes, who of course represent their system of faith in a much more favorable light than their Protestant opponents, and know how to idealize it, so that to a deep, earnest spirit it becomes powerfully imposing.

"Dr. Nevin gave expression to his newly gained ideas in the *Mercersburg Review*, established by his pupils, edited by him, and read extensively beyond the Reformed Church, more particularly in the Episcopal. He there developed, in a series of essays and reviews, full of life and spirit, and always going back to fundamental principles, the doctrine of the Person of Christ." [3]

It was in 1844 that Dr. Schaff, still a young man, arrived from Germany to assume his duties as Professor of Church History and Biblical Literature in the Theological Seminary of Mercersburg, Pa. He was just at the beginning of his theological career in the University of Berlin, and was, says Dr. Appel, "a gift from the Fatherland to the daughter Church on this side of the ocean, and we may add, to the country at large, destined to serve as an important link connecting the theological science of this country with that of Germany." [4] He came determined to use as his chief argument, the theory of historical development which, in the hands of the Catholic Möhler, had struck in Germany and everywhere, strong blows at Protestantism and brought about the reinstatement of the Catholic Church to a position of leadership.

On the eve of his leaving Germany, many Protestant leaders of the new German theology rejoiced with Dr.

[3] Appel, Life of John W. Nevin, pp. 412, 413, 414.
[4] Life of Nevin, pp. 200, 201.

Schaff over his call to America. Among others who wrote to him, was Dr. Dorner, whose work on the Atonement has ever attracted so much attention. Of Dorner, Andrew Lang wrote in the *Forum*:

"Dorner's position, however, notwithstanding his protest, is simply the Roman Catholic doctrine of purgatory somewhat rationalized."[5]   Dr. Dorner wrote to Schaff:

"Especially do I ask you to give attention to the Trinitarian and Christological controversies and the development of the theory of the Atonement."[6]

On his way to the United States, Dr. Schaff spent some time in England, visiting. He met Drs. Jelf, Stanley, Pusey, Maurice, and Jowett. He described Maurice as of a German temper of mind, and said of Jowett that he seemed to have more sympathy with German theological views than anyone else he met there. Pusey spoke strongly against the sect divisions in America, "expressing the wish that the bishops of the Anglican Church and the Roman Catholic Church alone had the ground."[7]

On his arrival in this country, and at his inauguration into the office which he accepted within the German Reformed Church, Schaff made an address entitled, "The Principles of Protestantism." His speech was so revolutionary that, as soon as it was translated into English and circulated, it produced a storm of criticism. It brought forth charges of Romanizing and Tractarian tendencies. "The address involved the church irreversibly in the doctrinal agitation which went on within its pale for a quarter of a century."[8]

Some attribute to this address the opening note of the Mercersburg Movement. Others say it began with the tract written in the preceding year by Dr. Nevin, entitled, "The Anxious Bench." This tract was a terrific denunciation of the system of revivals held in the evangelical churches and pointed out the Sacramental System as a

---

[5] *The Forum*, June 1887, p. 336.
[6] David Schaff, Life of Philip Schaff, p. 75.
[7] Life of Schaff, p. 88.
[8] Idem, p. 107.

refuge from fanaticism. Nevertheless the inaugural address of Dr. Schaff resulted in his being tried for heresy. He was formally acquitted; so he and Dr. Nevin went back to the Theological Seminary to vindicate themselves and promote their views among the rising generation. Dr. Berg, pastor of the First German Reformed Church of Philadelphia, bore the brunt of opposing the Catholic tide which evidently now had set in, in America, as it had before in Germany and England. From a converted Catholic priest he had heard that the professors of Mercersburg were insidiously instilling Romanizing poison in their classroom teachings. He tried several times to bring about a change, but finding the Synod obdurate, he went over to the Dutch Reformed Church, taking with him the larger part of his congregation.

The time spent by Dr. Schaff at Mercersburg was approximately twenty years. "The Mercersburg period of Dr. Schaff's career," says his son, "coincided with the rise and development of the Mercersburg theology." In 1864 he removed to New York, and for six years was connected with the New York Sabbath Committee, whose aim, says his son, "was not to defend the Sabbath as a religious festival, but as an institution recognized by civil legislation." During this time he traveled all over the United States, north and south, seeking by documents, by editorials, and from the pulpit and platform, to enforce Sunday Laws.

In 1870, Dr. Schaff connected with the Union Theological Seminary where he taught for over a quarter of a century. It must not be thought, however, that his revolutionary influence upon American theology was limited to his stay at Mercersburg. In his later writings and correspondence, we find those peculiar doctrines which certain German theologians expected him to promote in the United States, and which he urged, at times with insistence, upon the Revision Committee.

Dr. Schaff's teachings endorse the papal hierarchy of the Middle Ages. He magnifies the priesthood until "its ministers have more than earthly power; its sacraments have inherent objective efficiency." [9]   Dr. Schaff's conception of theology rests upon the doctrine of historical development. In his life's work, called "The History of the Apostolic Church," begun in 1853, may be found his scheme of doctrines. His theories in this book were so startling that several of America's leading theological reviews denounced them as anti-Scriptural, and anti-Protestant. In classifying the sources of history, he puts in first rank the "official letters, decrees, and bulls of Popes," pronouncing them "pure, original utterances of history." [10]

"Through the misty drapery of Dr. Schaff's philosophy, every essential feature of the papal system stands forth with a prominence so sharply defined, as to leave doubt impossible, and charity in despair," said one Reviewer. [11]

The following quotations from contemporary writers of standing present the danger of Schaff's teachings:

"It is quite time that the churches of our country should awake to the extent and tendencies of this movement in the midst of American Protestantism. After a series of advances and retractations, strongly resembling the tactics of the Tractarian party in England, we have at length a bold avowal of the 'primacy of Peter,' the fundamental and test doctrine of the Papacy, followed by a concession of every vital point of Christianity— Church, Ministry, Worship, Sacraments, and the Right of Private Judgment—to Romanism, and that too, *while the name and the forms of Protantism are* (as far as possible) *studiously retained.*" [12]

Remember, these are not the teachings of a Catholic, but of the great modern leader in American theology, President of both American Revision Committees which produced the American Standard Revised Version. One of his tendencies is described as follows:

"The first of these which we shall mention is the 'primacy of Peter,' which Dr. Schaff pronounces 'a subject

---

[9] *Princeton Review*, Jan. 1854, p. 189.
[10] *New Brunswick Review*, May 1854, p. 20.   [11] Idem, p. 23.
[12] Idem, p. 62.

of vast importance,' and justly observes that 'the claims of the Papacy are well known to center here.' Dr. Schaff fully asserts 'the primacy of Peter,' and devotes about thirty pages of his work to the proof of it, and the exposition of its relations to the Christian church and its history." [13]

We shall now see that Dr. Schaff's anti-Scriptural doctrine of the "Person of Christ," modifies all doctrines and destroys Inspiration:

"As the conception of Christianity as a principle or life, the divine-human life of Christ, leads to unscriptural views of His person; modifies essentially the scheme of redemption, and the mode of its application; involves the theory of organic development, with all its consequences; so, finally, it includes a new and thoroughly anti-Protestant view of the Church." [14]

Or, as this writer says in another place on Dr. Schaff's conception of Christ:

"It involves the doctrine of organic development, which overturns all the established views of the nature of revelation and of Christian doctrine. Revelation can no longer be understood as the supernatural objective communication of divine truths, but the elevation of human nature to a higher state, by which its intuitions of spiritual objects become more distinct." [15]

What an indictment of this modern doctrine of the Person of Christ! This teaching transfers the revelation of God from the Bible to the feelings, emotions, intuitions, and human judgment of the individual. It places a church composed of such individuals above the written Word of God. May we not here direct the reader's attention to this startling truth, that rejecting the infallibility and inspiration of the Bible leads to seeking refuge in another infallibility. Among Hindus and others, this is the infallibility of the individual; among the Papists, it comes to the infallibility of the Church.

We further quote, from a monthly magazine of stand-

---

[13] *New Brunswick Review*, May 1854, p. 23.
[14] *Princeton Review*, Jan. 1854, pp. 182, 183.   [15] Idem, p. 180.

ing, to show that Dr. Schaff's system of doctrines is truly papal, and that he was disloyal to the faith he professed:

"The Church of Rome has committed it (treason). She has denied the sovereignty of her Lord, and appropriated His royal attributes to Peter, in order, from that shadowy source, to derive them, by her fictitious 'succession,' to herself. She alone, of all the nominal churches of Christ, has done this, and a heavy reckoning she will have for it.

"Dr. Schaff has taken his position in this system so boldly and distinctly, that he quite spares us the invidious office of giving him or his theory an odious name. . . .

"He has determined, too, to write a 'history of the Christian church' on this system. He has thus laid the foundation of it. We shall have occasion to see hereafter that he carries up the whole building plumb and true to the ground-plan, and 'after the pattern showed him' by the most approved masters of papal church-building." [16]

"That such a work should have proceeded from the bosom of the Protestant church, and from a chair of ecclesiastical history in a church especially renowned of old for its learned and powerful champions of reformed Christianity, is a portentous fact. It is, to say the least, not less so, that it has somehow gained the strongest testimonials from several of the most respectable and influential Protestant journals. The Papacy has never won a victory but by *stealing a march*. Her tactics have fairly been successful this time. This book is circulating through the Protestant church with an imprimatur from authorities which no American Protestant has been in the habit of questioning. One of them goes so far as to recommend that Dr. Schaff's book (then only published in German) be translated and introduced as a textbook into our theological seminaries. It would be well, as a preparatory measure, in case that were done, to apply to the 'General of the order of Jesus' to send us over professors to teach it. Our Protestant professors would (till properly initiated and trained) betray some awkwardness in laying down the primacy of Peter as the foundation of the church of Christ, drawing the waters of history from such sources as bulls of the Popes, and

---

[16] *New Brunswick Review*, May 1854, pp. 60, 61,

weaving together beautiful legends and oral traditions
into an osier-work of church history, instead of piling
up, as heretofore, the solid granite of historical fact, and
the pure marble of Christian doctrine. Our students of
divinity, too, for whose 'benefit' Dr. Schaff's work is
especially intended, would be sorely puzzled when set to
learn 'beautiful legends' by heart, to search among 'bulls
of the Popes' for 'doctrine and government,' and to take,
for the first lesson in Church History, 'the Primacy of
Peter.' A sad change must come over our Theological
Schools when this 'broad road leading Rome-ward' is
substituted for the 'old path.' " [17]

It may be urged that Dr. Schaff at times spoke against
the Papacy. This point is noticed by the following
writer:

"It is quite true that Dr. Schaff has said some hard
things of the Papacy. He speaks of the 'extravagant
claims,' 'the deadly coils of the Papacy.' But we have
not yet forgotten that Mr. Newman pronounced the Roman Church 'impious,' 'blasphemous,' 'gross,' 'monstrous,'
'governed by the Evil One,' 'bound by a perpetual bond
and covenant to the cause of Antichrist,' which 'we
ought to flee as a pestilence.' Yet a short time after, be-
held him at the feet of a Romish priest, exclaiming, 'I
ask your blessing,' and 'withdrawing' before the world
'these expressions and the arguments derived from them.'
His peace was easily made.... Dr. Schaff has said, also,
handsome things of Protestantism. He has used Protestant phrases, and made Protestant observations not a
few. *If Dr. Schaff had written a book of unmixed Romanism, it would have found few readers in this country.*" [18]

THE AMERICAN REVISION COMMITTEE

As in England, so in America, two Companies were
formed for Revision, one for the Old Testament, one for
the New. Bishop Ellicott and Dr. Angus of the English
Revision Committee requested Dr. Schaff to take the
initiative and a leading part. In consultation with them,
he selected the American members. The Episcopalians,

[17] *New Brunswick Review*, May 1854, pp. 61, 62. [18] Idem, p. 322.

having declined to nominate members from their body, Dr. Schaff filled out the list. He drew up the provisional draft of the Constitution, made arrangements for the organization and first meeting. During the fourteen years of their labors, Dr. Schaff was the life and soul of the work. He often traveled to England, meeting with Ellicott, Westcott, Hort, and others to smooth out difficulties and save the day in delicate situations. "For the American share in the work," says Dr. T. W. Chambers, a member of the American Old Testament Committee, "the Christian public is indebted to Philip Schaff more than to all other persons together." [19]

The American Committees entered upon their work prejudiced in favor of the Vulgate. They considered the Bible of the Papacy more accurate than the King James. "But the text which the Protestants used," said the final editor of the American Version, "was in many cases, it is now acknowledged, less accurate than that represented by the Vulgate." [20] This attitude of mind certainly would be one desired by Catholics. We have evidence that Dr. Schaff felt at liberty to read his Roman prepossessions into the Sacred Text. In his Church History he translated that famous passage in Matt. 16:18, more in favor of Peter being the first Pope than even papal writers, thus: "Thou art a rock, and upon this rock I will build my church." One writer, reviewing his "Church History," said, "Dr. Schaff has laid his hand on the text itself. With unparalleled audacity he has translated Matt. 16:18, 'thou art a *rock*, and on this *rock*, etc., as if 'Peter' and the 'rock' were expressed in the original by the same word. Bellarmine has not ventured to do this, nor any other Romanist within our knowledge." [21] Could one who had such papal leanings and who dared to mistranslate the Scripture in his own history, be considered safe as a leader in translating all of the rest?

---

[19] Life of Dr. Schaff, p. 389.
[20] Dr. Riddle, Story of the Revised New Testament (American), p. 28.
[21] *New Brunswick Review*, May 1854, p. 57.

The sacerdotal leaning of Dr. Schaff can be further seen from the fact that the American Committee changed, at his personal insistence, the rendering of the English Revision Committee of Acts 20:28, from "overseers" to "bishops." The report of this incident, by his son, we give in full:

"The final Revision,—Paul's address to the elders, Acts 20:28,—as it came from England in 1879, contained 'overseers' in the text and 'bishops' in the margin. In Dr. Schaff's own copy he has written on the margin 'Bishops in the text in all passages, and overseers in the margin (moved by Schaff and adopted unanimously April 30, 1880). The discussion was long.' The printed copies of the Revision, it will be seen, contain the American change and read: 'Take heed unto yourselves, and to all the flock, in the which the Holy Ghost hath made you bishops.' " [22]

Dr. Schaff was on such good terms with the Papacy that he sought and obtained unusual privileges to study Vatican documents. His biographer writes: "Through Cardinal Hergenröther, the Cardinal librarian, he received almost unrestricted access to the Vatican Library and Archives. The latter is a distinct department, containing the papal correspondence, encyclicals, regesta, and other documents pertaining to the curia." [23]

What Greek text was followed in the American New Testament Revision Committee, may be gathered from the report given by Dr. Schaff of his visit to the home of Bishop Westcott, Durham, England, 1869. He said,— "Westcott and Hort's Greek Testament I think will suit me exactly." [24]

Dr. Riddle tells us that in discussing the readings of the Greek New Testament to be adopted, that, "while in the vast majority of cases the preferences of the English Revisers were approved, this was due to independent judgment." [25] Dr. Riddle further informs us that the

---

[22] Life of Dr. Schaff, p. 380.   [23] Idem, p. 417.   [24] Idem, p. 245.
[25] Dr. Riddle, Story of American Revised Version, p. 30.

Versions, English and American, are in substantial agreement.[26]

While time does not permit to study theologically the individual members of these two committees, it is evident that Dr. Schaff carried into the committees, the atmosphere of his doctrines and European contacts. All the serious changes in the English Revised, which so greatly aroused public hostility, also appear in the American Revised. In the New Testament Company, in which the most critical questions came up, Dr. Ezra Abbott was accounted the most competent in problems of textual criticism. He was a Unitarian. As a Unitarian he differed on some points from his fellow Revisers. Of him Dr. Riddle writes,—"Dr. Ezra Abbott presented a very able paper on the last clause of Romans 9:5, arguing that it was a doxology to God, and not to be referred to Christ." [27]

He succeeded in getting his view into the margin. In the article by Dr. Abbott on Bible Texts, in Schaff-Herzog's Encyclopedia, he claims that the early church was not so bent, as those of this generation, upon preserving the exact words of the original autographs of the apostles. Who will believe that those who lived nearest the apostles cared less for the sacred writings than we do now? To make such an arbitrary—and in the very nature of things, unreasonable—statement indicates too low an estimate of the sacred words for us to trust him as a qualified Reviser. Unitarians and Romanizers may serve to revise the Bible for others, but not for evangelical Protestants.

Thirteen colleges and universities located along the Atlantic seaboard had members of their faculties on these two Revision Committees. What the result has been of linking America's educational institutions with European theology, which Dr. Schaff set out to do, may be seen in the letter written him by the famous Dr. Weiss of the Berlin University. He says:

---

[26] Idem, p. 73.   [27] Idem, p. 39.

"If to-day the famous theological seminaries in the United States have become nurseries of theological science, so that the old world no longer gives to them alone, but receives from them instruction in turn, this is owing chiefly to your activity." [28]

If the influence of Dr. Schaff's scheme was so revolutionary upon all the theological seminaries of the United States, what must have been his influence and that of his Revision activities upon the American Revised Version? Will not this explain the peculiar acceptability of the American Revised Version to those who lean toward advanced and liberal theology?

Cardinal Newman and Dr. Schaff drank their inspiration from the same fountain,—from the higher critical theology of Germany,—at the same time both pagan and papal. As to the results of Newman's life and the Oxford Movement, let a quarterly *Review* testify:

"He (Newman) had left the leprosy of Popery cleaving to the very walls of Oxford, to infect the youth of England, through an unknown future." [29]

As to the effect of Dr. Schaff, the Mercersburg theology, and his doctrines, let the same witness testify again:

"Our examination has extended only to a little beyond the middle of Dr. Schaff's work (i. e. his History of the Apostolic Church). But the positions he has already advanced, are such as to lay the whole truth and grace of God, and the whole liberty, hope, and salvation of the human race, at the feet of the Roman Papacy." [30]

Under such influences were born the English and American Revised Versions.

---

[28] Life of Dr. Schaff, p. 467.

[29] *New Brunswick Review*, Aug. 1854, p. 322.

[30] *New Brunswick Review*, Aug. 1854, p. 325.

CHAPTER XV

The Rising Tide of Modernism and Modern Bibles

"The Revisers had a wonderful opportunity. They might have made a few changes and removed a few archaic expressions, and made the Authorized Version the most acceptable and beautiful and wonderful book of all time to come. But they wished ruthlessly to meddle. Some of them wanted to change doctrine. Some of them did not know good English literature when they saw it. . . . There were enough modernists among the Revisers to change the words of Scripture itself so as to throw doubt on the Scripture." *Herald and Presbyter (Presbyterian), July 16, 1924, p. 10.*

B ECAUSE of the changes which came about in the nineteenth century, there arose a new type of Protestantism and a new version of the Protestant Bible. This new kind of Protestantism was hostile to the fundamental doctrines of the Reformation. Previous to this there had been only two types of Bibles in the world, the Protestant, and the Catholic. Now Protestants were asked to choose between the true Protestant Bible and one which reproduced readings rejected by the Reformers.

A New Protestantism Which is Not Protestant

The new Protestantism arose from the new doctrine concerning the Person of Christ. The deep love of all Christians for Christ makes them ready listeners to any teachings which seem to exalt Jesus and increase the glory of Christ. For this reason Protestants easily fell in with the new doctrines concerning Christ which were entirely different from those held by the Reformers. The new Protestantism rejected the sole authority of the Scriptures. They held that the church was instinct with a mysterious life which they called the Person of Christ.

They taught that this life came into all humanity when Jesus was manifest in the flesh; not simply the flesh of Jesus of Nazareth, but in the flesh of all humanity. They held that this life was progressive, and therefore, from time to time, it led the church to new doctrines. The Bible was secondary. This life was communicated through the sacraments, and the participants in the sacraments graduated from one experience to a higher experience. So Christ had two bodies,—His own body in which divinity and humanity were united, and His "theanthropic" life common to all believers, which life constituted the body of the church, or Christ's second body.

This new Protestantism captured most of the Church of England, permeated other Protestant denominations in Great Britain, and flooded the theological seminaries of America. One college professor, alarmed at the atmosphere of paganism which had come into American universities and denominational colleges, investigated them and reported that "ninety per cent or more teach a false religion as well as a false science and a false philosophy." [1]

False science teaches the origin of the universe by organic development without God, and calls it evolution. German philosophy early taught the development of humanity through the self-evolution of the absolute spirit. The outstanding advocates of this latter philosophy, Schelling and Hegel, were admitted pantheists. [2] Their theory was applied to theology in the hands of Schleiermacher whose follower was Dr. Schaff, and whom Dr. Schaff characterizes as "the greatest theological genius" since the Reformation. He also said, "There is not to be found now a single theologian of importance, in whom the influence of his great mind is not more or less to be traced." [3] The basis of Schleiermacher's philosophy and theology was acknowledged by such men as Dorner to be "thoroughly pantheistic." [4]

---

[1] Confessions of a College Professor, *Sunday School Times*, Phila., p. 18.
[2] *Princeton Review*, Jan. 1854, p. 168.   [3] Idem, pp. 169, 170.
[4] Idem, p. 170.

One definition of pantheism is the belief that "the totality of the universe is God." God is in the grass, the trees, the stones, earth, man, and in all. Pantheism confounds God with matter. Gnosticism is essentially pantheistic. "Dr. Schaff says there is 'a pantheistic feature which runs through the whole system' of Popery." [5] Both Gnosticism and Pantheism are at war with the first verse of the Bible which reads, "In the beginning God created the heaven and the earth." This verse places God before matter, makes Him the Creator of matter, and hence apart and distinguished from the material universe.

Modernism, or the new Protestantism, is essentially pantheistic and therefore anti-Scriptural and anti-Protestant. Schaff says that by following this new theology, modern evangelical Germany is as widely separated from the Reformation as the Reformation was from Roman Catholicism. The Reformers taught that every child of God is in immediate contact with Christ and grows in grace and the knowledge of God through the Word and through the Spirit. The new theology taught that Christianity was not "a system of truth divinely revealed, recorded in the Scriptures in a definite and complete form for all ages," but that Christianity is Christ. The church is the development of Christ very much as in this false philosophy, the universe is the development of God. This, of course, is pantheistic, though perhaps all who profess this teaching are not avowed pantheists. The new theology changed the Protestant conception of Christ; then very naturally it changed all the fundamental doctrines and consequently made the Bible secondary as the fountain of faith, while nominally giving to the Bible its customary usages. However, like the Gnostics of old, this new theology would not scruple to change sacred passages to support their theology.

THE GLORIFICATION OF THE VATICANUS AND SINAITICUS

Why was it that at so late a date as 1870 the Vatican and Sinaitic Manuscripts were brought forth and ex-

---

[5] *Princeton Review*, Jan. 1854, p. 167.

alted to a place of supreme dictatorship in the work of revising the King James Bible? Especially when shocking corruptions of these documents betray a "systematic depravation"? On this Dean Burgon says: "The impurity of the texts exhibited by Codices B and (ℵ) is not a matter of opinion, but a matter of fact. These are two of the least trustworthy documents in existence. ... Codices B and (ℵ) are, demonstrably, nothing else but *specimens of the depraved class thus characterized.*" *

Dr. Salmon declares that Burgon "had probably handled and collated very many more MSS. than either Westcott or Hort" and "was well entitled to rank as an expert.'" Nevertheless, there has been a widespread effort to belittle Dean Burgon in his unanswerable indictment of the work of Revision. All assailants of the Received Text or their sympathizers feel so keenly the powerful exposures made by Dean Burgon that generally they labor to minimize his arguments.

Concerning the depravations of Codex (ℵ), we have the further testimony of Dr. Scrivener. In 1864 he published "A Full Collation of the Codex Sinaiticus." In the Introductions he makes it clear that this document was corrected by ten different scribes "at different periods." He tells of "the occurrence of so many different styles of handwriting, apparently due to penmen removed from each other by centuries, which deform by their corrections every page of this venerable-looking document." Codex (ℵ) is "covered with such alterations, brought in by *at least* ten different revisers, some of them systematically spread over every page."

Each of these manuscripts was made from the finest skins and was of rare beauty. "The Codex Sinaiticus of the fourth century is made of the finest skins of antelopes, the leaves being so large, that a single animal would furnish only two. . . . Its contemporary, the far-

---

⁶ Burgon, Revision Revised, pp. 315, 316.
⁷ Dr. Salmon, Some Criticism of the Text, p. 23.

famed Codex Vaticanus, challenges universal admiration for the beauty of its vellum." [8]

Evidently these manuscripts had back of them royal gold. They were reasonably suspected to be two of the fifty Greek Bibles which the Emperor Constantine ordered at his own expense. Why should ten different scribes, through the centuries have spread their corrections systematically over every page of the beautiful Sinaiticus? Evidently no owner of so costly a document would have permitted such disfigurements unless he considered the original Greek was not genuine and needed correcting.

As the Vaticanus and Sinaiticus are evidently the product of Gnosticism, what would be more natural than that the Catholicism of Cardinal Newman and the Gnosticism of his followers, who now flood the Protestant churches, would seek, by every means possible, to reinstate in leadership, Gnosticism's old title-papers, the Vaticanus and Sinaiticus?

THE GNOSTICISM OF THE REVISERS

Cardinal Newman believed that tradition and the Catholic Church were above the Bible. Westcott and Hort, great admirers of Newman, were on the Revision Committee in strong leadership. Dean Stanley believed that the Word of God did not dwell in the Bible alone, but that it dwelt in the sacred books of other religions as well. [9] Dr. Schaff sat in the Parliament of Religions at the Chicago World's Fair, 1893, and was so happy among the Buddhists, Confucianists, Shintoists, and other world religions, that he said he would be willing to die among them. [10] The spirit of the Revisionists on both sides of the ocean was an effort to find the Word of God by the study of comparative religions. [11] This is the spirit of Gnosticism; it is not true faith in the inspiration and infallibility of the Bible.

---

[8] Scrivener, Introduction, Vol. I, p. 23.   [9] Stanley, Essays, p. 124.
[10] Life of Schaff, p. 486.
[11] G. F. Nolloth, The Person of Our Lord, p. 3.

Modern Bibles

How far the new theology has been adopted by the editors of the many different kinds of modern Bibles, is a question space does not permit us to pursue. In the main, all these new editions conform to the modern rules of textual criticism. We have already mentioned Fenton, Goodspeed, Moffatt, Moulton, Noyes, Rotherham, Weymouth, Twentieth Century, the Polychrome, and the Shorter Bible. To these the names of others might be added. The Fenton Farrar translation opens thus in Genesis, first chapter:

"By periods God created that which produced the Solar Systems; then that which produced the Earth. . . . This was the close and the dawn of the first age."

Here is plenty of scope for evolution, Gnosticism, and the æon theory.

The latest sensation is "A New Commentary," by Bishop Gore (formerly of Oxford, and a descendant of the Tractarians), and others. According to this publication David did not kill Goliath, Noah never had an ark, Jonah was not swallowed by a whale, the longevity of Methuselah was an impossibility, and certain Gospel miracles are regarded with skepticism.

"Every theological seminary of standing in this country, we are told," says one of the most widely read weeklies of America, "has been teaching for a quarter of a century almost everything contained in the new Commentary." [12]

Under these circumstances, how can these theological seminaries regard the Hebrew and the Greek of the Bible as dependable or attach to them any degree of inspiration?

When Doctors Westcott and Hort called "vile" and "villainous" the Received Text which, by the providence of God, was accounted an authority for 1800 years, they opened wide the door for individual and religious sects

---

[12] *Literary Digest,* Dec. 29, 1928.

to bring forth new Bibles, solely upon their own authority.

It will be necessary to cite only two texts to show why the Protestants cannot use the Douay or Catholic Version in its present condition.

Genesis 3:15 reads: "I will put enmities between thee and the woman, and thy seed and her seed: she shall crush thy head, and thou shalt lie in wait for her heel."

This rendering opens the way to exalt the Virgin Mary as a redeemer instead of her divine Seed.

Heb. 11:21 reads: "By faith Jacob dying, blessed each of the sons of Joseph, and adored the top of his rod." What is this, if it is not image worship? One has only to read the 13th chapter of Daniel in the Douay, a chapter which does not exist in the King James, to be shocked at one of the corruptions of the Word of God, which the martyrs rejected. What becomes, then, of the statement that all versions are good, and that all versions contain the true, saving Word of God? The numerous modern Bibles, translated from the Westcott and Hort text, or from one built on similar principles, are no better in many respects than the Douay.

Will not God hold us responsible for light and knowledge concerning His Word? Can we escape His condemnation, if we choose to exalt any version containing proved corruptions? Shall we not rather, avoid putting these versions on a level with God's true Bible?

And what is the practical result of this tide of modernism which has largely engulfed England and is sweeping the theological schools and popular Protestant churches in America? It renders such a missionary useless in the foreign field. He will find that the heathen have been in possession of a philosophy like his for 3,000 years. He is no more certain of his ground than they are. It is sad to see the heathen world deprived of the Bread of Life because of modernism.

Uniformity in expressing the sacred language of the one God is highly essential. It would be confusion, not order, if we did not maintain uniformity of Bible language in our church services, in our colleges and in the memory work of our children. "For God is not the author of confusion, but of peace, as in all churches of the saints." *I Cor. 14:33.* It is not those who truly love the Word of God, who wish to multiply various versions, which they design shall be authorized for congregational use or exalted as authority for doctrine. Let the many versions be used as reference books, or books for study, but let us have a uniform standard version.

NOTE: How revolutionary have been the effects of that movement in England which embraced Ritualism and Revision, let the following statements from a book just off the press (1929), by H. L. Stewart, entitled, "A Century of Anglo-Catholicism," speak:

"Condemned or sanctioned, the Movement is now admittedly beyond all stopping. What seemed chimerical a hundred years ago seems irresistible to-day. Four bishops, out of forty-three, are still definitely hostile." [13]

"On the other hand, two thousand two hundred Anglican priests have lately published their unalterable conviction about the Sacrament in terms which no honest man can pretend to think different in any essential respect from those of the Church of Rome." [14]

Speaking of Reservation, the practice of consecrating the sacramental elements some time in advance of the hour when they are to be used, and of worshiping them, H. L. Stewart gives good authority to indicate over 800 churches and institutional chapels "where the sacramental Elements were not only reserved but adored." And, "One finds in *Crockford's Clerical Directory* for 1927, a forecast that ten years of further decline like that of the ten just ended would wipe the Church of England out of existence." [15]

In referring to the Prayer Book controversy, which lately has repeatedly convulsed England and which arose from the new Prayer Book so arranged as to make a ritual like the Catholic legal in the Church of England, this new volume says:

"Mr. Rosslyn Mitchell told the House of Commons that if the English clergy were armed with the Alternative Prayer Book, they could make England Roman Catholic within a generation." [16]

Speaking of the controversy in England between Higher Criticism and belief in the Bible, he further says:

"Making its normal speed of progress, according to the rate at which new thought travels westward, it has now reached America, to divide the churches of the United States into Modernist and Fundamentalist." [17]

---

[13] p. **VI.**   [14] p. **826.**   [15] p. **862.**   [16] p. **844.**   [17] p. **198.**

CHAPTER XVI

Conclusion

BARREN rock, mountain solitude, and lonely wilderness have all contributed their brave sons to defend the Word of God, and, if need be, to die that it might be kept unadulterated. He who hath chosen the weak things of this world to confound the mighty, would not permit man to be robbed of that simplicity of the divine Word which made the untampered Scriptures a peculiar treasure.

The moral law within the heart is compelling. One great philosopher felt this when he said, "There are two things in the universe which awe me: the glory of the heavens above and the majesty of the moral law within me." God did not leave mankind to struggle in ignorance with the awful impressiveness of the law within, without revealing Himself in His Word as the moral Governor of the universe. The supreme lessons of the Bible only can reach the deeper feelings of the heart. The Bible is the absolute standard of right and wrong. In the Word dwells spiritual life the most perfect. Jesus said, "It is the Spirit that quickeneth; the flesh profiteth nothing: the words that I speak unto you, they are spirit, and they are life." *John 6:63.*

The Psalmist wrote: "Thou hast magnified thy Word above all thy name." The created worlds magnify the exalted name of the Eternal. But God has magnified His Word above all these. It is an unhappy hour when humanity lightly esteems the Bible; for there God reveals Himself more than through the material universe. A man is no better than his word; if one fails to command confidence, so does the other. Heaven and earth shall pass away, but God's Word shall never pass away.

In the Bible is revealed the standard by which we shall be tried when the judgment day comes. From the garden of Eden until now, one standard and one only has been revealed. Inspiration declares that this revelation has been under the special protection of all power in heaven and in earth. "The words of the Lord are pure words," says the Psalmist, "as silver tried in a furnace of earth, purified seven times. Thou shalt keep them, O Lord, thou shalt preserve every one of them, (margin) from this generation forever." *Psalms 12:6,7.* Lonely mounds in distant lands mark the graves where fell those who forsook home and civilization that the Word of God might live.

We believe in Jesus Christ as the divine Teacher, because unlike Mohammed and others, He did not come unheralded. There were fifteen hundred years of prophecy pointing forward to His coming among men. A perfect transmission of these predictions was necessary if they were to be fulfilled in every specification.

There is nothing which so stirs men to the holiest living as the story of Jesus Christ. Yet only within the lids of the Bible is that story found. At the cost of great sufferings, God yielded up His son. The history of the ages which prepared for this holy event, and the story of our Redeemer's life are all found within the same volume. These priceless records have been the object of God's infinite solicitude.

The divine Saviour and the holy apostles spoke beforehand of events which would occur even to the end of time. Of what value would such a prophetic revelation be, if it were not to guide those who would pass through the predicted scenes, and if it were not to warn the wicked and encourage the good? This value, however, would be destroyed if the words foretelling the events, the meaning of the events, and the prediction of rewards and punishments were so tampered with that the force of the divine utterance was destroyed. Moreover the very fact that the Word could make such a prediction not only stamps the Word as divine but condemns as wicked, yes, points out as being the predicted apostasy, that system which would either tamper with the Word, or make the Word secondary. The writing of the Word of God by Inspiration is no greater miracle than the miracle of its preservation.

The pathetic question of Pilate, "What is Truth," is not more pathetic than the error of those who say that only by balancing one version against another, or by examining the various manuscript readings,—those of apostates as well as those of the faithful,—can we arrive at approximate truth.

Left to ourselves we stumble through the darkness guided only by the little lamp of reason. But when we accept the Bible, a great light shines upon our path. History and prophecy unite to confirm our faith. Daniel, and John, the apostle, point out the four great empires which succeeded one another,—Babylon, Medo-Persia, Greece, and pagan Rome. After these arose a cruel, anti-Christian power, the Papacy, from whose terrible persecutions the church fled into the wilderness. As Daniel and John predicted, the Papacy trod underfoot the Truth, the Word of God. From false manuscripts she issued a volume which she chose to call a Bible, but added tradition and elevated it to a greater inspiration than the Scriptures themselves.

Eating the bread of poverty and dressed in the garments of penury, the church in the wilderness followed on to serve the Lord. She possessed the untampered manuscripts of holy revelation which discountenanced the claims of the Papacy. Among this little flock, stood out prominently the Waldenses. Generation after generation of skilled copyists handed down, unadulterated, the pure Word. Repeatedly their glorious truth spread far among the nations. In terror, the Papacy thundered at the monarchs of Europe to stamp out this heresy by the sword of steel. In vain the popish battalions drenched the plains of Europe with martyr blood. The Word lived, unconquered.

Let Gilly tell us how the Waldenses survived the fury of the Papacy:

"They occupy a mountain district, . . . and yet from this secluded spot, have they disseminated doctrines, whose influence is felt over the most refined and civilized part of Europe. They . . . speak the same language, have the same patriarchal habits, and simple virtues, and retain the same religion, which was known to exist there *more than a thousand years ago.* They profess to constitute the remains of the pure and primitive Christian church, and those who would question their claims cannot show either by history or tradition that they ever subscribed to the popish rituals, or bowed before any of the idols of the Roman Church. . . . They have seldom been free from persecution, or vexatious and intolerant oppression, and yet nothing could ever induce them to conform, even outwardly, with the religion of the state. . . . In short, there is no other way of explaining the political, moral, and religious phenomenon, which the Vaudois have continued to display for so many centuries, than by ascribing it to the *manifest interposition of Providence,* which has chosen in them 'the weak things of this world to confound the things that are mighty.'" [1] (Italics Mine.)

The Redeemer said: "Thy word is truth." Rome, the Papacy, did as the prophet Daniel wrote, she "cast down the truth to the ground." While Rome was cruelly persecuting the church in the wilderness, was she also the divinely appointed guardian of the true Word of God? God placed the answer to this question in prophecy. And now the Revised Version, built almost entirely on the Vatican Manuscript, kept in the Pope's library, and upon the Sinaiticus, found in a Catholic monastery, (types of manuscripts upon which the Vulgate was built), comes forward and proposes to set aside the text of our Authorized Bible.

---

[1] Gilly, Excursions to Piedmont, pp. 258, 259.

The Authorized Version was translated in 1611, just before the Puritans departed from England, so that they carried it with them across stormy seas to lay the foundation of one of the greatest governments the world has ever known. The Authorized Version of God's Holy Word had much to do with the laying of the foundation of our great country.

When the Bible was translated in 1611, God foresaw the wide extended use of the English language; and, therefore, in our Authorized Bible, gave the best translation that has ever been made, not only in the English language, but as many scholars say, *ever made in any language.*

The original Scriptures were written by direct inspiration of God. This can hardly be said of any translation. Nevertheless, when apostasy had cast its dark shadow over the Western lands of opportunity, God raised up the men of 1611. They were true Protestants. Many of their friends and associates had already fallen before the sword of despotism while witnessing for the Holy Word. And in a marvelous way God worked to give us through them an English version from the genuine manuscripts. It grew and soon exercised a mighty influence upon the whole world. But this was an offense to the old systems of the past. Then arose the pantheistic theology of Germany, the ritualistic Oxford Movement of England, and the Romanizing Mercersburg theology of America. Through the leaders, or associates of the leaders, in these movements, revised versions were brought forth which raised again to influence manuscripts and versions long discarded by the more simple, more democratic bodies of Christianity, because of the bewildering confusion which their uncertain message produced.

Again the people of God are called upon to face this subtile and insidious program.

It is difficult for them to expose the systematic depravation without being misunderstood, and without being charged with attacking the genuine, while seeking to expose the erroneous mixed with the genuine. They recognize that these modern versions can be used as books of reference even if they cannot be put on a level with the Received Text.

Paul said, in Acts 17:28, "As certain also of your own poets have said, For we are also his offspring." Paul quoted good sayings from the pagan poets, but did not use these Greek writers as authority. It is as unthinkable to forbid excellent quotations from pagan and heathen scholars as it would be to place their writings on a level with the pure Word of God. Likewise, parts of modern versions edited by scholars may be used with care in considering Bible verses from another angle. This fact, however, is taken advantage of, to claim divine inspiration for all the rest, and sow confusion among the churches of believers.

Through the Reformation, the Received Text was again given to the Church. In the ages of twilight and gloom, the corrupt church did not think enough of the corrupt Bible to give it circulation. Since the Reformation, the Received Text, both in Hebrew and in Greek, has spread abroad throughout the world. Wherever it is accurately translated, regardless of whatever the language may be, it is as truly the Word of God, as our own Authorized Bible. Nevertheless, in a remarkable way, God has honored the King James Version. It is the Bible of the 160,000,000 English speaking people, whose tongue is spoken by more of the human race than any other. German and Russian are each the language of 100,000,-000; while French is spoken by 70,000,000. The King James Version has been translated into many other languages. One writer claims 886. It is the Book of the human race. It is the author of vastly more missionary enterprises than any other version. It is God's missionary Book.

We shall need the Lord Jesus in the hour of death, we shall need Him in the morning of the resurrection. We should recognize our need of Him now. We partake of Him, not through some ceremony, wherein a mysterious life takes hold of us. When we receive by faith the written Word of God, the good pleasure of the Lord is upon us, and we partake of Him. Through this Word we receive the power of God, the same Word by which He upholds all things, by which He swings the mighty worlds and suns through the deeps of the stellar universe. This Word is able to save us and to keep us forever. This Word shall conduct us to our Father's throne on high. "The grass withereth, the flower fadeth; but the Word of our God shall stand forever."

> "The starry firmament on high,
> And all the glories of the sky,
> Yet shine not to thy praise, O Lord,
> So brightly as thy written Word.
>
> "The hopes that holy Word supplies,
> Its truths divine and precepts wise,
> In each a heavenly beam I see,
> And every beam conducts to Thee.
>
> "Almighty Lord, the sun shall fail,
> The moon her borrowed glory veil,
> And deepest reverence hush on high
> The joyful chorus of the sky.
>
> "But fixed for everlasting years,
> Unmoved amid the wreck of spheres,
> Thy Word shall shine in cloudless day,
> When heaven and earth have passed away."

ERRATA

Page 33. *Read* Desanctis *instead of* DeSanctis.

Page 73. *Read* June *instead of* July (footnote).

Page 79. *Read* Remonstrant *instead of* Romonstrant.

Page 105. *Read* DeWette *instead of* DeWitte.

Pages 114, 116. *Read* Thirlwall *instead of* Thirwall.

Page 69. Credit first paragraph of quotation to F. J. Firth, "The Holy Gospel," pp. 17, 18.

Page 21. "Soviet Museum at Moscow." Latest authoritative information confirms the report that the priceless treasures of Leningrad have been removed recently to Moscow, but leaves uncertain whether or not Codex Aleph was removed.

Meek and Mighty The Man Moses
A compilation of Ellen G. White's writings on the life of Moses from *The Signs of the Times* and *Patriarchs and Prophets*.

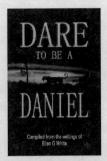

Dare to be a Daniel
A compilation of Ellen G. White's writings from *The Youth's Instructor* and other sources on the life of Daniel.

Other Titles from TEACH Services, Inc.

The Youth's Instructor Articles
A compilation of about 470 of Ellen G. White's articles that were originally published (1852–1914) in magazine form. Facsimile.

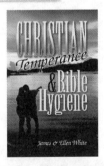

Christian Temperance & Bible Hygiene
This collection of writings by James and Ellen G. White will both inspire and instruct you in temperance and hygiene from a Biblical point of view.

We'd love to have you download our catalog of titles we publish at:

www.TEACHServices.com

or write or email us your thoughts, reactions, or criticism about this or any other book we publish at:

TEACH Services, Inc.
254 Donovan Road
Brushton, NY 12916

info@TEACHServices.com

or you may call us at:

518/358-3494

Produced in partnership with
LNFBooks.com